Adrian Graffy

Trustworthy and True

THE GOSPELS BEYOND 2000

D0313056

the columba press

First published in 2001 by
the columba press
55A Spruce Avenue, Stillorgan Industrial Park,
Blackrock, Co Dublin

Reprinted 2006

Cover by Bill Bolger
The cover picture is The Evangelist Mark from Ms 139 (12th century)
in the Chester Beatty Library, Dublin. Used by kind permission.
Origination by The Columba Press
Printed in Ireland by Colour Books Ltd, Dublin

ISBN 1 85607 332 7

Contents

Preface

'I saw heaven opened, and there was a white horse, and the one sitting on it was called trustworthy and true.' (Revelation 19:11)

Among the many visions of the Book of Revelation the white horse and its rider are easily missed. The scriptural allusions which follow identify the rider as the Messiah. He is also called 'the Word of God', echoing that most significant idea of John's gospel. That Messiah, the Word of God, is described as 'trustworthy and true' *(pistos kai alethinos)*. Yes, we might say, Christ himself is to be trusted. Christ himself is the Way, the Truth and the Life. But what about the gospels?

The twentieth century witnessed enormous developments in the study of the scriptures. Assisted by numerous advances in techniques of communication, understanding of the Bible has been greatly facilitated. A variety of views have been expressed about the Bible. As for the gospels, new views have been expressed and some have questioned their reliability. Such questions are delicate, even threatening for believers. If modern methods of study have shown the gospels to be unreliable, how can the believer discover Jesus? Would it not be better to shun all contact with such new methods? If so much of the gospel tradition is the result of later reflection, how can the gospels be trusted to provide a true portrayal of Jesus? What can we find out from the gospels about Jesus? Is it still possible to describe the four gospels as 'trustworthy and true' as the third millennium of Christianity begins? Or are we fooling ourselves, and trying to fool others? This book takes an honest look at the four gospels, for when the issues are faced in this way it soon becomes clear that, far from undermining belief in Jesus, modern approaches in fact enliven reading of the gospels. Not only are the gospels 'trustworthy and true', but each one of them makes a vital contribution to Christian faith and life.

This book is dedicated to my mother and father who introduced me to the gospels.

Introduction

It is undeniable that Jesus of Nazareth made an extraordinary impact on the people of his day, both those who accepted him as sent from God, and those who considered him in a less positive light. Both the writers of the New Testament and non-Christian authors testify to his impact. Those who accepted him as sent by God began to tell others of this man. They began to preach about one who not only came as a prophet of God and worker of mighty deeds, but as one who was quite unique. It was their experience of Jesus risen from death that was fundamental. Disciples of Jesus encountered him after his death. In trying to make sense of this they began to see him in a new light. God had done something extraordinary in Jesus of Nazareth. They sought to make sense of it all by reference to the Old Testament. They understood him better as the Messiah of God, God's anointed, even though Jesus had apparently been reluctant to accept such a title. Jesus was considered to be Son of God in a unique sense. Since God had spoken through this man as never before, he was also a great prophet. More than this, he was the Word of God. Due to their experience of Jesus risen they had a new confidence, a confidence they had lacked while Jesus was with them, a new conviction. They received a new spirit, a dynamic spirit such as the prophets had foreseen.

The good news about Jesus was proclaimed by travelling preachers. They spoke about the extraordinary impact of Jesus, his preaching of the kingdom of God, his amazing deeds of healing, but above all they spoke about his death and that God had raised him from death. The missionary journeys of the apostles and the traditions found in the Acts of the Apostles testify to this. Christian communities were born in various parts of the eastern Mediterranean, even as far west as Rome. At what point some of these traditions about Jesus were put in writing we cannot be sure. What modern study has shown to be plausible is that different traditions about Jesus existed in this stage of oral preaching and were gathered only later and put into written form. Perhaps the story of Jesus' suffering and death was the first tradition to be written down. Collections of parables may have been put in writing, and collections of stories about the powerful works Jesus performed.

At some point a new form of writing arose, which we have come to know as a 'gospel'. The Greek term *euaggelion* refers primarily to news which is carried by a messenger. The same term is used both of the preaching of Jesus and of the preaching of the good news by St Paul. It is not surprising that the term came to be used also for the written form of such good news that we have in the gospels. The evidence suggests that these documents were compiled in the second half of the first century AD. Our gospels show signs of developing communities of Christians and developing ideas about Jesus and his teaching. They witness both to the life and deeds of Jesus and also to a growing understanding of Jesus among his followers.

As time went on and writing about Jesus continued new gospels developed in new and sometimes strange ways. Even those who disagreed radically with the accepted view of Jesus, for example those groups now known as Gnostics, wrote gospels. Just as in Judaism it had become necessary to establish a canon, a list of books which were considered to provide true teaching, so among Christians it was necessary to identify which were the authentic gospels, not merely because they contained reliable traditions about Jesus' life, but more importantly because they set down an understanding of Jesus which corresponded to the faith of the community. In this way four gospels emerged as the foundation of Christian faith.

Even a cursory reading of the gospels will reveal similarities between the three gospels known as 'synoptic', those according to Matthew, Mark and Luke, and quite a different presentation from the fourth gospel, the one entitled 'according to John'. The basic pattern of a ministry of Jesus in the north, around Galilee, followed by a journey to Jerusalem, where he is arrested, tortured and executed, is found both in the shortest gospel, that of Mark, and in those of Matthew and Luke. By contrast, the gospel of John has Jesus often in Jerusalem and rarely in Galilee. Deeper scrutiny of Mark, Matthew and Luke shows that much of Mark's material is also to be found in Matthew and Luke. Furthermore, not only is the material often similar, but it is quite obviously copied. A comparison between these three gospels makes it very plausible that Mark's short gospel was adopted and added to by both Matthew and Luke. Comparison of identical material often reveals a different perspective in a later gospel. A later evangelist may well enhance the presentation of one of Jesus' deeds to stress the divine power at work in Jesus. A later evangelist may increase the store of Jesus' wise teachings by discovery of new traditions or by development of existing ones.

As regards the synoptic gospels, given this name due to their shared perspective, it is clear that Mark was the gospel used by the subsequent evangelists. Both Matthew and Luke preserved and adapted Mark's material, as well as adding material which is common to them but not found in Mark, and also material found only in Matthew or Luke. Naturally enough, both Matthew and Luke produced longer gospels as a result, but more significantly their gospels brought in later reflection on Jesus and more developed understanding of him. Such new understanding was inspired by the Spirit powerfully at work among the first followers of Jesus. Furthermore, each gospel was in some way affected by the situation of the community for whom it was written. The gospel of Mark emphasises the suffering of Jesus and the persecution of his followers. Matthew's gospel is particularly interested in presenting the teaching of Jesus to Jews. The gospel of Luke has a special interest in Jesus' care for the poor and marginalised, which might suggest this was a special problem in the community for which this gospel was written.

The genius of Mark is perhaps seen above all in the way he constructs his gospel. He gathers the traditions about Jesus in Galilee into the first part of the gospel. These include stories of Jesus' mighty deeds, his parables, and his encounters with the religious authorities. Mark then has Jesus travel the way to Jerusalem, the way to the place of the cross, and Jesus speaks of his coming death at stages along the way. The ministry and subsequent events in Jerusalem are then narrated. The other synoptic evangelists must have been so taken by this simple structure of Galilee ministry, journey to Jerusalem and Jerusalem events that they adopted it for their gospels too. They used it as the basic framework for the new traditions they added to the gospel record. Luke extended the journey to Jerusalem from three chapters to ten. Matthew inserted considerable blocks of the teaching of Jesus into his gospel.

And what of the gospel according to John? As with all the four gospels, we need to be aware of the ancient titles given to the gospels. *Kata iohannen*, 'according to John', is not the equivalent of 'written by John'. We are dealing with the gospel traditions preserved and promoted within the community with which John was associated. Maybe John founded the community, maybe he just preached there. And the same is true of each of the gospels. Mark's gospel is linked to a certain Mark who may have been Peter's assistant. Matthew's gospel arose in the church which had Matthew as its founder or patron. Luke's gospel was somehow associated with Luke, a companion of Paul, who seems to have also written the Acts of the Apostles. As for John, then, a very different collection of traditions was nevertheless accepted and kept in the canon by the church. Even though it contained quite a different account of the ministry of Jesus, the gospel of John was considered to provide new and precious insights into the truth about Jesus. What then can we mean by describing the gospels as 'trustworthy and true'? On the basis of historical memories of Jesus, new and developing understandings of Jesus, his life and death, and his abiding legacy, are recognised by the church and offered to believers as the good news.

What then is a gospel? Christians are often misled and develop unreasonable expectations of the written gospels. The gospels, as the diversity between them clearly shows, are not the very words and very deeds of Jesus, exact in all their details. They are accounts of Jesus, but accounts in which the significance of the protagonist is set forth by using historical traditions about him as a foundation for explanation of his identity and his achievement. In this way the gospels show similarities to ancient lives of leaders and teachers contemporary to Jesus. The gospels cannot be divorced from the true life of Jesus. But neither can they be divorced from developing understandings of Jesus in the early decades of Christianity. The Spirit of Jesus was guiding the church to a fuller understanding of what God had done in Jesus of Nazareth.

We will begin our survey of the gospels by examining the synoptic record of the ministry of Jesus, leading to his death and resurrection. We take Mark as our guide, examining how the later synoptic evangelists, Matthew and Luke, have developed his material. This thematic journey through the basic synoptic record will be completed in the first seven chapters of this book. In chapters eight, nine and ten we will examine the particular contributions to the synoptic tradition made by Matthew and Luke. Three chapters will then be dedicated to a survey of the gospel of John. Translations of all biblical texts are by the author.

CHAPTER 1

Baptism and Temptation

Mark's opening verses

The opening words of the earliest written gospel might be translated: 'Here begins the good news about Jesus, the Messiah, the Son of God.' (Mark 1:1) This headline grabs the attention. Here is something worth reading. Mark, however, does not begin his gospel with stories about Jesus' birth and infancy, as are found in Matthew and Luke. Neither does this evangelist begin with a poetic meditation on Jesus' origins, as found in the gospel of John. Mark nevertheless in these opening verses makes most significant statements about Jesus. Mark calls what he is writing 'gospel' or 'good news'. This is what the Greek term *euaggelion* means. It is used by Mark of the preaching of Jesus about the kingdom (Mark 1:14), and Paul uses it when he summarises the good news about Jesus which he received and which he has passed on. (1 Corinthians 15:1) It is used in a similar way in the first verse of Mark chapter 1.

Here begins the good news about the man called Jesus. His name is not unique to him. The Old Testament hero we know as Joshua and the wise man called Jesus ben Sira, whose wisdom is recorded in the book of Ecclesiasticus, are perhaps the most well-known other bearers of this name, which is traditionally interpreted as 'Yahweh saves' (Hebrew *yehoshua*, abbreviated as *yeshua*). The evangelist immediately gives this Jesus special status by describing him as the Messiah, or 'anointed one' (Greek *christos*), and as Son of God. Mark's opening verse is a celebration of faith. This Jesus is the Messiah. This Jesus is the Son of God.

Judaism in the first century AD had various hopes and some

15

of these concerned a God-given Messiah. Hopes expressed in some of the prophets, particularly Isaiah of Jerusalem who had lived in the eighth century BC, and in some psalms, had fuelled speculation about the role of this anointed one. Would he be a leader who would establish justice and peace on earth? Would he be a liberator who would after centuries of foreign oppression rid Israel of pagan rule once and for all? Would he be a chosen priest of God? Would his coming be a sign of the end-times? As the gospel proceeds it will become clear what kind of Messiah Jesus is. At this point Mark simply expresses the faith of the early believers, who called themselves 'Christians', that Jesus was the Christ, the Messiah. The evangelist also gives Jesus the title 'Son of God', a title which seems to go back to Jesus himself, and speaks of Jesus' awareness of a special relationship to the Father. Even this earliest gospel suggests the unique relationship of Jesus to his God.

Mark rather abruptly follows this opening title with two pieces of Old Testament scripture. This evangelist, unlike his successor Matthew, does not often quote from scripture. The fact that he does so here surely illustrates a concern to anchor this new good news to the continuing story of God's dealings with the Jewish people recorded in the Hebrew scriptures. The words he chooses are from the books of the prophets Malachi and Isaiah (Malachi 3:1 and Isaiah 40:3). The fact that Mark reports them as being from Isaiah alone suggests that the two quotations had become so associated in Christian use and understanding that they were treated as one. Both quotations speak of a messenger, one who comes to prepare the way. This messenger would announce the imminent coming of God. The messenger Mark refers to, and regards as the fulfilment of these prophetic words, announces the arrival of God's anointed one, the Messiah who is the Son of God. The evangelist suggests in this way that the hopes of the faithful, nurtured through the centuries by prophets and psalms, are now realised in Jesus.

John the witness

Both Old Testament texts spoke of one who would come before the Lord, called a 'messenger' in the Malachi text and a 'voice in the wilderness' in the Isaiah verse. This messenger, this voice, the one who prepares the way, is identified by Mark as John the Baptist. John begins a ministry of preaching and baptising at about the time Jesus emerges from Nazareth and begins to preach and heal in Galilee. The suddenness of John's arrival might recall the sudden appearance of the prophet Elijah in the first book of Kings. Mark does in fact want his readers to see John as fulfilling the role of a new Elijah. The prophet Malachi had identified the messenger to come as a new Elijah who would preach a return to God as Elijah did. (Malachi 3:23/4:5) This new prophet preached repentance (Greek *metanoia*) and forgiveness of sins, the sign of which was immersion in the waters of the river Jordan. John the Baptist drew crowds from Jerusalem and from all the countryside of Judah. Mark stresses John's similarity to Elijah even in his clothing. His 'garment of camel-skin and leather belt' reflects the clothing of Elijah (2 Kings 1:8). He lives on desert food, for Elijah had food provided on his wilderness journeys.

John therefore was a prophet preaching repentance, who drew people to a new life and symbolised this with a ritual of washing. The later synoptic writers, Matthew and Luke, will fill out this presentation of John giving an account of his challenging preaching as he addressed scribes and Pharisees, tax-collectors and soldiers (Matthew 3:7-10; Luke 3:7-14).

The portrayal of John as preacher of conversion and social prophet is the basis on which the evangelists build their picture of John as witness to Christ. The John who preaches and baptises in the wilderness, the John who will baptise Jesus amid the crowds who throng to hear John and receive his baptism, this John is presented by the evangelists as a witness to the true identity of Jesus. As the gospel tradition develops, John the Baptist becomes more and more clearly the one who bears witness to Jesus, the one who points him out. This process is seen most clearly in the fourth gospel, where John the social preacher and baptiser is transformed into John the witness to the Messiah. In the fourth gospel John the Baptist even declares that Jesus is 'the Lamb of God, who takes away the sin of the world.' (John 1:29)

This process of witnessing to Jesus begins in Mark's gospel. The Baptist describes the coming one as 'the stronger one' (Mark 1:7). This curious title suggests a conflict, a need for courage and strength. This description of the one who is to come suggests a coming battle with the forces of evil, a battle which for Mark begins when Jesus encounters Satan (Mark 1:13), a battle due to continue in his exorcisms and other works of healing. John also makes clear that Jesus is greater than he is. He himself is no Messiah. He feels unworthy even to serve God's anointed. He speaks of a new baptism which Jesus will bring. John the preacher and baptiser has become John the witness to the coming Messiah. In the gospel tradition John the Baptist proclaims Jesus as the fulfilment of Old Testament hopes, as the one who comes to confront evil and as the herald of the kingdom of God.

The baptism of Jesus
The first appearance of Jesus in the earliest gospel states: 'Jesus came from Nazareth of Galilee, and was baptised by John in the Jordan.' (Mark 1:9) The most ancient tradition begins with Jesus performing an extraordinary act of humility. The tradition of the baptism of Jesus has given rise to much reflection, to elaborate gospel accounts, and to artistic masterpieces. At its heart, however, lies a simple religious act of submission on Jesus' part and profound solidarity with the ordinary people who came to hear the preaching of John. Christian attention has tended to avert its gaze from the baptism itself and to focus on the elaborations. The action of Jesus of course presented a problem for Christian believers, perhaps even an embarrassment. Jesus, who was heralded as the Lord, the sinless one whose death had reconciled sinners, surely did not need to undergo such an act of penance. And yet he did. The baptism of John seems to have been a

purificatory rite such as those regularly practised by the Essenes, the community who lived at Qumran by the Dead Sea in the time of Jesus. But John's baptism was received only once to mark a new beginning in the life of an individual. Jesus associated himself with this preacher who called for a change of heart, a new way of living, and preparedness for a new intervention of God.

It comes as no surprise then that even the earliest gospel account available to us moves quickly from Jesus' act of anonymous humility to something which reflects his unique status. Mark tells of Jesus' vision. It is useful to recall here the visions of the prophets as they responded to God's call. Isaiah in the temple, Jeremiah as a young boy, Ezekiel by the river Kebar, the three great prophets are recorded as having visions of God to challenge them as they began to preach the word (Isaiah 6; Jeremiah 1; Ezekiel 1-3). In this respect, as in so many others, we discover a profound similarity between Jesus and the prophets. Jesus, the ultimate prophet, has his inaugural vision too.

Mark makes it clear that this vision is seen by Jesus and accompanied by the voice of God. Just like the prophet Ezekiel, Jesus sees the heavens opened. While Ezekiel beholds 'visions of God' (Ezekiel 1:1), Jesus sees the spirit, like a dove, descending on him. This powerful symbol implies that Jesus is the Messiah, the one filled with the Spirit according to the words of the prophet Isaiah: 'The spirit will rest upon him.' (Isaiah 11:2) Such a vision was expected in contemporary writing to set apart the anointed one, the one sent by God. What Mark presents as a private vision of Jesus will be presented as seen by other witnesses as subsequent gospels develop the story.

The vision is accompanied by a voice. This voice from heaven, God's voice, is addressed to Jesus: 'You are my beloved son. With you I am well pleased.' (Mark 1:11) It is not surprising that these words of God recall words of scripture. In the second psalm God marks out the king for special favour with the words: 'You are my son.' (Psalm 2:7) Once more it is implied that Jesus is the anointed king, the Messiah. But there is more. The second phrase used by God recalls God's words to the servant in the first of the servant songs in the second part of the book of Isaiah: 'This is my servant ... I delight in him.' (Isaiah 42:1) Jesus is both Messiah and servant. He is the one who comes as God's anointed to fulfil Israel's yearning for a king who is to rule in peace and justice. But he is also the servant who will suffer rejection and death. The servant of the Lord is portrayed thus in later poems of Second Isaiah.

The vision and the voice are a new layer of the tradition built on the foundation of the baptism of Jesus. As expected in contemporary thought, the Messiah is designated as such by God. As expected in contemporary thought, he receives the Spirit in abundance. What is unexpected is that this Messiah is also a servant. He comes as prophet of the kingdom to do God's will, even if this leads to suffering and death.

The baptism story is further elaborated in subsequent gospels. Matthew provides a dialogue between John and Jesus designed to answer Christian concerns about John baptising the Messiah. John says: 'I need to be baptised by you.' (Matthew 3:14) This is clearly a catechetical addition to the tradition. Yes, Jesus is superior of John, but Jesus freely chose to undergo John's baptism. In Matthew's account too the words of the Father undergo a subtle development, for God says: 'This is my beloved son.' (Matthew 3:17) The words of God are no longer a personal statement to Jesus. They become a public introduction of Jesus to the world. In the gospel of Luke we find further editing of the baptism story. John the Baptist is imprisoned by Herod Antipas, the tetrarch of Galilee, before the account of the baptism of Jesus is given (Luke 3:20). When the baptism is reported in Luke 3:21 there is no mention of John and attention moves rapidly to the prayer of Jesus and to the opening of the heavens. Luke, like Matthew, prefers to focus on Jesus' unique status than on his self-abasement. Luke presents the Spirit as descending 'in bodily form'. (Luke 3:22) There is no doubt that the vision of Jesus is now a vision for all to see.

The gospel of John portrays John the Baptist as witness and

eliminates any mention of the baptism of Jesus by John. Nevertheless, the Baptist declares that he saw the Spirit descend on Jesus (John 1:32). The humiliation of baptism is put aside completely in the fourth gospel in order to focus on the Baptist's witness to Jesus. John the Baptist 'came as a witness, in order to witness for the light.' (John 1:7) The two tendencies we saw at work in the transformation of the baptism tradition in the synoptic gospels clearly operate in John's gospel too. John's gospel also avoids the embarrassment that Jesus should undergo such a rite and from one who was naturally considered inferior to Jesus. John's gospel also moves away from the private vision of Jesus to a public spectacle visible to all. The baptism scene as such no longer exists. It is replaced by repeated declarations about Jesus from the mouth of John the Baptist. A significant but problematic historical tradition has been transformed by statements of the faith of early Christian believers.

The encounter with Satan

Mark's story of the testing of Jesus in the desert is extremely brief. The Spirit which had descended on Jesus drives him into the desert. It was an ancient belief that the desert was a place of evil. Jesus, the stronger one, empowered by the Spirit, goes directly into the dwelling place of evil. The next verse of Mark's account reads: 'He was in the desert for forty days, being tested by Satan. He was with the wild animals and the angels served him.' (Mark 1:13) What does Mark intend here? He does not even report how Jesus fared in his testing by Satan. What is the sense of the presence of the wild animals and the service by angels? Matthew and Luke, as we shall see, provide some answers to these questions in their more detailed accounts, but they seem to be able to make no sense of the wild animals and omit all reference to them.

As the text stands, Mark tells us of an encounter of Jesus with Satan. The rest is enigmatic. We may well be able to shed some light on his brief statements with material from the Old Testament. In the book of Deuteronomy, Moses invites Israel to reflect on their experience in the desert. He says to the people: 'Remember how the Lord your God led you for forty years in the desert, to humble you, to test you and to know your heart.' (Deuteronomy 8:2) For Israel the wilderness was a place of trial. Is Jesus shown here reliving the experience of his people? As they spent forty years, he spent forty days. We might also recall that Moses spent forty days on Sinai seeking the presence of God, or that Elijah travelled for forty days to the same mountain, this time called Horeb, to be confirmed in his work as prophet (Exodus 34:28; 1 Kings 19:8). Jesus, the new prophet, is portrayed here, like them, as spending forty days in barren solitude where the presence of God and the presence of evil cannot be hidden. Prophets such as Jeremiah had their trials and temptations (Jeremiah 20:9). Mark tells us that Jesus had his.

The evangelist may intend us to see another parallel. Jesus is tested as Adam was tested. The letters of Paul demonstrate that Christians reflected on Jesus as the new Adam (Roman 5:12-21). While Adam had brought sin and death into the world, Jesus, the new Adam, brings grace and life. Mark speaks of Jesus as tempted, but also as suffering no harm from wild animals. Does Mark suggest by this detail that Jesus is able to re-establish the harmony of creation, the harmony between human beings and the animals portrayed in the book of Genesis? We might recall that the great messianic poem of Isaiah already referred to, which presents the Messiah as full of the Spirit, goes on to describe the re-establishment of peace in creation which the Messiah brings. Isaiah declares: 'The wolf dwells with the lamb, the panther lies down with the kid, calf and lion cub feed together, and a small boy leads them.' (Isaiah 11:6)

Mark seems to be suggesting here that Jesus, the new Adam, by his resistance to Satan, will re-establish the conditions of paradise lost by the first Adam. When we discover that contemporary retelling of the story of Adam and Eve also spoke of angels providing food for them in paradise, and recall Mark's statement that angels served Jesus in the desert, such an understanding of these enigmatic verses seems even more likely. Jesus' encounter with Satan and his resistance to Satan open the way to the re-establishment of the conditions of paradise.

It may be that Mark simply aims to present Jesus as a just man protected by God, as described in the book of Job (Job 5:22-23). Or is Mark simply presenting Jesus as a prophet provided for in the desert, as Elijah was (1 Kings 19:5-8)? The parallel with Adam, however, remains attractive. These two short verses are clearly full of allusions and contain numerous pointers to how Christians might deepen their understanding of Jesus as he begins his public life. The surface statements about Jesus carry deeper truths about his person and significance.

The brief enigmatic nature of these verses in Mark is transformed in the gospels of Matthew and Luke, who both record a more detailed tradition of three specific temptations laid in Jesus' path by the devil. Matthew and Luke use 'devil' (Greek *diabolos*) rather than Mark's 'Satan' (Greek *satanas*), which is adapted from the Old Testament name. It has been suggested that the longer accounts found in Matthew and Luke may owe something to conversations of Jesus with his disciples. It may be, on the other hand, that the verses are the fruit of early reflection on the challenging and humbling theme of the testing of the Son of God. Matthew and Luke have recorded identical temptations, though Luke places last Matthew's second temptation, which is located at the temple in Jerusalem. Two of the temptations aim to seduce Jesus into an abuse of his powers as Son of God. He is tempted to use the power the Father gives him for selfish and unworthy ends. A third temptation is to gain power by collusion with Satan.

The first temptation, that the Son of God after forty days of fasting should use his power to turn stones into bread, is so reasonable and so cunning. Surely no one would object to such a use of his special powers. But Jesus does not yield. He does not abandon his fast. He does not deviate, nor succumb to a selfish use of God's gifts. His reply to the devil is: 'Man shall not live by bread alone.' (Matthew 4:4; Luke 4:4) With these words from the book of Deuteronomy, Jesus takes his stand against the devil.

Jesus is tempted then to use power in a spectacular way. He could throw himself from the pinnacle of the temple and be saved by God's angels. This is a temptation to put God to the test, to use power in order to impress. Jesus replies with a further citation from Deuteronomy: 'You shall not test the Lord your God.' (Matthew 4:7; Luke 4:12) The final chilling temptation is that Jesus should collude with Satan to gain power over the nations of the earth. This final temptation is based on a lie, the lie that Satan already controls the nations. The temptation is to collude with the lie and to change sides. Jesus, free to collude, does not collude. He resists the lies of Satan. He does not succumb to evil. With a final quotation from Deuteronomy he sends Satan off: 'You shall worship the Lord your God, and you shall serve him alone.' (Matthew 4:10; Luke 4:8)

The temptations described in the gospels of Matthew and Luke should not embarrass Christians. They are a precious illustration of the vulnerability of Jesus. They no doubt give us a unique insight into the fidelity of Jesus throughout his life and ministry. The Son of God enters fully into the wonderful and terrible freedom God gives to human beings. The temptations to self-centred or spectacular use of God-given powers could seem so reasonable, so justifiable. Even his disciples could tempt Jesus to similar deviation from the true path. Peter will be rebuked with the same words, 'Get behind me, Satan!', which Matthew attributes to Jesus in the temptation account (Matthew 4:10 and 16:23). The temptation to collaborate with Satan is the most pernicious of all. It is the temptation to accept Satan's lies and to collude with evil. To yield to such a temptation would open an easier way, but Jesus takes his stand for goodness and truth. The temptation story leaves no doubt that he is the stronger one, come to confront evil in all its forms (Mark 1:7; Matthew 3:11; Luke 3:16).

The detailed temptation account in the two later synoptic gospels has a powerful catechetical message. The way of Jesus is the way of his disciples. Temptations to self-centredness and greed, and to spectacular display to win the world's admiration, must be rejected by Christians. The third millennium of Christian discipleship is an opportunity for Christians to ask whether this is so in our lives and in our churches. The most insidious cancer is, however, collusion with lies and evil. The Jesus of the temptation story throws down a major challenge to Christians and to the churches that they be people of goodness and people of truth.

The Son of God is shown in the gospel stories of the baptism and the temptation to be the one who in the power of the Spirit challenges evil and lies in the world of his day. It is his followers, from the first disciples onwards, who take up that challenge as the centuries of Christianity continue.

CHAPTER 2

The Kingdom and the Mighty Works

The structure of a gospel

The traditions concerning the baptism of Jesus belong at the beginning of the story of Jesus' ministry. His contact with John the Baptist can be understood as a preparation for his public appearance. The baptism is an anointing with the Spirit for the road ahead. The tradition of the temptations shows that, with the strength of the Spirit, Jesus confronts the power of evil. After this Mark records words and deeds of Jesus which may well have come to him in no particular order. The earliest evangelist gave the gospel its structure. It is this first evangelist who, with considerable skill, devised its form. His inspired layout of the first gospel was then adopted and modified by Matthew and Luke.

Fundamental to Mark's structuring of his story of Jesus is the gathering together of traditions belonging to different geographical locations. Mark devises a gospel in which an initial ministry in and around the northern region of Galilee is followed by the journey of Jesus to Jerusalem and his ministry, death and resurrection there. This simple structure is then used by Matthew and Luke. The layout of the synoptic gospels stands in contrast to that found in the gospel of John, which features several journeys of Jesus to Jerusalem. This diversity is an excellent example of how the evangelists compiled the traditions they received into gospels in different ways. The historical core of the gospel traditions lies in the various pieces of tradition and not in their ordering in each gospel. The ordering is part of the editorial activity of each evangelist. We cannot know whether the healing of Jairus' daughter in Mark chapter 5 came before the healing of the blind man in chapter 8. Nor do we need to know. Of course certain events, particularly those at the beginning and ending of Jesus' public life, have a clear place in the story, but many autonomous traditions will have been allocated places in their gospels by the evangelists for logical rather than chronological reasons. They would usually not have been aware of the relative historical order of the events remembered in the tradition.

Mark's inspired structuring of his gospel has a profoundly catechetical purpose. Jesus is called to a ministry of word and deed and initially many listen and follow. Jesus then must take the road to the place of suffering and death. This pattern in the life of Jesus is lived also by the followers who are called to take up their own cross. (Mark 8:34) The structure of the gospel provides the disciples of Jesus with a challenge and an example. They too will find life by the cross.

The prophet's manifesto
Each evangelist chooses very carefully the opening words of Jesus in his public ministry. The first words of Jesus in Mark's gospel story appear in Mark 1:15. 'The time has been fulfilled and the kingdom of God has come near. Repent and believe the gospel.' Matthew begins his account of Jesus' ministry in a similar way. (Matthew 4:17) Luke, by contrast, places first the story of a visit of Jesus to the synagogue in Nazareth during which Jesus reads from the scroll of the prophet Isaiah. In Luke Jesus' first words are: 'The Spirit of the Lord is upon me, for he has anointed me. He has sent me to bring good news to the poor.' (Luke 4:18) While in Mark and Matthew Jesus simply announces the kingdom, Luke has Jesus describe some features of its arrival.

Jesus' manifesto is therefore that 'the kingdom of God' has come. What does he mean? Where does the expression 'kingdom of God' originate? The idea that God is king over all the earth, and holds sway particularly over Israel, is not uncommon in the Old Testament. We might recall here how Samuel objected to the people's demands that they should have a king like every other nation by reminding them that God was their king. (1 Samuel 8:7) The prophet Isaiah declares that his eyes have seen 'the king' in his vision in the temple. (Isaiah 6:5) That God rules as king is often stated in Israel's psalms. (Psalm 93:1 and 95:3) The Greek term for 'kingdom of God', *he basileia tou theou*, found in the gospels, renders the Hebrew concept of *malkut yahweh*. It is rightly pointed out that 'kingdom of God' may not be the best rendering of the phrase. It is translated more precisely as 'reign of God' or 'rule of God', for it concerns not a territory but an activity of God. God's *malkut*, God's rule, is a theme found in the Psalms and in the writings known as apocalyptic. (Psalm 145:12-13; Daniel 2:44)

Apocalyptic writing, as the Greek word *apokalypsis*, meaning 'revelation', indicates, is designed to uncover or to reveal secrets of the future. A visionary sees a vision in which details of the end-time are shown. In the book of Daniel, which contains the principal examples of apocalyptic literature in the Old Testament, prominent among these revelations is the arrival of the *malkut*, the reign or kingdom of God. In Daniel chapter 2 Daniel interprets Nebuchadnezzar's dream about the whole course of history. The dream foresees God's triumph over all the powers of the earth and the establishment of an eternal kingdom (Daniel 2:44). The idea of the kingdom, expressed in this way, is a concept of the future when God is expected to intervene in the world's affairs to abolish evil and reward the just. It is this idea which Mark suggests is fundamental to Jesus' preaching. He puts it alongside the idea of the 'time' (Greek *kairos*), another concept with apocalyptic overtones. The coming of the kingdom of God, expressed as the 'kingdom of heaven' in Matthew's gospel out of reverence for the name of God, is the constant theme of the preaching of Jesus.

The kingdom and Jesus
That God should rule over creation and over human beings seems quite straightforward. The idea is broad and many-faceted. The gospels explore different aspects of the kingdom. It

is a kingdom experienced both on earth among human beings and in heaven, the dwelling-place of God. It is a kingdom experienced during the lifetime of Jesus and a kingdom awaited in the future. It is a kingdom which can be entered by some, but which others will try to enter in vain. The kingdom of God is understood as a powerful presence for those with ears to hear, but also as something which can be disregarded and rejected.

Jesus' statement that 'the kingdom of God has drawn near' is itself ambiguous. We need to recall that the gospels are written in Greek, in the international form of the Greek language known as *koine*, which had become widespread from the time of Alexander the Great, who died in 323 BC. Jesus himself spoke Aramaic. We cannot be sure what precisely Mark intended with these Greek first words of Jesus about the kingdom. It is virtually impossible to reconstruct the original Aramaic statement of Jesus. What is beyond doubt is the frequency and variety of words about the kingdom, and the basic fact that the coming of the kingdom of God is understood to be related to the ministry and work of Jesus. With Jesus the kingdom has come near. The words of Jesus in Mark 1:15 will be carried forward by the disciples, who are sent out to proclaim the same message. (Matthew 10:7; Luke 9:2; Luke 10:9)

The impact of the kingdom can be experienced in the works of Jesus. As Jesus begins his preaching and healing activity he is acclaimed and pursued. It is not long before Mark records the interest of religious officials in the activities of this new prophet. In chapter 3 Mark tells us of the arrival of a delegation of scribes from Jerusalem to question Jesus. The scribes were no doubt sent by the religious authorities. It is their opinion that a prophet who shows such power in working exorcisms and healing must be in league with Satan. A fuller account of the dialogue between Jesus and these scribes is given in the gospels of Matthew and Luke. (Matthew 12:25-30; Luke 11:17-23) It is in Luke's gospel that Jesus states: 'If by the finger of God I cast out devils, then the kingdom of God has overtaken you.' (Luke 11:20) The work of this prophet is not simply to proclaim the presence of the kingdom. He also demonstrates that presence by powerful deeds. Jesus is unique in this respect. Miracles worked in the early church, as reported in the Acts of the Apostles, are worked in the name of Jesus. The bringing together of kingdom preaching and mighty deeds is found in Jesus alone.

Jesus' words about the kingdom are many and varied. One saying, only found in Luke's gospel, has had a considerable impact. When asked by the Pharisees when the kingdom is to come, Jesus maintains that it does not come 'with observation'. People will not say 'It is here!' or 'It is there!' For, says Jesus, 'the kingdom of God is among you.' (Luke 17:20-21) Jesus repeatedly refuses to speculate about the time of the full establishment of the kingdom. He is indeed using apocalyptic imagery, but detailed apocalyptic calculations are not in order. The time of the end is not known. His followers are to live in hope and preparedness.

But what precisely is Jesus saying in his reply here? The kingdom of God, he maintains, 'is among you'. The Greek phrase *estin entos humon* has often been rendered 'is within you'. Such a concept of the rule of God in individual hearts does not fit with the New Testament idea of the kingdom, however diverse this may be. The kingdom is not an inward reality or inner condition. What Jesus more probably says here is that the rule of God is present and available among or in the midst of the hearers of his message and the witnesses of his deeds. Christian tradition has understandably reinterpreted the saying in reflecting on Paul's concept of the presence of the Spirit of God dwelling in the believer. (Romans 8:9) Disciples are urged by Jesus in this saying to recognise the present challenge of the kingdom rather than speculate about its full realisation at some unknown point in the future.

The sayings examined so far have stressed the presence and the availability of the kingdom of God in the life and ministry of Jesus. Other words of Jesus in the gospels direct us towards the future complete establishment of the reign of God. Many of the parables of the kingdom, to which we shall return, lay stress on growth, from small beginnings to completion, under the mysterious power of God. The Lord's Prayer, in both Matthew's and Luke's versions, is the prayer for the coming of the kingdom. (Matthew 6:10; Luke 11:2)

Does Jesus ever give a precise time for the full coming of the kingdom? Is the urgency of his preaching about the kingdom directed to an imminent event? This appears to be the case in the isolated saying of Jesus in Mark 9:1: 'Amen, I say to you, there are some of those standing here who will not taste death until they see the kingdom of God coming in power.' The saying is loosely attached to the preceding words of Jesus concerning the challenge of discipleship. Many scholars have affirmed that Jesus held the mistaken belief that the time of the end and the kingdom of God would be established soon. He was proved wrong by the passage of time. We should recall here Jesus' repeated insistence that his disciples should be constantly prepared for the day of the end and should not engage in speculation regarding days and times. The saying in Mark 9:1 clearly stands in tension with such advice. For this reason it is more plausible to consider the saying as an additional word attributed to Jesus by an early Christian teacher.

The problem was that of a community in which the first generation of believers was gradually dying out. Would Jesus return before they had all died? What would happen to those who had died? Paul addresses a similar issue in his early letter, the first to the Thessalonians. Paul speaks of the end coming soon and affirms that some of his company, who will still be alive at the time, will be brought to join those who have died so that all will be with the risen Lord. (1 Thessalonians 4:17) Both Paul and the unknown speaker of Mark 9:1 declared their belief in an imminent establishment of the kingdom, within the lifetime of the first believers. They were anxious about the delay in Christ's return. The genuine teaching of Jesus was not so definite. Jesus constantly stressed the urgency of accepting the challenge of the kingdom, but his words about its complete realisation are expressed in vaguer terms and in prayer. The time is not known.

The mighty works of the kingdom

The deeds of Jesus are closely related to his preaching. His extra-ordinary deeds are referred to in the synoptic gospels as 'acts of power', or 'mighty deeds'. The Greek term *dynameis* is used constantly to refer to actions of Jesus in which the power of God is considered to operate. Jesus affirms the presence of the power of God in his kingdom preaching. Jesus confirms that presence in his mighty deeds.

That a prophet should also perform extraordinary acts of healing, even of raising the dead, is not unheard of. The first and second books of Kings contain the traditional stories concerning Elijah and his lesser disciple Elisha. (1 Kings 17-2 Kings 13) The miracles of both bear some resemblance to those recorded of Jesus. They healed the sick, they raised the dead, they provided food which did not run out. It is with these prophetic traditions from the Old Testament that we discover the closest similarity. But we know too of other miracle traditions from the lands of the eastern Mediterranean in Jesus' day.

Parallels are often drawn with the deeds recorded of the first century AD itinerant philosopher and miracle-worker, Apollonius of Tyana. His eloquence as an orator and teacher and his power to heal those considered possessed are celebrated in his life-story, written in the third century by Philostratus. The length of time between Apollonius' life and the writing of his story raises major questions about its historical reliability. Stories about miracle-working rabbis from the time of Jesus suffer from the same problem, that long periods have elapsed between the life of the rabbis and the recording of the traditions.

It is undeniable that contemporaries of Jesus also performed strange deeds of healing. Jesus himself refers to the exorcisms of Jewish teachers of his day. (Matthew 12:27) He also expected his disciples to go out and heal. (Mark 6:7, 6:13) In the case of the gospel records, the gap between the life of Jesus and the writing of the traditions is relatively short and there is abundant written material to consider. The synoptic miracle stories provide reliable evidence of Jesus' healing work. Some enhancement of the traditions may, nevertheless, have taken place in order to accentuate the healing power of God at work in Jesus. The non-canonical apocryphal gospels clearly contain fictional miracles. It would have been strange if, given the impact of Jesus' life, such elaborations of the historical record had not taken place.

Jesus' mighty deeds are a firm part of the traditions with a reliable historical basis. The first-century Jewish historian Josephus also speaks of Jesus as a worker of extraordinary deeds. About one third of Mark's gospel is concerned with miracles, either accounts of these deeds, or disputes about them, or general summaries of Jesus' miracle-working activity. All the mighty deeds can be seen as evidence of the presence of the kingdom, but it is in the exorcisms that the encounter between Jesus, the prophet of God's kingdom, and the forces of evil is most evident.

Exorcisms and healings

The first mighty deed of Jesus in the earliest gospel is the healing of a possessed man. Here the evil effect of Satan is challenged and overcome. The man in the synagogue at Capernaum is described as having an 'unclean spirit'. (Mark 1:23) With such a description and with little else to go on, it is not possible to have a precise idea of the man's condition. The gospels show that all kinds of sickness, both of the mind and of the body, were considered to be the work of Satan, and there is no clear distinction of physical and mental illness. In Luke's gospel the enfeebled condition of a woman who has been ill for eighteen years is blamed on possession by a spirit, and Jesus declares that 'Satan has held her bound'. (Luke 13:11,16) Later in the gospel of Mark it is implied that an 'unclean spirit' makes the epileptic boy deaf and dumb. (Mark 9:25) The phrase 'unclean spirit' seems to be interchangeable with 'devil' or 'demon' (Greek *daimonion*), understood as a manifestation of evil in the sickness, physical or mental, suffered by the individual. Jesus is the stronger one whose mighty deeds challenge such evil with the power of God. All his healings point to the coming of the kingdom, for evil is confronted and vanquished.

In the latter part of the first chapter of Mark, and beginning with the healing of the possessed man in the synagogue, the evangelist has presented a typical day of the ministry of Jesus in the town which seems to have become a centre for Jesus' activity. (Mark 1:21-39) Other cures are recounted. The fever leaves Simon's mother-in-law. Many sick and possessed people are healed. After the description of this day of teaching and healing in Capernaum, the evangelist tells us that Jesus does the same throughout Galilee. This first chapter concludes with the healing of another individual considered unclean, in this story a leper.

The most dramatic account of an exorcism is found in Mark chapter 5. The story of the Gerasene demoniac is long and detailed. It is remembered above all because of the stampede of a herd of pigs into a lake. This feature may well distract readers from the essence of the tale. Jesus ventures across the sea of Galilee and into a pagan land. A man 'with an unclean spirit' lives among the tombs. (Mark 5:2-3) He is deranged and has the strength to break any fetters. He howls and gashes himself. This story shows that no human misery is beyond the reach of Jesus' compassion and no evil beyond his strength. It is customary in stories of exorcisms that some kind of dialogue takes place between the possessed person and the healer. This seems to involve a struggle to gain power, one over the other, by extracting knowledge of the opponent's name. In this case the name 'Legion' has an added significance, for it points to the perceived presence of a multitude of devils. (Mark 5:9) And what of the pigs? In most of the stories of Jesus' exorcisms the question of the fate of the unclean spirits or devils is not mentioned. Here, in similarity to some ancient stories of exorcism, and perhaps due to the enormous power of the spirits considered to inhabit the man, the narrator is keen to consider this issue. Unclean spirits go into unclean animals. They end up where they belong, in the chaos of deep waters. What are we to say of this feature of the story? Are we to consider it as a reliable historical report? A definite answer cannot be given, for we are already aware that miracle stories were elaborated in the tradition. Whatever the case, the pigs should not distract us from the fundamental point, the healing by Jesus of a desperately sick man. His transformed state is stressed by the evangelist. (Mark 5:15) He is sent by Jesus to tell people what God has done for him. (Mark 5:19) It is quite plausible that this element of the story gave added impetus to the outreach of the early preachers into Gentile areas.

Jesus' exorcisms may be dramatic and the frequent reference to them underlines his mission to confront evil as he proclaims the coming of the kingdom. But the healing of other ills, the curing of leprosy, the return of sight to the blind, hearing to the deaf, mobility to the paralysed, are also seen as examples of the triumph of good over evil. One such miracle is the healing of the deaf and dumb man in the seventh chapter of Mark. What is extraordinary about this miracle story is the use by Jesus of several different techniques for healing. Jesus puts his fingers in the man's ears and touches his tongue with spittle. (Mark 7:33) The use of spittle applied as a remedy for healing is found again in the cure of the blind man at Bethsaida. (Mark 8:23) Both miracles show Jesus using techniques similar to other ancient healers. In this respect these two miracles and the healing of the man born blind, in the ninth chapter of John's gospel, when Jesus uses a paste made of earth and spittle, are different from all the other miracle stories of Jesus.

In the story of the deaf and dumb man Jesus also sighs, and pronounces in Aramaic the word *ephphatha*, translated as 'Be opened'. (Mark 7:34) In the story of the healing of the blind man at Bethsaida, the cure seems to take place in stages. Jesus uses spittle, and lays hands on the man twice. 'I can see people but they look like trees walking about,' says the man. (Mark 8:24) Finally the cure works. With all these features it is understandable that both these miracle stories were dropped by later gospels, in which the evangelists were keen to stress the extraordinary power of Jesus the healer. Such techniques similar to those used by pagans and such repeated attempts at a cure were not, it seems, considered appropriate to their picture of Jesus.

Jesus is thus presented as a healer who can restore health to the sick in mind and body. He is also recorded as having the power to raise the dead.

There are three such stories in the gospel tradition: the raising from death of the twelve-year-old daughter of Jairus narrated at great length in Mark chapter 5 (and with parallels in Matthew chapter 9 and Luke chapter 8), the raising to life of the son of the widow of Nain in Luke chapter 7, and the story of the raising of Lazarus in the fourth gospel. This last story will be examined later.

The straightforward way in which the raising of Jairus' daughter is narrated suggests that it is seen to be much like the other deeds of healing of Jesus. Jesus uses the Aramaic words *talitha kum* ('young girl, arise') (Mark 5:41), just as he had used the Aramaic expression *ephphatha* in healing the blind man at Bethsaida. And yet, the miracle is witnessed privately by the specially chosen disciples, Peter, James and John, and the girl's mother and father. (Mark 5:37, 40) To early Christians the words used of the raising of the little girl in Mark 5:41-42 would be familiar as those used in Christian preaching about the resurrection of Jesus. It is noteworthy that similar resurrection vocabulary appears in the account of the healing of the epileptic boy: 'Jesus raised him up and he arose.' (Mark 9:27) New life is bestowed in all kinds of ways. The story of the raising of the widow's son at Nain (Luke 7:11-17) has certain similarities with a story about Elijah in 1 Kings chapter 17, in which the prophet restores the life of the son of the widow of Zarephath. Clearly here there is a deliberate demonstration that Jesus has equal or greater power than Elijah. Luke had already shown Jesus comparing his healing ministry to that of Elijah and Elisha in his address in the synagogue at Nazareth in Luke chapter 4.

What are we to make of these reported deeds of Jesus? These stories of the raising from death of Jairus' daughter and of the young man at Nain do not provide sufficient detail for a full evaluation of what exactly happened. The gospel accounts do not set these raisings of the dead apart from the other miracles. The Jesus who demonstrated such diverse healing power was also acknowledged as one who could raise the dead. Is the obvious catechetical importance of these stories in their relevance to faith in the resurrection of Jesus and of Christians firmly founded on historical deeds of Jesus? We cannot give a definitive reply to this question. And yet, that Jesus raised the dead is part of a catalogue of healings which are among the most strongly attested traditions about Jesus.

Both the gospels of Matthew and Luke report a story about John the Baptist sending messengers to Jesus. From his prison he asks: 'Are you the one who is to come or are we to expect another?' (Matthew 11:3; Luke 7:19) The reply of Jesus lists his acts of healing and ends with reference to the raising of the dead and the good news being preached to the poor. The complete list of the deeds of Jesus has a coherence about it. All Jesus' activities are signs of the coming of the kingdom. Jesus does not reply directly to the Baptist's question. His focus is not on himself and his role or identity. The focus is on what God is achieving: the building up of the kingdom.

This text also allows a profound insight into the life of John the Baptist. The one who is presented as a witness to Jesus in the opening chapters of all four gospels is genuinely perplexed that this new and greater prophet does not, like John, focus on God's coming judgement, but offers healing and new life to all. The message sent back to John by Jesus ends with what might be understood as a challenge: 'Blessed is the one who is not scandalised by me.' (Matthew 11:6; Luke 7:23) The God of Jesus, a God of healing and hope, eclipses the God of justice preached by John. The dialogue has a ring of truth about it. Both Matthew and Luke allow the section to end without fully resolving the issue of John's questioning.

Other miracle stories

The miracles considered so far have all, in a broad sense, been healings. Individuals have been the beneficiaries of a powerful transforming act of God through the ministry of Jesus. These miracles have also been 'epiphanies', manifestations of the power of God at work in Jesus. There are other miracles in which the aspect of epiphany seems to dominate. In these miracle stories what Jesus actually does for people is overshadowed by focus on Jesus himself. There is some similarity here with the fourth gospel's description of miracles as 'signs', for John's signs point to aspects of Jesus' person and work.

The tale of the stilling of the storm is found in all three synoptic gospels. A remarkable feature of this story is the similarity with what is told of the prophet Jonah in chapter 1 of the book of Jonah. Both Jonah and Jesus embark on a journey by boat. The boat is in danger from a storm at sea. Both Jonah and Jesus continue to sleep soundly. They are woken up by the others on board, who appeal to them for help. While Jonah tells the crew to throw him into the sea, Jesus rebukes the storm with a command reminiscent of exorcisms. In both stories the storm is stilled. The crew on Jonah's boat and the disciples of Jesus are filled with awe. 'Who then is this?' ask the disciples of Jesus. (Mark 4:41) These close similarities between the two stories, which are maintained in the versions of the stilling of the storm in Matthew chapter 8 and Luke chapter 8, suggest that the focus of the tradition is on the person of Jesus as one greater than Jonah. This comparison recalls the saying of Jesus: 'There is something greater than Jonah here.' (Matthew 12:41; Luke 11:32) Is the tradition therefore to be understood as a catechetical story about the identity of Jesus, a prophet greater than Jonah? Is there any historical foundation to the tale? It is quite plausible that a historical tradition about a crossing of the Sea of Galilee by Jesus and the disciples has become the basis of this teaching about the greatness of Jesus.

The story of the stilling of the storm also provides an example of how Matthew edits Mark's traditions. Comparison of the version in Mark chapter 4 with that in Matthew chapter 8 shows several intriguing changes. Matthew alters Mark's great storm (Greek *lailaps*) to something like an apocalyptic earthquake (Greek *seismos*). Mark's cry of the disciples to their 'teacher' (Greek *didaskalos*) becomes an appeal to the 'Lord' (Greek *kyrios*).

In Matthew's version they cry out: 'Lord, save us!' (Matthew 8:25) Matthew superimposes on the story of Jesus' power to still the storm an image of a struggling community appealing to its Lord for salvation in the face of danger.

The story of the walking on the water has similar features. The focus here is even more strongly on the person of Jesus. A minor stilling of rough seas is mentioned but nothing is made of it. (Mark 6:48,51) The focus is on a manifestation of Jesus and on the disciples' reaction. Jesus is described as 'walking on the sea'. (Mark 6:48) It is worth recording that other significant figures, such as the Buddha and the Persian king Xerxes, have similar traditions recorded of them. In Jesus' case there is a clear allusion, as in the stilling of the storm, to the power of the God of Israel over creation. In one of the poems of Job, God is described as 'walking on the waves'. (Job 9:8) The power of God over sky and sea is again celebrated in the final verses of Psalm 77. The implication here is surely that Jesus shares the status of God. Other biblical figures worked healings and even raised the dead, as Jesus did. God alone has power over the seas and over creation. Jesus' words to the disciples, 'It is I!' (Greek *ego eimi*), confirm what is implied by Jesus' actions. (Mark 6:50) They echo the self-identification of God to Moses in Exodus 3:14. We are dealing here with a tradition which even in the earliest gospel suggests the divine status of Jesus. In Mark's account the disciples do not understand and are described as having 'hard hearts'. (Mark 6:52)

Once again, in the story of the walking on the water, Matthew adapts Mark's account. It is only in Matthew's version that Peter impetuously requests to walk on the sea too. (Matthew 14:28) The one who is to be praised later by Jesus for his God-given insight, when he declares Jesus to be Messiah and Son of God, is portrayed here as a man of little faith who doubts the power of Jesus. A further difference Matthew brings to the story is that, in contrast to the lack of insight of the disciples in Mark, at the end of the story in Matthew all the disciples worship Jesus as the Son of God. (Matthew 14:33) They thus anticipate Peter's declaration of faith in Jesus. Luke omits all mention of this tale,

maybe because he sees no relevance in such a heroic portrayal of
Jesus. There is a brief account of the miracle in John chapter 6. As
with Mark and Matthew, it comes immediately after the feeding
of the five thousand.

There is an ancient connection between these two miracles.
When Mark, at the end of the story, speaks of the disciples' hardness of heart (Mark 6:52), he mentions that they had not understood about the loaves. Mark alone makes this explicit connection between the multiplication of bread and the walking on the
water. But Matthew and John also place the two miracle stories
together. This twinning of the two traditions, and particularly
Mark's reference to the disciples' lack of understanding of what
they had experienced in the two events, are evidence that the
bread miracle should also be seen as an epiphany. The Jesus
who walks on water like the creator God also provides bread for
the multitude like the liberator God of Exodus.

It seems indeed that the two great exodus traditions of the
crossing of the Sea and the provision of the manna are being remembered. (Exodus 14-16) The God who rescues and provides
is to be seen now in Jesus. As we have seen, Jesus' reassuring
words to the disciples, 'It is I', also recall the exodus story. In addition to this, the 'hardness of heart' of the disciples recalls use
of similar language as the followers of Moses complained to him
during their desert journey. Jesus acts as the God of the exodus
acts. He has the status of God in his power over the waters. He
also imitates God in providing more than abundant food for the
people. Jesus reflects not only the power of God over the elements, but also God's caring concern for the people. Mark introduces his first story of the loaves with an allusion to Jesus as a
shepherd, a shepherd who guides and who provides. (Mark
6:34) This strong image of God in the Old Testament is found
here for the first time in the gospel tradition.

There are several versions of the bread miracle tradition.
Mark records two traditions, in which first five thousand and
then four thousand people are fed. The stories, in chapter 6 and
chapter 8, show very close resemblance. The description of the

disciples of Jesus on the second occasion, as completely unaware of what Jesus might do to satisfy the crowd's hunger, is a clear sign that we have here two versions of the same tradition. Mark sets one version on the shores of the Sea of Galilee clearly in Jewish territory, but the second seems to be set in pagan land. Mark's ordering of events before the second miracle suggests Jesus may be outside Galilee. The two reports of one tradition point to Jesus' mission to both Jew and Gentile. Later on, Mark even has Jesus reprove the disciples that they understood neither of the two separate bread miracles. (Mark 8:19-20)

Like Mark, Matthew records two stories (Matthew 14:13-21, 15:32-39). Like Mark, he has Jesus challenge the disciples for their lack of insight. By contrast, Luke and John report only one miracle. (Luke 9:10-17; John 6:1-15) All these versions seem to suggest a particular meal of Jesus with the crowds at which food seems to have been multiplied due to an extraordinary intervention of Jesus.

It seems right to consider the multiplication of loaves and fish as another epiphany miracle, in which the focus is on the person of Jesus. Jesus provides bread for the people.

Another feature of the bread miracle must not be neglected. There is a clear similarity between the actions of Jesus in taking, breaking and giving the bread and his actions at the Last Supper. No doubt Christian celebration of the eucharist influenced the way in which the miracle story was told. In John chapter 6 the miracle is the occasion for Jesus' teaching about himself as the 'bread of life'. The symbolism of the miracle, that God through Jesus gives life in abundance for the people, is clearly also relevant to Jesus' action at the Last Supper and to the Christian eucharist.

A final biblical connection must not be forgotten. In 2 Kings chapter 4 Elisha is recorded as providing food for one hundred people with twenty loaves. Such provision of food which does not run out is a feature of the ministry of the two miracle-working prophets, Elijah and Elisha. Once again there are similarities between Jesus and these two prophets.

It is clear by now that within the miracle traditions of Jesus there are two fundamental types: healings and epiphanies. With the epiphanies the emphasis is on a manifestation of Jesus' status and power. Jesus does what God does. Such miracles prepare for the fourth gospel's understanding of the signs of Jesus as revealing his glory as the Son of God. Both the healings and the epiphanies have truths to present concerning the person of Jesus. Both healings and epiphanies are based on historical deeds of Jesus. In both healings and epiphanies, teaching about Jesus builds on historical tradition. It is sometimes the case that the focus on the person of Jesus makes it difficult to detect what the historical basis of a tradition might be.

Two stories generally considered as miracles must also be mentioned, two stories which understandably cause some embarrassment. The story of the cursing of the fig tree by Jesus is found during the Jerusalem ministry in Mark chapter 11. Matthew chapter 21 records the same tradition and even enhances this story of Jesus' power. While the fig tree in Mark's story is found to have withered on the day after Jesus curses it, in Matthew's version it withers at once. (Mark 11:20; Matthew 21:19) This tradition is best kept separate from the miracle stories and better understood as a symbolic action of Jesus. Prophets regularly performed symbolic actions, often in order to speak of God's judgement. Jeremiah publicly smashes an earthenware pot to declare God's punishment on the people and the city in Jeremiah chapter 19. For the prophets the fruitless fig tree or vine is a frequent image. Jesus the prophet curses the fig tree, which represents a people who do not produce the fruit God desires. The action of cursing the fig tree is similar to Jesus' action in the temple, which immediately follows his curse in both Mark and Matthew. Both point to God's displeasure and to judgement. Luke omits this uncongenial action of Jesus. His parable of the fruitless fig tree in chapter 13 makes a similar point in a more comfortable way.

Finally, we should consider briefly a tradition concerning Peter found only in Matthew. When the collectors of the half-shekel temple tax (Greek *didrachma*) come to Capernaum, Jesus suggests that, to pay the tax for them both, Peter catch a fish. In its mouth he will find a shekel (Greek *stater*). This strange tale in chapter 17 of Matthew's gospel ends at this point. We do not know what, if anything, happened next. The tradition is best understood as an isolated piece of teaching about God's providence and the need for the disciples to rely on God. The shekel in the mouth was perhaps spoken of with tongue in cheek.

Our survey of the miracles of Jesus shows their fundamental connection with his preaching of the kingdom. Jesus, who announces God's powerful intervention in his preaching, confirms it in his deeds. But the accounts of his deeds point also to the person of Jesus. As so often in the gospels, fundamental historical traditions are the vehicles for a developing understanding of Jesus.

The healing work of Jesus continues among his disciples. When Jesus sends out the twelve, they, like Jesus, cast out devils and heal the sick. (Mark 6:13) Only Luke tells us of a mission of seventy disciples by Jesus. On their return they rejoice that they share Jesus' power to heal. Jesus exclaims: 'I saw Satan fall like lightning from heaven.' (Luke 10:18) The healing ministry of the followers of Jesus, reported in the gospels and in the Acts of the Apostles, has continued for two thousand years. Sometimes they facilitate dramatic and inexplicable cures. More often they assist people in bearing their continuing pain. The power of God works still in the disciples of Jesus to heal and to confront evil. Such healing acts are enduring signs of the presence of the kingdom of God.

CHAPTER 3

Discipleship and Parables

Come, follow me

Mark opened the account of Jesus' public ministry with his declaration about the coming of the kingdom. Mark follows this with the call of the first disciples. (Mark 1:16-20) The call is dramatic and no delay is allowed. It is reminiscent of the story of Elijah's call of his disciple Elisha. As Elisha is abruptly summoned from his ploughing by Elijah in 1 Kings chapter 19, so the first four disciples are called from their fishing boats. There is an obvious catechetical point here. Response to the preaching of the kingdom and to the call of Jesus, the prophet of the kingdom, is a matter of urgency. Luke is perhaps closer to the historical truth when he places the call of the disciples after the initial preaching and miracles of Jesus. Indeed, Luke has Peter experience an extraordinary catch of fish at Jesus' command before he is called away with his companions to be a disciple. (Luke 5:1-11)

A more fascinating scenario is provided in the fourth gospel. The evangelist has John the Baptist direct Andrew and another disciple to Jesus. (John 1:35) They approach him as a teacher and stay with him. Andrew then brings along his brother, Simon Peter. John's gospel seems to provide a more plausible version of how the early disciples became attached to Jesus than Mark's abrupt account. Did Jesus meet his first disciples when he was in the company of the Baptist? Since John the Baptist is presented as pointing to Jesus as the awaited one, it is logical that he should direct his disciples to Jesus. The question remains, though, whether this is simply another way of portraying the Baptist as forerunner of the Messiah. The gospel accounts of the calling of the first disciples all display the blend of historical memory and catechetical retelling already familiar to us.

The call to sinners

To return to the synoptic tradition, we find in Mark chapter 2 further developments concerning the disciples. After the call of the first four disciples, Mark inserts in chapter 1 his typical day's ministry in Capernaum during which this evangelist records some typical acts of healing of Jesus. Jesus is accompanied by James and John together with Simon and Andrew. (Mark 1:29) Once we come to the second chapter of Mark's gospel, we find renewed emphasis on the disciples. The chapter is very carefully constructed. At its heart lie three stories involving the disciples and leading to a challenge by Jesus to contemporary religious ideas and practices. These three stories concern Jesus' association with sinners, the question of fasting, and the observance of the sabbath. (Mark 2:13-17, 18-22, 23-28) These stories are flanked by miracle stories which have connections with the controversies.

The first miracle story, the healing of the paralytic in Mark 2:1-12, raises the issue of the forgiveness of sins since, in addition to healing him, Jesus declares the man's sins forgiven. (Mark 2:5) Jesus is not only the healer of bodily ills. He brings healing of the spirit as he announces God's forgiveness to sinners. The objection of the scribes that Jesus declares the forgiveness of sins prepares for the first of the three stories of controversy, which concerns the welcome afforded by Jesus to sinners. At the end of the section Mark places the healing of the man with the withered hand. (Mark 3:1-6) This healing work, which Jesus performs on the sabbath day, raises the issue of sabbath rules and connects with the third story of controversy which immediately precedes it. Mark demonstrates considerable skill in this section (Mark 2:1-3:6) in weaving together the stories of two more healings with the three stories of controversies over religious practice. The healings of Jesus are also signs of forgiveness and freedom.

The first of the three controversies is provoked by Jesus' call of another named disciple. He saw Levi son of Alphaeus sitting at the customs house, and he called him. (Mark 2:14) That the name Levi does not appear in Mark's list of the twelve in chapter

3 should remind us that there is a certain fluidity about the names of the twelve in the synoptic tradition and that the fourth gospel contains no such list. As far as the call of Levi is concerned, while Luke reports it in similar fashion, Matthew reads 'Matthew' in place of 'Levi'. (Matthew 9:9) It seems likely that an original tradition about a tax collector called Levi, reported by Mark and Luke, was adapted to provide a story about the call of the evangelist in the gospel according to Matthew. Nothing more is ever heard of the willing tax collector Levi, except in the controversy story which follows his call. Levi acts as host to Jesus and his companions. Mark emphasises that Jesus had with him 'many tax collectors and sinners' and that 'they followed him'. (Mark 2:15)

The prominence given in the gospels to tax collectors needs some explanation. An elaborate system of taxes and tolls was in operation in Jesus' day both in the province of Judaea which was ruled by Roman prefects and in Jesus' own region of Galilee which came under the control of Herod Antipas the tetrarch. In addition to a poll tax levied on men and women there was a tax on land, and various taxes on sales and inheritance as well as toll fees for crossing borders. These Roman taxes in operation in Judaea were probably imposed in Galilee by Antipas. In addition to this there were the Jewish tithes on crops, the temple tax and the mandatory sacrifices to be offered in the temple. Responsibility for tax collection was farmed out to officials who bid for such positions. It is evident from the writings of the historian Josephus and from Jewish writers that tax collectors took their own profit. To be a tax collector was to be regarded as dishonest. Levi in his tax office by the shore of the lake would no doubt profit from the travellers journeying from the Mediterranean coast inland to Syria. The repentant prayer of the tax collector (Greek *telones*) in Luke chapter 18 forms the heart of the parable of the Pharisee and the tax collector. The story of the conversion of the chief tax collector (Greek *architelones*) Zacchaeus in Luke chapter 19 is another example of a complete change of life following a meeting with Jesus.

In Mark chapter 2 the tax collectors are associated with the more general category of 'sinners' (Greek *hamartoloi*). The term no doubt points to those regarded as sinners due to their life-styles. It is these people who flock to Jesus. In answer to the question of the scribes about the company he keeps, Jesus gives his first brief parable: 'It is not the healthy who need the doctor, but the sick.' (Mark 2:17) The message of the kingdom and the healing work of Jesus challenge both sickness and sin. He offers a new start to those whose lives are in any way blighted by evil. The complaint of the scribes that 'he eats with tax collectors and sinners' echoes through the gospels. It is Jesus' fundamental challenge to the religious attitudes of his day. The sinners are the first to enter the banquet of the kingdom. This is a continuing challenge to those who stand for Jesus and his good news of for-giveness.

Mark continues with two more controversies involving the disciples. Jesus is quick to counter the complaint that his disci-ples do not imitate the disciples of the Pharisees and those of John the Baptist in their practice of fasting. Jesus delivers another brief parable. Those who assist a bridegroom would not think of fasting while in his company. (Mark 2:19) There follow two of Jesus' sayings about the newness of the preaching. A new cloak cannot be used to patch up an old one. (Mark 2:21) New wine requires new wineskins. (Mark 2:22) The third controversy con-cerns behaviour on the sabbath. The apparent triviality of the disciples' action in plucking corn as they cross a cornfield is designed to underline the legalistic excesses of some Jewish teachers. For Jesus the priority is always to place the human need first. His healings on the sabbath emphasise that 'the sab-bath was made for man'. (Mark 2:27)

The challenge of discipleship
Mark's story continues with Jesus selecting twelve of his disci-ples. Mark says that Jesus distanced himself from the crowds by going up a mountain, summoned some to accompany him, and 'made the twelve'. (Mark 3:14) This solemn and detailed intro-

duction suggests an action of some importance. This gospel will refer frequently to the twelve but speak also of 'the disciples'. The later term 'apostles' has only one certain use in Mark (6:30). There is a symbolism in Jesus' selection of twelve of his followers. This is another example of a symbolic action such as the prophets of the Old Testament performed. The twelve reflect the traditional twelve tribes of Israel. They suggest the completeness of the new community begun by Jesus, and the establishment of a new people of God. It is the twelve who will be sent out to preach repentance. (Mark 6:7) It is they who are given special teaching on discipleship. (Mark 9:35; 10:32) It is they who will accompany Jesus in Jerusalem. (Mark 11:11) It is they who will share the supper on the night he is arrested. (Mark 14:17) The frequent references to 'the disciples' suggest a larger group. Discipleship is open to all. The choosing of the twelve is a symbolic action.

Mark chapter 3 continues with a curious reference to the relatives of Jesus. The Greek expression *(hoi par'autou)* means something like 'those from his home'. These people are so astounded at the following he has provoked that they determine to seize Jesus. 'He is out of his mind,' they say. (Mark 3:21) Both Matthew and Luke omit this negative tradition. This judgement on Jesus and his behaviour is followed by reference to the opinion of the scribes from Jerusalem who consider Jesus possessed. (Mark 3:22) This may well be implied in the words of the relatives. When the relatives arrive and wish to see him, Jesus makes a very significant statement about family ties and discipleship. Looking at those gathered around him, he says: 'Here are my mother and my brothers.' (Mark 3:34) It is those who do the will of God who are the family of Jesus. (Mark 3:35) A similar striking reply is given in Luke's gospel when a woman in the crowd heaps blessings on the mother of Jesus. Jesus replies: 'Blessed rather are those who hear the word of God and keep it.' (Luke 11:28) This should not be understood as a rejection of his mother by Jesus. As in the Mark tradition, Jesus points out that true greatness lies not in blood ties but in faithfully doing the will of God.

Discipleship has it difficulties. The first suggestion of the disciples' problems appears in Mark chapter 4. In this chapter Mark gathers together a collection of parables. In an interlude after the parable of the sower, with which the chapter begins, Jesus makes some very significant statements about his use of parables. To these we shall return later in this chapter. In Mark 4:13 Jesus seems to express frustration at the disciples' slowness to understand the parable. In fact, the slowness of the disciples becomes a regular theme in the next few chapters. After the narration of the miracle of the loaves and the walking on the water, Mark affirms that the disciples did not understand. 'Their hearts were hardened,' he says. (Mark 6:52) This is a Semitic way of saying that their minds were not open to true understanding. All these negative references to the disciples are omitted by Matthew and Luke, and a further reprimand from Jesus in Mark 8:17-21 is softened by Matthew. (16:8-12) This is a fascinating instance of the development from Mark to the later synoptic gospels. While Mark shows remarkable honesty in the portrayal of the disciples, and even seems to stress their faults, Matthew and Luke present them in a more positive light.

The major challenge for the disciples comes when Jesus begins to speak of the fate he foresees for himself in Jerusalem. There is a new tone to the synoptic gospels when Jesus begins his journey to Jerusalem. As he begins to travel to the place where prophets are killed, he starts to speak of what he foresees to his disciples. In Mark's account Peter has just made his declaration that Jesus is the Messiah. (Mark 8:29) That the Messiah should suffer and be put to death is not in Peter's vision. Peter's objections earn the rebuke from Jesus, 'Get behind me, Satan!' (Mark 8:33) The temptation to take the easy path was already suggested in the temptation story of Matthew and Luke. There, as here, it is rejected by Jesus in very clear terms. Jesus then proceeds to speak of the cross his followers are to carry. (Mark 8:34) Matthew's account of the first time Jesus speaks of suffering and death has a similar objection from Peter and an equally clear rejection by Jesus. But when Jesus speaks of his death in Luke, no difficulty of the disciples is recorded.

As the journey continues, Jesus speak for a second and third time about his suffering. (Mark 9:31 10:33-34) The sense of foreboding increases as Jesus approaches Jerusalem. On both occasions in Mark the disciples avoid the issue and change the subject, preferring to talk about their own positions of greatness and about the rewards in store for them. Jesus teaches them about the humility of the child (Mark 10:15), about the danger of riches (Mark 10:23), and about the call to service. (Mark 10:43-44) Their slowness to understand is the opportunity for Mark to record various pieces of teaching about true discipleship as the journey to Jerusalem progresses. Even Luke records the disciples' failure to understand Jesus' words about his suffering, but he excuses them by saying that the truth 'was concealed from them'. (Luke 9:45, 18:34) For Luke, God did not intend them to understand at this stage.

Mark's honesty and Luke's idealised portrait of the disciples are contrasted most clearly in the narratives of the passion, to which we shall return in a later chapter. Mark does not shrink from recording the slowness to understand and the faults of the disciples, as if to encourage Christians who knew only too well their own faults and those of their companions. Luke meanwhile stresses the fidelity of the disciples of Jesus in order to encourage similar fidelity amid trials among the people for whom he writes. Mark's realism is in contrast to Luke's idealism. Both provide powerful gospel messages about discipleship for today.

Teaching in parables
The most remembered and cherished features of the public life of Jesus as recorded in the gospels are the miracles and the parables. Miracle stories and parables have fed people's faith, their art and their lives since the beginning. As with the miracles, the parables too have connections with the prophets of the Old Testament. At this point we will consider some general issues concerning the parables of Jesus and survey the parables found in Mark, most of which are recorded in Matthew and Luke too. The parables of Matthew and those of Luke will be considered in the relevant later chapters.

The commonly held perception that a parable is a story with a religious or moral message is very close to the truth. The Hebrew term *mashal*, which is the nearest equivalent term to 'parable' in the Old Testament, has a wide variety of meanings. The book of Proverbs, attributed to king Solomon, and containing collections of wise poems and wise sayings, is the book of *meshalim*, the plural form of *mashal*. A *mashal* is a piece of instruction, a rule, a lesson, a popular saying, a proverb. The same word is used by the prophet Ezekiel for more substantial pieces of writing. Ezekiel uses the term *mashal* and he uses the term *hidah*, which is best translated 'riddle'. Ezekiel's poem of the eagles in chapter 17 is described in both ways. The meaning of a riddle is not always obvious. It might present a challenge to the reader. It might not be easy to understand. This is a feature to be aware of when considering the parables of Jesus. Ezekiel's poem about the eagles is in fact an allegory, though this term is not used in the Bible. In an allegory the different actors in the story, in this case the vine and the two eagles, represent different people, in this case the people of Judah, the king of Babylon and the pharaoh.

Possibly the finest parable of the Old Testament, and the one most similar to the story-parables of Jesus, is the parable of David's prophet Nathan in 2 Samuel chapter 12. The rich man who steals the poor man's lamb to produce a meal for a visitor is a potent accusation to David who, having many wives, has stolen Uriah's wife, Bathsheba, and arranged for the killing of Uriah. In the parables of Jesus we find short sayings like those in the book of Proverbs and we find the occasional allegory, but the most effective and memorable of Jesus' parables are those which, like the parable of Nathan, convey a challenge.

There may be some doubt as to whether a parable is intended as an allegory. It is quite obvious in the parable of the wicked tenants in Mark chapter 12 that the different individuals, sent by the owner to demand his share of the produce, stand for the prophets sent by God to the people. Allegorical elements are intrinsic to the story. The same is surely true of the parable of the

sower, in which different receptions of the preaching of the
gospel are illustrated. Christian interpreters have, however,
sometimes gone to unwarranted lengths in the interpretation of
parables. For St Augustine the good Samaritan is Christ, the
man who fell among thieves is Adam, and the innkeeper is St
Paul. These are only three elements of his elaborate allegorical
treatment of the parable. Such interpretations seem excessive,
but they are rooted in a commitment to deriving the maximum
spiritual nourishment from the text. The interpreter, as indeed
the reader and the preacher, is called to discover the meanings
of the text. This is not always easy, for parables may be like riddles.
They may be enigmatic. There is always more to discover. The
parables of Jesus are understandably treasured and much loved.
They communicate simply and powerfully, but they might also
confuse.

Mark's collection of parables
Various short sayings, in which an image is used to illustrate a
situation, can be discovered early on in Mark. In chapter 2 Jesus
speaks of sinners as needing a doctor, of his presence as that of a
bridegroom at a wedding, of the need for a new garment and
new wineskins. Answering the scribes' accusations in chapter 3,
that he performs exorcisms in league with Satan, he evokes the
images of a divided kingdom, a divided household and of the
plundering of a strong man's house. A more substantial collection of parable material is to be found in chapter 4, both short
sayings and the more familiar story-parables.

We should not imagine that Jesus taught all the parables
found in Mark chapter 4 on one occasion. Parables would have
been a major component of early Christian preaching about
Jesus. It is the evangelist who has collected the parables together
and constructed this section of teaching in parables. It begins
solemnly with Jesus teaching a huge crowd from the boat. He
then teaches the twelve in private with some rather difficult
words about the purpose of parables. (Mark 4:11-12) As the
chapter continues Jesus seems to be addressing the crowd again.

The parable of the sower is given first place. 'Listen! Look at the sower going out to sow!' (Mark 4:3) This first image is a familiar one for Jesus' listeners. In Galilee people lived from the land and others from fishing in the Sea of Galilee. Wheat and barley sown in the autumn would produce a crop before the fierce heat of summer. Though ploughing was done with the help of animals, sowing was done by one man scattering seed. The parable stresses that the seed is scattered in all directions with a certain lack of care. It stresses the different receptions of the seed, which falls by the path, on rocky ground, among thorns. The climax comes with the abundance of the harvest reaped from the good ground. Farmers would be fortunate to derive a five-fold harvest from the seed sown. In this parable the seed produces thirty, sixty, and one hundred times the amount sown. (Mark 4:8) Such amounts were inconceivable. The story is of no ordinary sowing and no ordinary harvest. This parable is one of a few which the gospel tradition itself interprets as allegories. Jesus explains in detail the different receptions given to the seed, which is the word of the preaching.

It may well be that the explanation of the parable found in Mark 4:13-20 owes something to early preachers' experience of the various reactions to the gospel. They knew how the seed of the gospel sown in people's heart could be removed by the temptation of evil, just as the seed was devoured by birds from beside the path. They knew that the faith of believers might grow enthusiastically only to be scorched by trials and persecutions, just as the seedlings on rocky ground were burnt up by the sun. They knew that commitment to the gospel could be choked by the cares, riches and cravings of life, just as the young growth was strangled by thorns. But the preachers of the gospel were also aware of the extraordinary effects of the preaching. Where the seed found fertile soil it increased and multiplied in an astounding way. The parable of the sower, while describing failure and infidelity, gives the greatest emphasis to the triumph of the word in the hearts of steadfast believers. The generosity of the sower, despite risks and losses, produces an extraordinary harvest.

In Mark's collection of parables in chapter 4 Jesus then re-
verts to brief sayings, such as we met in Mark chapter 2. What
does a person do with a lamp? It is not to be hidden under a
measure or under a bed. It is placed on a stand to bring light to
hidden places. The light of the preaching here in Mark 4:21 is
just one use of the image of light. For Matthew the disciples
themselves will be lights. (Matthew 5:14) John applies the symbol to Jesus. (John 8:12) The saying about the measure in Mark
4:24 seems best interpreted in reference to judging and being
judged. It reappears with this meaning in the Sermon on the
Mount. (Matthew 7:2) The following verse never fails to make
an impact. 'The one who has will be given more. From the one
who has not, even what he has will be taken away.' (Mark 4:25)
This saying is reported by Matthew and Luke and used again in
Matthew's parable of the talents and Luke's parable of the
pounds. As far as a person's human and spiritual gifts are concerned, the rich get richer and the poor get poorer. The illogicality
of the second part of the saying gives it the alluring quality of a
riddle. How can one who has nothing lose what he has? Yet the
saying conveys an undeniable truth. Once again the underlying
theme is that of growth. We either grow or decline. We cannot
stay the same.

After these challenging short sayings of Jesus, we come to
two parables of the kingdom, parables in which the situation
described teaches something about the coming of the kingdom.
The first of these, the parable of the seed growing secretly, is
found only in Mark. (Mark 4:26-29) Like the parable of the
sower, it is a parable of growth. But the emphasis is different.
Both parables point to the triumph of the seed which is the
word, but in this parable the focus is on the secret way in which
the seed inexorably produces a harvest. The man sows the seed
but he knows nothing of the secret processes of growth. This
parable is clearly not an allegory. It is the whole process of mysterious, irreversible growth, not the individual stages of development, which is the focus of the parable. A second kingdom
parable is found in all three synoptic gospels. The mustard seed,

smallest of all seeds, grows into a great tree, which provides shelter for the birds of the air. (Mark 4:30-32) The emphasis here is on the contrast between insignificant beginnings and surprising growth. These two parables of the kingdom point to its mystery and to its assured success. They are images of the growth of the Christian community with a power not its own. While the popularity of the image of the mustard seed is understandable, it is more difficult to explain why only Mark preserves the parable of the seed growing secretly. Perhaps the detailed account of the germination and growth of the seed was thought to have allegorical significance. This apparently difficult parable was then disregarded by Matthew and Luke.

Mark concludes his collection of parables in chapter 4 with a general statement about Jesus' parables. Jesus uses parables to teach the crowd, but explains his teaching to the disciples while they are alone. (Mark 4:33-34) A similar but more difficult statement of Jesus in 4:11-12 seems to reflect the fact that the parables need explanation and may be misunderstood. True, they are designed to express truths about life in the kingdom, but there is always need for the listener to decipher the meaning. 'Let the one who has ears to hear listen,' says Jesus. (Mark 4:9, 4:23) Jesus was aware that the message of a prophet, of one who speaks the truth of God, will not always be heeded. He was aware of the difficulties of the great prophets of Israel. In particular the failure of the prophet Isaiah to turn minds and hearts back to the God of Israel seems to have been a yardstick for Jesus. In the difficult words in 4:11-12 Jesus quotes from the story of Isaiah's call. (Isaiah 6:9-10) It is important to realise that this story was part of the tradition about the prophet written down by his disciples. It is written as a record of his preaching ministry and its difficulties. The prophet is instructed by God to harden hearts, to close minds. These verses of the story are often quoted in the New Testament to show that God fully expected the lack of response, the hard hearts and closed minds, which the preaching of Jesus and of his followers encountered. The parables delivered to the crowds, with their riddles and challenges, are presented as achieving such a result. Those outside the group of believers are given only parables, for they do not have open eyes, open ears, open hearts and minds. It is the true disciples who will understand the mystery of the kingdom. (4:11-12) Despite failures and setbacks the seed sown by the sower will triumph.

The use of the words from Isaiah chapter 6 by the gospel writers is not easy to understand. It speaks of God's overriding providence in all that goes on in the preaching of Jesus and his disciples. God is aware that the message will often fall on deaf ears, and the enigmatic nature of the parables is understood to provoke this. But it is also true that the parables remain the most effective teaching tool of Jesus and his disciples. Many will hear and will respond. The power of the parables will again be apparent when, in later chapters, we consider the parables found in Matthew and in Luke.

CHAPTER 4

Rejection and the Journey to Jerusalem

Rejection by his own

In what we have seen so far of the gospel records of Jesus there have been some similarities between Jesus and Israel's prophets. Jesus, like the prophets, was called to preach. Jesus, like the prophets, gathered disciples. Jesus also shared the prophetic fate of misunderstanding and rejection. In Mark chapter 2 we saw the first reports of conflicts between Jesus and the religious authorities of his day. Jesus was viewed with disapproval because he shared meals with sinners, because he and his disciples did not practise fasting, and because they were judged to violate the sabbath. In Mark 3:6 there is the first reference to plots against Jesus. After his healing of the man with the withered hand on the sabbath day 'the Pharisees went out and immediately plotted against him with the Herodians how they might destroy him.' (Mark 3:6) Religious and political people banded together against this prophet. The fate of a prophet is rarely a happy one. The greatest of Israel's prophets, Elijah, Isaiah and Jeremiah, had to tolerate misunderstanding and even persecution.

Mark gives clearest emphasis to the rejection of Jesus in the Galilee ministry when Jesus visits Nazareth, his home town. Mark and Matthew place the story well within their accounts of the Galilee ministry. (Mark 6:1-6; Matthew 13:53-58) Luke, for reasons we shall examine in a later chapter, places his rather different account of the visit of Jesus to Nazareth at the very beginning of the ministry. (Luke 4:16-30)

Mark has already stated in chapter 1 that Jesus came from Nazareth, a hill village some fifteen miles away from the Sea of Galilee. There is no doubt, therefore, that he intends us to under-

stand Jesus' return to his home as a return to Nazareth. The reception of Jesus by the people in the synagogue of Nazareth is
similar to that given him on his visit to the synagogue in
Capernaum. They are impressed by his teaching, but in this
story the mood quickly changes.

A series of questions are thrown up against him. The tone is
negative and carping. 'Where does this man get all this?' (Mark
6:2) How does this local man come by such wisdom, and such
extraordinary power to heal? They know well who he is, yet the
account continues with more rhetorical questions. 'Isn't he the
carpenter, the son of Mary?' (Mark 6:3)

The fundamental stumbling block against their accepting
Jesus is his origin in their very village. Mark says that 'they were
scandalised because of him.' (Mark 6:3) They took offence and
could not accept him. He means that Jesus' common origins,
that he was a carpenter, that his family was from their village,
became an obstacle, a stumbling block (Greek *skandalon*), to their
acceptance of him on his return. There is a firm tradition that
Jesus practised the trade of a carpenter, which would involve
making furniture and perhaps even ploughs and yokes.
Matthew alters Mark's text and refers to Jesus as 'the son of the
carpenter'. (Matthew 13:55) It seems that Matthew considers
such a trade inappropriate for Jesus, the prophet and teacher.
The reference to Jesus as 'son of Mary' suggests that Joseph is no
longer alive. The reference to brothers and sisters of Jesus still
gives rise to debate and disagreement. (Mark 6:3) Christians
from the earliest centuries have believed that the mother of Jesus
had no further children after Jesus. The brothers and sisters
mentioned in this text have traditionally been understood as
cousins. This is the normal understanding of the text among
Catholics. Given the very ordinariness of Jesus, the people of
Nazareth cannot regard him as a prophet sent by God. For
Mark, as for the other synoptic gospels, rejection at Nazareth
prepares us for rejection by the people of Israel as a whole.

Jesus alludes to the fate of the prophets. 'A prophet is only
rejected in his own town, by his own relatives and in his own

house.' (Mark 6:4) Jesus the prophet faces the fate of a prophet. As the ministry progresses Jesus foresees not only rejection, but execution. Jesus will not be the only prophet in the gospel story to be put to death.

The death of John the Baptist

In the synoptic gospels John the Baptist is already in prison when Jesus begins his preaching. The fourth gospel provides a somewhat different account and suggests Jesus worked in association with the Baptist and his disciples. (John 3:22-24) Only Mark and Matthew give a report of the death of the Baptist.

Mark and Matthew take advantage of an interlude in the gospel story, when Jesus sends out the disciples to preach and heal, to insert the story of the martyrdom of John. (Mark 6:17-29; Matthew 14:3-12) The Jewish historian Josephus confirms that the Baptist died by execution at the command of Herod Antipas, son of Herod the Great, and tetrarch of Galilee. According to Josephus, Antipas had John killed because he advocated rebellion. The gospels on the other hand state that John was executed due to the displeasure of Herodias, Antipas' second wife. John had reproved Antipas because he had abandoned his first wife and had taken the wife of one of his brothers. There is some uncertainty concerning the precise identity of this brother of Antipas, which is not surprising due to the complicated nature of family relationships among the Herods. Herod the Great had a total of ten wives. Josephus and Mark seem to disagree on the location of John's imprisonment and execution. Mark implies this was Galilee, while Josephus locates the events in the southern territories of Herod Antipas, at Machaerus, to the east of the Dead Sea.

The gospels have elaborated the historical record, possibly using material from the Elijah traditions. John has already been presented as a new Elijah when Mark spoke of his ministry of baptism and preaching of repentance. He even had him wear the same kind of clothes that Elijah wore. It is, therefore, quite plausible that the tradition concerning John's death was filled out by borrowing from the stories of Elijah. Just as the weak king of Israel, Ahab, was led astray by his pagan wife Jezebel in her opposition to the prophet Elijah, so was Antipas manipulated by his wife Herodias to bring about the elimination of John, the new Elijah. In both stories it is the women who take the lead against the prophets of God. Their husbands weakly collude. It is worth noting, however, that whereas Mark states that Herodias wanted to kill John, Matthew reports that Antipas himself desired John's death. (Matthew 14:5) Perhaps he is pointing out that Herod Antipas is no different from his father Herod the Great, who sought the death of the infant Jesus in Matthew chapter 2.

Why has Mark given such prominence to a story which does not even mention Jesus? John the Baptist is remembered above all as the prophet who baptised Jesus. Some gospel traditions, notably those in the first two chapters of Luke's gospel, go to great lengths to illustrate the relationship between John and the Messiah. Mark seems to do this by showing that as well as preaching, like Jesus, a message of repentance, John gave his life, like Jesus, as a witness to truth and justice. He did not hesitate to denounce the tetrarch's sins and suffered the consequences. Jesus' preaching of the kingdom will bring him to a similar fate. The early Christians would be aware that the prophets of Israel, and now John and Jesus, had suffered for their preaching. It was small wonder that they too as followers of Jesus would have to face persecution and even death.

Peter's faith

The opening chapters of the synoptic gospels give accounts of the Galilee ministry of Jesus. They recount his preaching, his miracles, and provide some record of controversies between Jesus and the religious authorities. The second major part of the story as told by Mark, and as adopted by Matthew and Luke, concerns the journey to Jerusalem. In these three gospels, Mark, Matthew and Luke, Jesus makes only one journey to Jerusalem during his public ministry. The evangelists have in fact gathered the traditions about Jesus' public activity into three sections: the Galilee ministry, the journey to Jerusalem, and the events in Jerusalem. This is a logical and literary arrangement and does not answer the historical question of how many times Jesus went to the holy city. It is much more likely that Jesus paid several visits.

The journey begins with a most significant incident reported in different ways by these three gospels. (Mark 8:27-33; Matthew 16:13-23; Luke 9:18-22) Jesus is in the region of Caesarea Philippi, a northern town, known in ancient times as Panias. It was renowned for its sanctuary of the Greek god Pan, the god of fields, feasts, flocks and shepherds. Visitors may still see the remains of the shrine to Pan. The sources of the Jordan river are close by. Philip the tetrarch, son of Herod the Great, rebuilt the town and renamed it, dedicating it to the Roman emperor Caesar Augustus. It thus became 'Philip's Caesarea'. It is a long way north of Jerusalem. The geographical distance symbolises the journey of preparation to be made by Jesus to the place of his death, and the challenge to the disciples to accompany him. As the gospels progress, each at its own pace, Jesus and his disciples approach Jerusalem. As they approach he will speak to them about his coming death.

But before the journey begins, in very deliberate fashion, Jesus puts a question to the disciples. The question is a gift for Christian preachers and catechists. Was such a question in fact asked by Jesus? It is so clearly a catechetical question that it may well have originated in the preaching of the early disciples about Jesus. Jesus asks the disciples: 'Who do people say I am?' (Mark 8:27) It seems a curious question until one remembers the multiplicity of beliefs among the Jews of Jesus' day concerning figures expected to come before the end of time.

Earlier in the gospel, Herod Antipas had speculated about the identity of Jesus. Is he John come back from the dead? Is he a new Elijah? Is he another prophet? (Mark 6:14-15) The disciples at Caesarea Philippi give similar answers to Jesus. Some people, they say, believe that Jesus is John the Baptist. Perhaps such people did not know that John had been executed at the command of Herod. They might have thought that such a great prophet had returned from the grave. The suggestion that Jesus might be Elijah would find its justification at the end of the book of Malachi, for Elijah was to return before the end of time. That Jesus might be a new prophet would fulfil expectations expressed in the book of Deuteronomy (18:18) that God would one day raise up a prophet like Moses. These answers are all inadequate, and it is Peter who will provide the right answer, declaring the faith of the Christian church. Peter answers by referring to another expectation of Jews of the time. Peter answers: 'You are the Messiah!' (Mark 8:29)

The Messiah question is a complex one. Not only were there multiple expectations about figures whom God might send to Israel. There was also a great diversity of beliefs concerning the Messiah. What precisely would be his role? How would he behave?

The messianic hope arose in the time of the monarchy of Israel. Once it was accepted that the people of Israel could have a king, that God could approve of such a move, the way was open to developing an ideology of the Messiah. The Hebrew concept of 'Messiah' becomes the Greek *christos*. Both terms mean 'anointed one'. The Messiah is God's chosen king, the guarantor of God's continuing solidarity. The foundation of such ideology comes in 2 Samuel chapter 7 where the tradition records the promise of God to David and his descendants for ever, from the mouth of the prophet Nathan. God promises solidarity to David and his sons. As time goes on the successors of David very rarely match up to the task of divinely appointed anointed ones who should promote justice and peace. They are for the most part not pleasing to God, as the books of 1 and 2 Kings record. Gradually hope of a future ideal Messiah is born. The fundamental features of such a king are, as portrayed in Isaiah, chapters 9 and 11, and in Psalm 72, that he will bring peace and justice to the world.

But what were the contemporary expectations of the Messiah

in Jesus' own day? What would Peter have been suggesting when he asserted that Jesus was the expected Messiah? Perhaps the most helpful clue comes from a first century BC document known as 'the Psalms of Solomon'. These psalms were attributed to Solomon, in the way that contemporary apocalyptic writings were attributed to great figures of the past, like Enoch and Daniel. The seventeenth psalm reflects the Roman takeover of Jerusalem in 63 BC, when the Roman general Pompey audaciously entered the holiest parts of the temple. The writer of this psalm prays for an end to the desecration of Jerusalem by pagan nations. A new son of David must come to remove the unrighteous rulers. This psalm develops in great detail ideas taken from the ideology of the Messiah in the prophets and in the psalms of the Old Testament. The idea that a coming Messiah would help Israel regain its independence was surely in people's minds. Other contemporary texts suggest other types of Messiah. The Essenes of the Qumran sect expected both a kingly and a priestly Messiah.

Peter's affirmation that Jesus is the Messiah, the Christ, is therefore open to a variety of meanings. This may well explain the strange reaction of Jesus in Mark 8:30. Jesus, says Mark, warned the disciples to speak to nobody about him. At any rate, this is the response given by Mark, and shared by Luke. Matthew too records Jesus' warning, but Matthew inserts at this point some significant words of Jesus to Peter.

Peter's declaration in Matthew 16:16 is a longer version of what was reported in Mark's gospel. Peter says to Jesus: 'You are the Messiah, the son of the living God!' This declaration is now a fuller profession of the faith of the early Christians. It echoes the opening title of Mark's gospel: Jesus is the Christ, and the Son of God. Such a development in Matthew's account enhances the faith of Peter and invites some kind of positive acknowledgement from Jesus. In Matthew's gospel alone Jesus commends Peter's God-given insight. It was not 'flesh and blood' which revealed this to Peter. God has enlightened him and revealed to him the truth about Jesus. (Matthew 16:17) Peter in his turn is given a task by Jesus to be the rock on which the community of believers is to be founded. (Matthew 16:18) There is a play here on the words for 'Peter' (Greek *Petros*) and the word for 'rock' (Greek *petra*). If the words were spoken originally in Aramaic the one word *kepha* signifies both Peter's new name 'Cephas' and 'rock'. The name given to him by Jesus suggests Peter's new role, a role appropriate to one who has faith.

Jesus goes on to speak of Peter receiving the keys of the kingdom of heaven. The different gospels give Peter pre-eminence over the other disciples in a variety of texts. John chapter 1 again records that Peter is given the name Cephas by Jesus. In Luke chapter 22 Peter is told that once he has overcome his own failure he is to strengthen his brothers. In the resurrection appearance in John chapter 21 Peter is instructed to shepherd the sheep. In this text in Matthew solemn words of commissioning are borrowed from the appointing of Eliakim as master of the king's palace which is narrated in Isaiah chapter 22. These words contribute to a developing understanding of the role of Peter and his successors in the church.

This text is important too in emerging ideas about the church, the community of disciples (Greek *ekklesia*). Only Matthew among the four evangelists uses the term. It denotes a gathering of believers, a new community. Matthew will use the word again to speak of the role of the community in matters of correction and discipline. (Matthew 18:17) Peter then is the rock of the believing community. Paul attributes such a role to Christ as foundation stone (1 Corinthians 3:11), and the book of Revelation sees the twelve foundation stones of God's city bearing the names of the twelve apostles. (Revelation 21:14) These different perspectives need not exclude each other. At this point in Matthew's gospel Peter's faith commitment is presented as a rock of support for believers. Earlier in the gospel, Matthew had shown the faith of the whole group of disciples as they acclaimed Jesus as Son of God. (Matthew 14:33)

The suffering Messiah

Mark treats Peter's declaration of faith in a different way. He does not develop Peter's role. He needs to clarify the Messiah issue. Jesus is obviously hesitant about Peter's claim that he is the Messiah. In fact from the very beginning of the gospel Jesus has shown a reluctance to be recognised with any kind of honorific title. He has shown a reluctance to be acclaimed when a healing has taken place. He rebukes the possessed and orders them not to reveal his identity. (Mark 1:34) He tells a leper to report his cure only to the priest, but public knowledge of it brings crowds flocking to Jesus. (Mark 1:45) Even Jairus and his wife are strangely told to tell no-one of their daughter's recovery. (Mark 5:43) This feature of the ministry of Jesus, sometimes referred to as the 'messianic secret', seems to be a genuine aspect of the ministry. Acclaim for his deeds could lead to acclaim as a messiah. Such acclaim could lead Jesus where he would not wish to go. Perhaps the clearest expression of the situation comes in John 6:15: 'Jesus, knowing that they would come to seize him and make him king, withdrew again to the hills by himself.'

This feature of the gospel story goes some way to clarifying Jesus' puzzling response to Peter's faith. But there is more. In contrast to popular ideas about the Messiah and his role, Jesus foresees for himself suffering and death. The evangelists deliberately juxtapose Peter's declaration that Jesus is the Messiah with Jesus' first statement about his suffering and death at the hands of others. The journey to Jerusalem is for Jesus a journey to the place of death. The journey for the disciples is a journey of struggling with the very idea of a suffering Messiah.

Jesus' first statement about his death provokes disbelief from the believing Peter. The one who had affirmed his faith in Jesus now challenges Jesus' words as ludicrous. While Luke omits any response from Peter or the others, Mark and Matthew give Peter's sharp reaction. It is Matthew who elaborates the scene more fully. As he, more than the other evangelists, had celebrated the faith statement of Peter, so now it is he who emphasises

Peter's rejection of the words of Jesus. 'May God forbid it, Lord. This must not happen to you.' (Matthew 16:22) Both Mark and Matthew record the stern rebuke of Jesus to Peter: 'Get behind me, Satan!' (Mark 8:33; Matthew 16:23) Messianic popularity, which can deflect Jesus from his prophetic witness, constitutes a temptation. It comes from Satan. As Satan offered popularity and power in the temptation story in the gospels of Matthew and Luke, so now an easier road offered by the first of the disciples is slammed by Jesus as a satanic suggestion. The dialogue between Jesus and Peter at this point emphasises Jesus' unwavering commitment to the way of God, and the difficulty Peter and the others will have in accepting the martyrdom of Jesus.

Matthew again offers us more in the final verses of the Caesarea Philippi scene. In Matthew alone, in the gospel in which Peter's faith has been praised as a gift of God, the rock-like Peter is now described as a stumbling block, an obstacle, a scandal (Greek *skandalon*). (Matthew 16:23) These contrasting images of the foundation stone and the stumbling block are reflections of the one person. Yes, people of faith provide support. Yes, they can be rock-like. But all leadership is tempted. All leadership struggles. The gospels will witness to this again most powerfully in Peter's denials, a tradition which is reported faithfully by all four gospels. The Peter of Matthew chapter 16 remains a strong symbol, a challenge both to faith and to honest acceptance of weakness. A remarkable parallel to the use of the images of 'rock' and 'stumbling block' can be tracked down in the first letter of Peter. Christ is the 'living stone' on which Christians may build. (1 Peter 2:4) But Christ is also 'a rock of stumbling' (Greek *petra skandalou*), for there will be those who refuse to believe. (1 Peter 2:8)

The evangelists Mark, Matthew and Luke each report three 'passion predictions' of Jesus (Mark 8:31, 9:31, 10:33-34 and parallels). This is a further feature of the editorial work of the evangelist Mark which Matthew and Luke have adopted. It is a most effective device to remind readers repeatedly of Jesus' commitment to the way of truth no matter what the consequences. It may well be that the words of Jesus have been elaborated in the tradition and edited, but it is eminently plausible that Jesus foresaw his own death. Such deep insight has been experienced by so many men and women who have foreseen the consequences of commitments to truth and justice. As the twentieth century ended, Oscar Romero was a fine reminder of this. Jesus' words contain not only foreboding, but also hope of resurrection. This feature too is surely an aspect of Jesus' own understanding. He trusted in the God of life who would receive him and raise him up.

A particular feature of these 'passion predictions' is that they mention specific groups who are involved in the arrest and condemnation of Jesus. The elders (Greek *presbyteroi*) are influential lay people who belonged to the Sanhedrin, the Jewish body which played an administrative and judicial role under the Romans, and before which Jesus appeared after his arrest. The chief priests are present and past high priests and members of high priestly families. Scribes had travelled to Galilee to investigate Jesus' ministry. They are experts on religion and the law. It should be noted that there is no mention of Pharisees here, nor is there in the trial of Jesus. The third passion prediction stresses the role of 'Gentiles' as the ones who torture and kill Jesus. (Mark 10:33) While the passion traditions of the gospels will direct guilt towards the Jews and away from the Romans, this speech seems to be more even-handed. Responsibility for the injustice of the death of Jesus cannot be attributed simply to one group. There was collusion in a deed which was both expedient and unjust.

One feature of these speeches is the frequent recurrence of the phrase 'son of man' (Greek *ho huios tou anthropou*) as Jesus speaks of his fate. This phrase occurs very frequently and almost exclusively on the lips of Jesus in all four gospels, but its meaning is difficult to establish. A great variety of theories have been proposed concerning its meaning. There seems no doubt that Jesus used this term to refer to himself. Clues to what he meant by it are to be found in the Old Testament. Jesus is fond of quoting words from Daniel 7:13 which include this phrase 'son of man' (Aramaic *bar enash*). We will examine his use of Daniel when we consider his preaching in Jerusalem in the next chapter of this book. The most prominent use of the phrase 'son of man' in the Old Testament is found in the book of Ezekiel. God constantly addresses the prophet as 'son of man'. The term stresses his divine calling and his vulnerability. For Jesus it is a humble way of referring to himself and his mission in all its features, but primarily in the sense of danger to his life which gradually increases. There is some evidence in Jewish writings that teachers used the term of themselves. In any case, Jesus' use is a clear allusion to his prophetic role, his being called by the Father, and to his acceptance of vulnerability. It is most appropriately used, therefore, when Jesus speaks of his coming death.

In the gospel of Mark the three passion predictions punctuate the journey to Jerusalem. On the second and third occasions when Jesus speaks of his coming death, the disciples' reaction resembles Peter's response at Caesarea Philippi. The disciples in Mark's gospel do not understand and are afraid to ask. (Mark 9:32) The evangelist cleverly follows the second and third predictions with arguments of the disciples about their relative positions as followers of Jesus. Like Peter, the other disciples too find the notion of a suffering Messiah, and of a suffering and dying Jesus, too painful. They turn to more comfortable topics. Matthew and Luke too speak of the disciples' distress and difficulty in accepting the words of Jesus. (Matthew 17:23; Luke 9:45, 18:34) Mark's journey to Jerusalem takes us from chapter 8 to the end of chapter 10. The passion predictions are placed alongside Jesus' continuing teaching on discipleship and two miracle stories, the healing of the epileptic boy and of the blind man of Jericho, Bartimaeus. Matthew and Luke considerably augment the amount of material in the journey narrative, adding more of the traditional teaching of Jesus. All three synoptic gospels place the strange and wonderful story of the transfiguration of Jesus between the first and second passion predictions.

The transfiguration

The narrative of the transfiguration is the most complex of gospel stories. At the same time it offers extraordinary christological and catechetical richness. It is found in all three synoptic gospels. (Mark 9:2-8; Matthew 17:1-8; Luke 9:28-36) The fourth gospel omits the story. In this gospel there is a sense that Jesus is always transfigured. His glory is perceptible throughout. We are well accustomed to detecting the catechetical aspects of a gospel story and seeing how the gospel traditions build on historical events of the life of Jesus, but to distinguish the historical and catechetical levels in the story of the transfiguration is no easy task. There are three parts to the story: the transformation in Jesus' appearance, the appearance of Elijah with Moses, and the cloud and heavenly voice. Each part presents difficulties of interpretation. Are we dealing primarily with a story about Jesus, or with a vision of the three disciples? The difficulties are such that some have suggested that this is really an appearance of the risen Christ and that it has been misplaced in the gospel story. Such an explanation is unlikely, since the stories of the appearances of the risen Christ do not stress his glorious transformation as the story of the transfiguration does. What we are dealing with here is an event of Jesus' ministry which so struck the disciples that it became the basis for extensive christological and catechetical development.

The key to understanding the transfiguration story lies in its immediate context. It follows directly from the first passion prediction of Jesus and his subsequent words to the disciples about carrying their cross as he is to carry his. (Mark 8:34) How are they to find the courage to do this? How are they to discover such strength? The chosen disciples will see Jesus transfigured as he seeks his God on the mountain. Their experience of the change in Jesus is the historical kernel of the transfiguration tradition. The human Jesus, who by now is convinced that in Jerusalem he will face rejection, abandonment, arrest, torture and crucifixion, meets God in prayer and is profoundly changed.

That Jesus should ascend to a high place to pray is not un-common or strange. The gospels all speak of Jesus' need for soli-tude and his retreating to desert or mountain places. (Mark 1:35; John 6:15) This scenario of a prophet meeting God on a moun-tain recalls similar scenes from Old Testament tradition. Moses and Elijah both sought God on the holy mountain. Elijah needed strength to return to confront again the Israelite king Ahab and his evil wife Jezebel. The Moses tradition in addition contains the extraordinary report of the transformation of the face of Moses through his encounter with God. (Exodus 34:29) This is the starting point for a retelling of the story of Jesus on the mountain on the model of Moses on Sinai.

The strange reference in Mark and Matthew (Mark 9:2; Matthew 17:1) to a period of six days reflects a similar reference in Exodus 24:16. After six days Moses ascends the mountain to meet God. Peter, James and John are with Jesus, while Moses was ac-companied by the elders of Israel for part of the journey up the mountain. (Exodus 24:1) The transformation in Jesus' appearance is presented in a variety of ways. Luke 9:29 significantly speaks of a change in the appearance of the face of Jesus. Both Mark and Matthew say 'he was transfigured' (Greek *metemorphothe*), indicat-ing a God-given transformation. Luke's account suggests an early understanding that what happened to Jesus on the mountain was similar to what had happened long ago to Moses on Sinai.

At this point the transfiguration story takes another step in its evolution. The transformation in the appearance of Jesus seemed to be a foretaste of the glory of the resurrection. Contemporary apocalyptic tradition spoke of the glorious gar-ments worn by those who were raised to new life. The transform-ation in Jesus' appearance includes in all three synoptic gospels the radiance of his garments. The story now illustrates not only the new strength Jesus received from God, but also his future glory. Jesus now resembles not simply Moses who had seen God, but the saints who had been raised to the life of the resur-rection. This development in turn leads to another, the other-wise strange presence of two prophets who had survived death.

The appearance of Elijah with Moses builds on this new dimension of the story and confirms the focus on the risen life
which awaits Jesus after his cross. It is somewhat strange that
Moses, to whom clear allusion has already been made as the one
who was transformed by his encounter with God on Sinai,
should now appear with Jesus. The story shows a step by step
development. The strengthening of Jesus leads on to a contem-
plation of the glory of Jesus, at which point Elijah and Moses appear as two prophets who had, it was believed, themselves been
raised up to glory. Elijah is mentioned first by Mark. The stories
of this prophet end in 2 Kings chapter 2 as he is taken up in a
chariot by God. The tradition about Moses' death is less clear.
Deuteronomy chapter 34 affirms that no-one could find the
grave of Moses. The belief arose that he too had not died, but
that like Elijah he had been taken up to God. The two prophets
are seen with Jesus in a tableau. The life of glory given to Moses
and Elijah will be the life given to Jesus too.

Jesus who faces his death in Jerusalem is strengthened by
prayer to the Father on a high mountain. The disciples witness
the profound change in his appearance, which seems to be a
foretaste of the glory of the resurrection, the glory which Moses
and Elijah are believed to share. The various stages of the transfiguration story assert one fundamental message, that God
brings to the glory of transformed life those who live lives of
faithfulness. The message of resurrection, which is already
prominent in the book of Daniel and which lies at the heart of
the preaching about Jesus and at the climax of the gospel story,
is the fundamental truth being conveyed in the complex narrative.

Such an extraordinary build-up in the story deserves a fitting
conclusion. The cloud of God's presence is seen on the mountain.
As Moses entered the cloud to meet God on Sinai (Exodus
24:18), so now the three prophets are enveloped in cloud.
Finally, as at the baptism scene, God speaks. God speaks of the
Son in the words already found in the baptism tradition: 'This is
my beloved son!' But God adds: 'Listen to him!' The voice of

God once again testifies to Jesus. As God approved of the Son as he underwent John's baptism of repentance in solidarity with sinners, so now God approves of the Son who commits his energy and courage to travel the road to the place of death. The transfiguration story is a rich, profound, many-layered testimony to Jesus as the Son who comes to do God's will and to lead the way from death to the life of glory. This is the kind of Messiah God sends. The road to Jerusalem will be travelled.

CHAPTER 5

Symbolic Actions and Teaching in Jerusalem

The entry into Jerusalem

For Mark, as for Matthew and Luke, the arrival in Jerusalem represents a climax in Jesus' ministry. For these synoptic gospels this is the first arrival of the adult Jesus in the holy city. The journey section, with its reminders of the coming passion and death, brings us to Jerusalem, the city which kills the prophets. (Matthew 23:37; Luke 13:34) The section of these gospels dealing with the Jerusalem ministry of Jesus is likewise filled with pointers to the death of Jesus. Not one passage in Mark's chapters 11-13 is without some relevance to the Messiah's death. The section is dominated by symbolic actions indicating messianic awareness and coming catastrophe, and by confrontations with groups of opponents. The section ends with the apocalypse in Mark chapter 13, which speaks of the end-time events and urges steadfastness and readiness. Matthew and Luke adopt Mark's material, enriching it once again with their own additions.

By placing all the traditions of Jesus' Jerusalem ministry together, the synoptic gospels achieve an extraordinary impact. Jerusalem, the city conquered by David, now sees the Messiah for the first time. Jerusalem, the place where God dwells in the holy temple, sees the one who challenges the temple and its worship. Jerusalem, the place where prophets have confronted rulers, priests, scribes and false teachers, Jerusalem, which has persecuted and killed prophets, will now deal with Jesus.

The synoptic gospels indicate that Jesus comes to Jerusalem at the time of a feast. It becomes clear as Mark's narrative continues that the feast of Passover is approaching. (Mark 14:1) Great crowds would gather for the three pilgrimage feasts of Passover,

Weeks (Pentecost), and Tabernacles. At such times the occupying Romans would send extra troops from the garrison at
Caesarea Marittima to Jerusalem. They would be present in
large numbers in Jerusalem and would be particularly alert to
potential disturbances. There could be tensions between pilgrims from the country and the people of Jerusalem. Coming
from the northern region of Galilee with a reputation for powerful preaching and mighty deeds, Jesus might easily be caught up
in such tensions. It was a dangerous time for a prophet to speak
out in Jerusalem. Many thousands of visitors came to Jerusalem
so that some had to lodge in villages around the city, like Jesus
and his disciples who spent the nights in Bethany. (Mark 11:11)

All four gospels recount the entry of Jesus into Jerusalem in
the days before his death. (Mark 11:1-11; Matthew 21:1-11; Luke
19:28-40; John 12:12-19) The fourth gospel too presents it as an
event of significance even though Jesus has visited Jerusalem
before. The three synoptic gospels include reference to Jesus
sending out two disciples to commandeer a colt which he would
ride into the city. This is presented as an example of Jesus' fore-
knowledge of events, but more significantly it points towards
the messianic significance of the incident. A king is expected to
commandeer whatever he needs. These features of the story are
not present in John.

The essence of the incident can be explained by reference to
the prophet Zechariah. This prophet speaks of an entry of Sion's
king, who is humble and rides on an ass. Zechariah 9:9 is quoted
by Matthew and John. (Matthew 21:4-5; John 12:15) In Matthew's
gospel it is one example of the many texts which the evangelist
quotes directly in order to point out their fulfilment in events
surrounding Jesus. John points out that it was only later that the
disciples reflected on the incident and connected it to the passage from Zechariah. How are we to understand the account? It
is best to see it as a deliberate symbolic action by Jesus. It is an
acting out of the prophetic text to show a certain style of being
the Messiah. Jesus has already implicitly challenged views
about the Messiah. Here he seems to adopt one particular strand

of the various messianic understandings present in Judaism. Was the incident as impressive as the gospels make out? It would seem that any number of disciples coming with Jesus to Jerusalem might incite such acclaim. There would doubtless have been others among the pilgrims to Jerusalem who had witnessed Jesus' activities in Galilee. Matthew has a telling cry from those accompanying Jesus. In reply to enquiries about the identity of the man on the donkey, they shout: 'This is the prophet Jesus from Nazareth in Galilee'. (Matthew 21:11)

Matthew alone has the curious feature of the two disciples bringing two animals to Jesus. This seems due to a misinterpretation of Zechariah 9:9. The prophetic text uses customary Hebrew poetic repetition and states that the king will ride 'on an ass, and on a colt, the foal of an ass'. Poetic convention as well as common sense might have suggested that only one animal was intended. Matthew shows the disciples bringing two animals, and apparently preparing them both for Jesus to ride. (Matthew 21:7) The laying of garments and branches on the road suggests some kind of royal welcome. John alone has the crowd wave palms, which were associated with religious processions. (John 12:13)

All the evangelists except Luke report the cries of 'Hosanna!' The word originates from the Hebrew word meaning 'to save', but seems to have become a general cry of religious fervour. Psalm 118 is also quoted to proclaim blessings on pilgrims arriving in the holy city. But the words here are given a messianic addition. Mark has the crowd shout: 'Blessed is the coming kingdom of our father David!' (Mark 11:10) Similar messianic acclamations are found in the other gospels. There is a clear suggestion here of a messianic movement centred around Jesus. That such a demonstration was not universally welcomed is suggested by material in Luke and John. In Luke's gospel some Pharisees in the crowd urge Jesus to restrain the enthusiasm of his disciples. Jesus replies: 'I say to you, if these remain silent, the stones will cry out.' (Luke 19:40) John's gospel concludes the scene with people discussing the raising of Lazarus. The

Pharisees are concerned that 'the world is running after him'.
(John 12:19)

It seems then that we are concerned here with a symbolic action of Jesus, which may have been dramatised in different ways
as the tradition developed. Even a fairly restrained action of
Jesus could well have been taken over by the enthusiasm of the
pilgrim crowds. The scene has both religious and political connotations. A messiah of whatever type would threaten both the
religious and the political establishment. This action seems to
have provoked hostile reactions from some. The subsequent
prophetic actions of Jesus recorded in Mark and Matthew will
provoke further reaction.

Further symbolic acts

Mark has Jesus enter the temple briefly on his first visit to the
city. While Matthew presents Jesus as immediately driving out
the traders from the temple, Mark reports that Jesus first returned to pass the night at Bethany. (Mark 11:11) Mark then presents two more symbolic actions. Approaching the city on the
second day, Jesus sees a fig tree which is in leaf and has not yet
produced fruit. (Mark 11:13) The incident reported here is a
clear case of a symbolic action. Luke does not record Jesus'
curse. It may be that his parable of the fruitless fig tree is designed to replace what might be considered an act of anger on
Jesus' part. (Luke 13:6-9) The fig tree with no fruit symbolises for
Jesus the failure of the people of Israel to respond to God's call.
Similar imagery is found among the prophets of the Old
Testament. Isaiah speaks of the pampered vine which produces
only sour grapes. (Isaiah 5:1-7) In Jeremiah chapter 8 God finds
no grapes on the vine and no figs on the fig tree. By contrast, in
Hosea chapter 9 God speaks of Israel's early love as like finding
grapes in the wilderness or early fruit on the fig tree. Such imagery clearly lies behind Jesus' curse of the fig tree on the road to
Jerusalem. In Mark's gospel the tree will have withered by the
next day, while Matthew stresses the power of Jesus in the immediate withering of the tree. (Matthew 21:19) The focus of the

passage is not on Jesus' power to curse, but on the judgement awaiting those who produce no fruit. The parable of the wicked tenants will take up the theme again as the Jerusalem ministry continues.

Mark places the driving out of the traders from the temple between the two parts of the story of the cursed tree. (Mark 11:12-21) He had used a similar technique with the stories of the raising of Jairus' daughter and the healing of the woman with the haemorrhage in Mark chapter 5. Both Matthew and Luke present the expulsion of the traders as happening on Jesus' first arrival in the city. Luke reduces the violence of Jesus and presents a brief summary of his actions. (Luke 19:45) John records the tradition at the beginning of the gospel and uses it to relate the destruction of the temple to the death of Jesus. (John 2:13-22) For John, this action of Jesus, like the entry into Jerusalem, feeds the disciples' reflection so that they discover deeper meanings.

Mark's account gives a full description of Jesus' violence. (Mark 11:15-16) Merchants are driven out. Tables and seats are overturned. The sellers and buyers no doubt provided animals and offerings for sacrificial worship. Money-changers made available the coinage necessary for the temple tax. The reason for Jesus' disruption of this seemingly necessary trade is to be found in the combined quotation from Isaiah and Jeremiah: 'My house shall be called a house of prayer for all the nations. You have made it a den of robbers.' While the quotation from Isaiah 56:7 seems to defend the right of Gentiles to pray in the court of the Gentiles, the very place which it seems the merchants had taken over, the words from Jeremiah 7:11 suggest some dishonesty of dealings within the temple, perhaps in the form of exploitation of captive customers. There is a deeper symbolism here, however. The latest of the prophets had spoken of the purification of the temple. Malachi announced that after the arrival of a messenger, the Lord would come suddenly to purge the temple. (Malachi 3:1-3) Zechariah furthermore had claimed that in the final days traders would be removed from the temple. (Zechariah 14:21) By his cursing of the tree and disruption in the temple, Jesus evokes the words of the prophets, pointing to judgement and to the time of the end.

The chief priests and scribes are now the ones to react. For Mark they begin in earnest to plot the destruction of Jesus. (Mark 11:18) It seems that this incident in the temple provided the religious leaders with sufficient pretext to take action against him. In John's gospel the intensification of plots to destroy Jesus is linked to the raising of Lazarus. (John 11:53) The events of entering Jerusalem, cursing of the tree and disrupting temple business could easily be used as a basis for the accusations reported to have been made in Jesus' trial before the Sanhedrin, that he claimed kingly status and that he took a stand against the Jerusalem temple. As the narrative in Mark and the other synoptic gospels proceeds, there are attempts to entrap Jesus and further controversies.

Confrontation and questioning

Mark's narrative continues with a challenge to Jesus from the chief priests, scribes and elders, those mentioned together as the enemies of Jesus in Mark 8:31, who will reappear at his trial. Jesus is required to provide an explanation of his behaviour: 'By what authority do you do these things?' (Mark 11:28) The question probably refers to the symbolic actions of Jesus earlier in the chapter, and particularly to the disturbance in the temple. Jesus cleverly avoids answering by challenging them in his turn concerning their attitude to John the Baptist. A direct answer to their question would do nothing to challenge their blindness. Jesus counters their question with a challenge of their whole attitude. The response of the leaders, that they do not know (Mark 11:33), reveals a deeper truth about their unwillingness to listen and unwillingness to learn. It is indeed true that they do not know.

The tension is heightened in all three synoptic gospels by the important parable which follows. Mark 12:1-12 contains the only substantial parable recorded by Mark outside chapter 4, where he had gathered some parables of Jesus together. It clearly belongs during the Jerusalem ministry for it is very confrontational. Matthew inserts before it the parable of the two sons, which is also set in a vineyard and conveys a similarly blunt challenge. (Matthew 21:28-32)

The parable of the wicked tenants is without doubt allegorical. It is built on the song of the vineyard in Isaiah chapter 5, but use of the Isaiah material is condensed into the first verse of Jesus' new parable. The owner of the vineyard showed painstaking concern for his vineyard. At the appropriate time he expected the tenants to provide his share of the produce. The messengers he sends are badly treated by them and they continue to withhold what is due. The parable combines the theme of not producing fruit with the added theme of the rejection of God's messengers. The vineyard owner finally sends his son. The tenants seize him, kill him and throw him out of the vineyard.

Some consider that the final part of the story which speaks of the rejection of the son may have been added by Christian preachers to complete the full story of Israel's rejection of its prophets. There seems to be no reason, however, why it could not have been the dramatic climax of the parable as told by Jesus himself.

The parable includes a further interesting feature in the punishment of the wicked tenants and the giving of the vineyard to new tenants. (Mark 11:9) This final section of the story may be better considered as a Christian addition. It reflects the Jewish people's rejection of the Messiah and their replacement by new people. Matthew's version emphasises this feature by his addition: 'The kingdom of God will be taken from you and given to a people (Greek *ethnos*) who produce its fruits.' (Matthew 21:43)

The quotation from Psalm 118, that the stone rejected by the builders has become the corner-stone, is even more likely to be a Christian addition. The psalm text is a popular one in the New Testament with its use of the image of the stone for Christ, the rejected Messiah. In addition to its use in this parable, it is found in Acts 4:11 in a speech of Peter and in 1 Peter 2:7. Luke's version of the parable develops the use of the stone image in similar fashion to 1 Peter. It becomes a stone to stumble over and a stone which crushes. (Luke 20:18)

All three synoptic evangelists agree that the point of the parable is plain to the listeners. But the authorities are afraid to take action against Jesus for fear of the people who hold him to be a prophet. The religious authorities need more evidence against Jesus. Luke elaborates the plan of the scribes and chief priests. They send spies who pretend to be honest but who intend to catch him out in what he says so that he can be denounced to the Roman governor. (Luke 20:20) This is precisely the intention which lies behind the first question put to Jesus.

'Should we pay the poll-tax to Caesar?' ask the Pharisees and Herodians. (Mark 12:14) The unholy alliance of Pharisees who were closer to the people and Herodians who were willing to collaborate with the occupying power, suggests collusion of unlikely collaborators in common opposition to this dangerous prophet. Mark has already suggested during the Galilee ministry that representatives of these two groups had joined forces in plotting to destroy Jesus. (Mark 3:6) Their question now is an obvious trap. Any encouragement not to pay the taxes enforced by the Romans in Jerusalem and Judaea, where they governed directly, could be interpreted as seditious. Unquestioning acceptance of Roman taxation, on the other hand, would show no sympathy with the just grievances of the people. As with the earlier challenge about his authority, so here Jesus counters the question with a question. He gives no simplistic answer to their simplistic question. To give to both Caesar and to God what each is due is an obvious but challenging solution. The curious conclusion that they were amazed at his reply strengthens the impression of a battle of wits between Jesus and his opponents. (Mark 12:17)

The Sadducees also challenge Jesus. (Mark 12:18-23) They raise an issue about which there was disagreement in the Judaism of Jesus' day. Speculation about the after-life had continued throughout the Old Testament period and clear statements of belief in the resurrection of the dead emerged in apocalyptic writings. The Sadducees, a priestly faction accustomed to collaboration with foreign occupation, maintained opposition to this belief. They took their stand on the books of the Law, the first five books of the Old Testament, and were reluctant to adopt new insights. Jesus, who preaches the coming of the kingdom of God, has implicitly and explicitly pointed to the life beyond death, most dramatically in the prediction of his own death. Jesus' reply to the clever question of the Sadducees urges them to look again at the scriptures they revere to realise that the God of Moses is the God of the living. The Sadducees' attempt to trap Jesus underlines priestly opposition to Jesus.

These questions show Jesus in dialogue with the teachers of Judaism. He has outwitted those who come to him in groups, the Pharisees, the Herodians, and the Sadducees. There is a subtle change in the third and final question put to Jesus.

An individual scribe asks a genuine question of Jesus. (Mark 12:28) There is here no trace of animosity but rather a genuine search for truth and enlightenment. The dialogue between Jesus and the Jewish scribe illustrates the tragic truth that there exists a most profound accord between Jesus and his contemporaries, and between Judaism and Christianity. To the scribe's question about the greatest commandment of the law, Jesus replies by quoting Deuteronomy chapter 6. The text presents the Jewish prayer known as the *Shema:* 'Listen, Israel, the Lord our God is one Lord, and you shall love the Lord your God with all your heart, and with all your soul, and with all your mind, and with all your strength.' (Mark 12:29-30) Jesus then quotes the commandment to love one's neighbour as oneself from the Holiness Code in Leviticus chapter 19. Asked about the one greatest commandment, Jesus combines two commandments as one. Love of God and love of neighbour are the two lungs which give life to Jews and Christians alike. They provide a summary of the Law. Jesus might have been expected to quote the 'ten words', the ten commandments so significant in Jewish and Christian tradition, some of which he had quoted to the rich young man in Mark chapter 10. For Jesus, it seems, when there is true love of God and love of neighbour, all is said. Jesus' genius places together these two laws of Moses. The fourth gospel will add the new commandment, in which love of neighbour is modelled on Jesus' own love. (John 15:12) The same tradition will once again place love of God and love of neighbour together. They are inseparable. (1 John 4:21)

While Matthew reports Jesus' reply to the scribe in a similar fashion, Luke describes the scribe as a lawyer, and places the encounter earlier in the gospel story as the introduction to the parable of the good Samaritan. Luke makes a significant change. In his version Jesus makes the lawyer answer his own question so that the lawyer recites the two commandments as one. (Luke 10:26-27) Is Luke perhaps reluctant to have Jesus interrogated? Or is this simply another way of presenting the profound accord between Jesus and his contemporaries?

Mark continues the dialogue between Jesus and the scribe. With wonderful insight Mark has the scribe repeat Jesus' teaching in perfect agreement. Jesus then says to the scribe: 'You are not far from the kingdom of God.' (Mark 12:34) It is extraordinary that at the point of escalating tension and growing danger to Jesus' life there should be such a moment of profound agreement and mutual respect between two seekers after what is true and what is good. Mark closes the series of questions put to Jesus with the statement, 'and no one dared to question him further.' (Mark 12:34) There is a poignancy in the agreement between Jesus and the scribe and a challenge. Should religious dialogue be the airing of entrenched positions taken by groups who set out to uncover one another's mistakes and failings? Or should it be the voicing of the convictions of those who have reflected on their traditions and live by their truth?

No further question is put to Jesus once he has finished his dialogue with the scribe. It is now the time for Jesus to teach. Mark emphasises this new stage by reminding us that Jesus is teaching in the temple. (Mark 12:35) He has responded to the challenges of the teachers of Judaism. Now Jesus challenges them in his turn.

Final teaching in the temple

The first piece of teaching from Jesus after the questioning has ended concerns underlying speculations about Jesus' messianic identity. (Mark 12:35-37) The text can easily confuse, especially if we focus exclusively on what David is supposed to have said about a future Messiah. How can such a lord be a son of David? The key to understanding here is to recall Jesus' constant reluctance to be involved in messianic speculation. These verses are simply a further challenge to fixed ideas in Judaism about the identity of the Messiah. God is not bound by human expectations and agendas. The Messiah sent by God will come as God wills, and will aim to do God's will. As always, Jesus is concerned not with stereotypes and fixed agendas. His concern is with values, the values emerging from faith and the call to love.

His challenge to fixed ideas leads on to a challenge to fixed ways based on false values. Here Jesus criticises the self-congratulating behaviour of the scribes. Both this section and the subsequent words about the poor widow are triggered by the people Jesus observes going about their business in the temple precincts. The scribes, the experts on religious law and among Jesus' principal opponents, parade in their robes to be greeted obsequiously by others. (Mark 12:38) They love the places of honour. They love status. They make lengthy show of prayers. These are the things they display, but Jesus' criticism goes straight to their lack of love. They are the ones who swallow the property of widows. Their ostentatious parade is sad. Their wickedness to the weak is to be condemned. (Mark 12:40) Mark is brief and restrained in this section. At this point Matthew will insert his prolonged diatribe of Jesus against the scribes and the Pharisees, a section which may owe something of its vehemence to worsening relations between the Jewish religious authorities and Matthew's community. (Matthew 23:1-36) Luke will include some of these traditions at an earlier point when Jesus has been invited to dine with a critical Pharisee. (Luke 11:37-52) But Luke preserves Mark's contrasting pictures of the parading scribes and the poor widow at the same point in the Jerusalem ministry. (Luke 20:45-21:4)

While the scribes devour the property of widows ,the widow
gives 'her whole life' (Greek *holon ton bion autes*). (Mark 12:44)
The teachers give false teaching in their outward show and in
their private evil lives. The widow gives a very different lesson.
Mark introduces this final piece of teaching of Jesus in the temple in solemn fashion. Jesus calls the disciples to him to speak to
them. He begins with the solemn words 'Amen, I say to you'.
(Mark 12:43) But the widow becomes the teacher. She embodies
the commands of love. She incarnates the gospel. She presents in
her action what Jesus will soon do, giving his whole life as she
gave hers. Religious leaders may sometimes wear long robes.
They may recite lengthy prayers and sit in the places of honour.
True testimony however must be the witness of their lives.

Jesus' apocalypse
The final piece of teaching of Jesus in Mark's gospel concerns the
future and the end. (Mark 13) It is of significance that in Mark
and in Matthew the last substantial address by Jesus to the disciples considers these themes. Matthew will add three related sections to his presentation of this material. (Matthew 24-25) This
special material of Matthew will be considered later. Luke gives
his version of the material about the end in chapter 21, but has
further teaching of Jesus in the context of the Last Supper. (Luke
22) John has an extended final discourse of Jesus. (John 13-17)
The final words of Jesus in each gospel have special significance
for each evangelist and have been compared to the final words
delivered by important Old Testament figures before they die.
Jacob speaks to his sons in Genesis chapter 49. Moses addresses
the tribes in Deuteronomy chapter 33. Jesus' discourse in Mark
chapter 13 is both a farewell discourse and an apocalypse.

We have already seen that fundamental to the preaching of
Jesus in the synoptic gospels is the apocalyptic concept of the
kingdom of God. It is presented in the book of Daniel as Daniel
looks to the final intervention of God. (Daniel 2:44) It would be
most surprising if Jesus had not used ideas and expressions
from the same book when speaking of the future and of the end.

An 'apocalypse' sets out to provide a 'revelation'. The Greek term *apokalypsis* is an exact equivalent of the Latin word *revelatio*. In the last centuries before Christ, apocalyptic literature developed from origins in the writings of the prophets and recorded secret visions of the future and the end. It was particularly linked to situations of persecution, such as the oppression of Jewish religion by the Seleucid rulers of Judah in the second century BC. Apocalyptic writing was cryptic. It could be understood only by the initiated. It featured bizarre animals and provided complex calculations of times. The fundamental message was one of hope. God's final triumph over evil and the establishment of the kingdom of God were assured.

Jesus' words, assembled in Mark chapter 13, consider future threats and dangers and proclaim the final gathering together of God's people. The evangelist has used various pieces of traditional teaching. It is possible that the material has been augmented in the light of experiences of early Christians. Jesus uses the imagery of the book of Daniel to speak of the future and to give encouragement to his followers.

All three synoptic gospels contain this new form of apocalypse and comparison shows that Matthew and Luke have added to and adapted the material they found in Mark. The chapter begins with Jesus leaving the temple and pronouncing the most serious of his words against it. He declares that 'not one stone will be left here on another, for all will be destroyed'. (Mark 13:2) It is important to situate these words in the ministry of Jesus and to disregard the fact that the temple was actually destroyed by the Romans some decades later. These words about the destruction of the temple relate to Jesus' symbolic actions of cursing the fig tree and driving out the traders from the temple. To those who put their trust in the temple rather than in righteous behaviour, Jeremiah had threatened judgement. (Jeremiah 7:1-15) He illustrated the threat of destruction by smashing a pot. (Jeremiah chapter 19) To those who now trust in the temple which has been beautifully restored by Herod the Great, Jesus announces its vulnerability and he too confirms his message with symbolic actions. Jesus, like Jeremiah, calls for a change of behaviour and for repentance. But it is relevant also to recall the words of Jesus to the Samaritan woman recorded in John chapter 4, that true believers are to worship in no temple but 'in spirit and truth'. (John 4:23) In the synoptic tradition the pronouncement against the temple led to accusations in the trial of Jesus, and has been understood in the tradition as prophetic prediction that Jerusalem would one day fall. The insight from John's gospel points to a deeper sense of Jesus' words about the end of the temple.

Having left the temple, Jesus goes to the Mount of Olives with four disciples. (Mark 13:3) This location is significant as the place of God's final battle in the prophecies of Zechariah. (Zechariah 14:1-4) While Luke omits this detail, Mark and Matthew locate the discourse of Jesus in this place. The disciples' question about the future introduces Jesus' long discourse. It is an invitation to perseverance with hope.

Jesus begins by speaking of the troubles disciples will have to face. He constantly tells them to 'watch out' (Greek *blepete*). The first danger is that of false messiahs. Many will be led astray by people coming and claiming to be the Messiah. A similar warning is repeated later in the chapter. (Mark 13:21-23) Jesus tells the disciples not to fear wars, earthquakes, and famines. He declares that such disasters 'must' happen. The Greek word *dei* is used here, which is literally translated as 'it is necessary that', and speaks of a certain inevitability. Jesus also teaches preparedness for persecution and betrayal. The Roman church, for which Mark probably wrote the gospel, experienced such betrayals of Christian by Christian. Disciples are to trust that the Spirit will inspire their defence. They are warned of the need to stand firm to the end. (Mark 13:13) It is in these verses that we may detect a certain amount of development of Jesus' words in the light of early Christian experience.

The disciples had asked Jesus about the time and the signs of the end. Jesus does not begin to answer their questions until he has delivered these general warnings and the encouragement to persevere. From verse 14 onwards, however, the language is different. There are clear uses of phrases from the book of Daniel. Jesus now teaches about specific events and signs, but still in vague terms. He speaks in apocalyptic style of signs that are to precede the end, but gives no indication of when the end will be.

In Mark 13:14 Jesus uses the phrase, 'the abomination of desolation' (Greek *to bdelygma tes eremoseos*) which is found three times in the book of Daniel. (Daniel 9:27, 11:31, 12:11) An abomination is something which severely insults God. The term is used of idols frequently in the writings of the prophets. An abomination of desolation suggests the punishment and destruction such an insult to God might provoke. The term is found again in the first chapter of the first book of Maccabees. The Seleucid king Antiochus Epiphanes IV unleashes in the second century BC a persecution of Jewish religious practices and sets up an abomination of desolation, a pagan idol, in the temple. The use of this cryptic language from the book of Daniel is accompanied in Mark chapter 13 by the editorial comment, 'let the reader understand'. It is nevertheless quite uncertain what Jesus means here. Suggestions about specific insults to God in the Jerusalem temple are inconclusive. Jesus uses the language of apocalyptic to speak of the ultimate insult to God. Does he have the temple's destruction in mind here? Luke at this point replaces the abomination with 'Jerusalem surrounded by armies'. (Luke 21:20) Luke seems to show awareness of the Roman siege of Jerusalem which lasted six months and led to the razing of the city and temple in 70 AD. He will speak explicitly of Jerusalem's end in Luke 21:24.

When the 'abomination of desolation' appears, the disciples should flee to the mountains. This element recalls the flight of faithful Jews when Antiochus Epiphanes had profaned the temple. More significant is Jesus' use of a second phrase from the book of Daniel. He says: 'Those days will be a time of distress such as has never been.' (Mark 13:19) Such time of distress precedes the resurrection of the dead in Daniel chapter 12. After the ultimate insult to God comes the period of extreme distress, but the days are limited, for God has control over the time.

The climax of the chapter comes with Jesus' third quotation from the book of Daniel. He precedes it with elaborate use of imagery concerning the end, which is derived from the prophetic writings. (Mark 13:24-25) The cosmos is in turmoil to signal the final events. Jesus then declares: 'they will see the son of man coming in the clouds'. (Mark 13:26) This text from Daniel 7:13 deserves careful attention.

Daniel chapter 7 contains a strange apocalyptic vision. It is in a sense the heart of the book of Daniel. The chapter narrates Daniel's vision of four strange beasts which symbolise successive empires in the region. The final beast has 'a little horn and a mouth full of boasts'. (Daniel 7:8) This horn represents the persecutor Antiochus Epiphanes IV. All the beasts are destroyed in their turn but the focus is particularly on the destruction of this last tormentor of the Jews. As the vision proceeds Daniel sees 'one like a son of man'. (Daniel 7:13) This figure comes on the clouds into the presence of God. He is given sovereignty, glory and kingship. The chapter continues with the explanation of the vision. The beasts represent the successive empires, but the 'one like a son of man' represents the 'people of the saints of the Most High'. (Daniel 7:27) The faithful who have been persecuted are rewarded with glory. The rulers of the world and the persecutor of God's people are punished. In Daniel chapter 12 their reward is made clear: the just are to rise to everlasting life. The apocalyptic visions of Daniel proclaim faith in the resurrection of God's faithful people.

The use of the 'son of man' text by Jesus in Mark 13:26 associates Jesus with the triumph of the martyrs of the Maccabean time, those who remained faithful and were put to death for their fidelity to their God. As they were vindicated by God, so will Jesus be. Jesus has already foreseen both his death and resurrection. His use of this text associates him with those to whom the promise of resurrection has been proclaimed in the book of Daniel. He will use the text again during his trial, when he affirms his trust in God in the face of death. (Mark 14:62)

Jesus foresaw his death and associated his death with the

deaths of faithful Jews, particularly those persecuted during the Maccabean period. Jesus trusts in the Father's power to raise him from death. It is not surprising that, as reflection on the person and deeds of Jesus continued, the text of Daniel 7:13 was understood to refer specifically to Jesus. Meanwhile in Judaism too the same text was being newly understood and associated with a coming messiah figure. In both contexts, therefore, the powerful image of 'one like a son of man', which began as a symbol of the people, became also a symbol of the Messiah.

Jesus' use of the Daniel text to speak of his own triumph does not exclude reference to the future of his own people. In clear continuity with the original sense of the text in Daniel chapter 7, Jesus declares that this son of man 'will send out the angels and gather the elect'. (Mark 13:27) The promise of resurrection is restated as the promise for all God's faithful, for all Christ's chosen ones. The text of Mark chapter 13 reaches its climax with a proclamation in symbolic terms of the resurrection faith. The risen one, raised by the Father, will gather the disciples when the end comes.

The final verses of Mark chapter 13 underline the need for preparedness amid ignorance of the time of the end. Jesus uses a brief parable about a budding fig tree to speak of the signs leading to the end. (Mark 13:28) At this point a saying introduced with an emphatic 'amen' seems to give a more precise prediction of the end-time. (Mark 13:30) But it is a dubious saying, perhaps added by a Christian teacher keen to answer a question which Jesus had never answered. Christians have been eager to know precise dates and times, but Jesus stressed the need to be always prepared. Jesus' words in verse 32 seem to confirm his own teaching: 'As for that day or the hour, no-one knows it, neither the angels in heaven, nor the Son, but only the Father.' This saying seems to echo the authentic teaching of Jesus. It places limits on the knowledge of Jesus and would not have been added later as Christians treated Jesus with ever greater reverence. Jesus does not tell his disciples about precise times. He encourages them to live as good servants, always ready for the master's return. (Mark 13:34)

The message of the apocalyptic discourse of Jesus is one of hope and of the ultimate victory of God. It expresses in a new form the fundamental hope expressed in the apocalyptic visions of Daniel. It brings encouragement amid persecutions and disasters. The new element in this apocalypse is the central role of Jesus, who brings his chosen ones to share the life which he himself inherits. The extensive use of imagery associated with the book of Daniel should not surprise us. Jesus preached the coming of God's kingdom. He used this image to speak of God's final victory over evil and constant care for people. At the Last Supper Jesus relates his own death to the coming kingdom. (Mark 14:25) He relates it here to the triumph of all those vindicated by God, who destroys the evil tyrant and raises the dead to the life of glory. Jesus expected his own followers to face persecution, even martyrdom. The events of his suffering, death and rising to life will be the crucial elements in their new faith. It is to these events that we must now turn. The journey from the time of great distress to the life of the resurrection, foretold for his disciples in Mark chapter 13, will be the road travelled by Jesus before them.

CHAPTER 6

Suffering and Death

The passion narrative
The New Testament reminds us constantly that the most important events of the life of Jesus in the understanding of his early
followers were his death and resurrection. They lie at the heart
of the preaching of the disciples as reported in the Acts of the
Apostles. Both Peter and Paul repeatedly proclaim: 'You put
him to death, but God raised him up.' The reported Pentecost
speech of Peter in Acts chapter 2 makes brief mention of the
wonders worked by Jesus during the ministry, but Peter moves
on swiftly to the death and resurrection. Details of the earthly
life of Jesus are of little importance in comparison to these crucial
events. Peter's later speech to Cornelius will acknowledge the
early ministry of Jesus with the words: 'he went about doing
good and healing'. (Acts 10:38) Again Peter moves on quickly to
proclaim the death and resurrection of Jesus. If we turn to the
earliest New Testament documents, the genuine letters of Paul,
we can trace almost no reference to the earthly life of Jesus before his death and resurrection. The death and resurrection of
Jesus lie at the heart of Christian preaching, for it is through
these events that Christians understand their own new life, their
own hopes, their own future.

It is therefore natural that all four canonical gospels present
these events as the climax and end of the gospel story. Given the
momentous nature of the events leading to Jesus' death, it is to
be expected that the last days of the life of Jesus and the processes
of his arrest and trial should receive considerable attention in
the tradition and in the written gospels. It has been suggested
that an early passion narrative may have existed before the first

evangelist compiled his gospel. But, as with the rest of the gospel, so in the story of Jesus' suffering and death, each evangelist will display his own style and reveal his own concerns, as well as using his own sources. The synoptic stories and the narrative in John show considerable similarities, but also significant differences. Many of these will be due to the particular concerns of the Christian communities for which these different gospels were written.

The passion narrative must provide an account of events, an account of the involvement of people such as Judas and Pontius Pilate. But it must also address the theological problem. Why did God allow Jesus to die? How is the death of God's Son to be understood? As with the rest of the gospel material, there is a historical basis with a catechetical and christological overlay. Each synoptic gospel has two chapters which are customarily called 'passion narratives'. Some would have the story begin in Gethsemane, but the accounts of the plots against Jesus and of the last supper are so closely associated with the suffering and death of Jesus that they too may be considered parts of the passion narrative. In this chapter we will focus on the narratives of Mark, Matthew and Luke, with only occasional references to the fourth gospel. We will consider that gospel's story of Jesus' suffering and death in a later chapter, once we have become more familiar with John's gospel.

The last supper

The passion story in Mark begins with a reference to the religious feasts of passover and unleavened bread. (Mark 14:1) Mark suggests that Jesus had come to Jerusalem for the feast. It was customary for pilgrims to arrive several days earlier in order to fulfil the requirements of purification. This was a time of increased tension due to the presence of thousands of visitors, and the consequent regular deployment in Jerusalem of Roman troops from their base in Caesarea Marittima. The chief priests and scribes are searching for ways of doing away with Jesus, but they consider the time of the festival to be a dangerous one. An

arrest at such a time of such a popular figure could provoke unrest among the ordinary people. (Mark 14:2)

The issue of plots against Jesus is left aside momentarily to
allow for the account of the anointing of the head of Jesus by an
unnamed woman at Bethany in the house of Simon the leper.
This account, found in Mark and Matthew, is quite distinct from
an account placed earlier in the ministry of Jesus in Luke's
gospel. Luke narrates the anointing of the feet of Jesus by a
woman who was a sinner. (Luke 7:37-38) We are dealing with
two different women, though both show extraordinary tenderness and reverence for Jesus. The incident in Luke's gospel portrays a woman who has known forgiveness and expresses her
gratitude in love. The anointing of the head of Jesus by the
woman at Bethany is seen by Jesus as a preparation for his coming death. (Mark 14:8) John's gospel also reports an anointing at
Bethany, this time of Jesus' feet, by Mary, the sister of Lazarus.
(John 12:1-8) This might suggest some confusion between the
Mark tradition and the account in John. These accounts provide
a tender and tragic interlude as Jesus' death draws nearer.
Anointed in love before his death, this anointed one will be crucified for claiming such a status.

Despite the decision of the religious authorities to do nothing
during the time of the feast, procedures against Jesus accelerate.
This is due to the intervention of Judas: 'Judas Iscariot, who was
one of the twelve, went to the chief priests in order that he might
hand him over to them.' (Mark 14:10) The text of Mark is laconic.
We are not told why Judas made such a decision. There is no
hint of such a development before this point. But there can be no
doubting the embarrassing historical fact that it was one of those
chosen by Jesus who actually arranged his arrest. Matthew's text
suggests Judas was driven by love of money. If they paid
enough, he would betray Jesus. (Matthew 26:15) Luke attempts
to answer the question by having Satan, who had been sent
away by Jesus after his temptation 'until the right time' (Greek
kairos), enter into Judas. (Luke 4:13, 22:3) Christians have struggled
with the issue of a betrayal by one who was specially chosen. It

speaks of the immense freedom given to the individual to respond or not respond with love for love. Mark stresses the delight of the chief priests at Judas' solution to their problem. (Mark 14:11) The betrayal itself seems to consist in making arrangements to deliver Jesus into their hands without inciting trouble.

Arrangements for the last supper are made earlier in the day. In a scene reminiscent of the procuring of the donkey he rode into Jerusalem, Jesus sends two disciples to prepare the passover meal. (Mark 14:13) Two related problems arise at this point. Was the meal which Jesus celebrated with the disciples really a passover supper? Did this last meal of Jesus with the disciples actually take place on passover eve? The Jewish feasts of passover and unleavened bread, feasts which together celebrate the exodus from Egypt and God's bringing the Hebrew people into freedom, fall during the Jewish month of Nisan. The day of passover begins at sunset, when 14th Nisan becomes 15th Nisan. In Jesus' time passover lambs would have been slaughtered in the temple a few hours earlier on 14th Nisan. The lamb would be the central feature of the meals celebrated that evening as the feast of passover began. The day was a solemn feast, when no work was allowed. (Exodus 12:16) The feast of unleavened bread, recalling the departure from Egypt with no time to wait for dough to be leavened, went from 15th to 21st of the same month of Nisan.

If Jesus did celebrate a passover meal with his disciples in the evening as 15th Nisan began, it is surprising that there is no mention of the central element, the passover lamb. Did Jesus then substitute a new observance during the passover meal? A crucial difficulty lies in the apparent non-observance of the command to do no work on the day of festival. Trials and interrogations would surely not have happened on a feast day. These difficulties in the account provided by the synoptic gospels seem to be solved by the fourth gospel. According to John the feast of passover began on the evening of the day on which Jesus died. John 18:28 states that the Jews would not enter the praetorium and have dealings with Pilate. They wished to avoid defilement. They were preparing to eat the passover meal that very evening. Jesus was dying on 14th Nisan at the very time when the lambs were being slaughtered in preparation for the passover meals to be celebrated that evening.

If John's chronology is correct the problem of non-observance of the feast day disappears, for 14th Nisan is not a day of festival. The meal on the night before Jesus dies is not a passover but a farewell meal with the disciples. This does not mean that the meal had no passover connotations as will be clear when we examine what Jesus said and did. The evangelists underline the fact that this is the final time Jesus will be at a meal with his friends. (Mark 14:25) That the synoptic gospels describe the meal as a passover could well be due to the fact that the feast was imminent and that Jesus' meal was somehow modelled on the passover meal. The understanding shown by St Paul of Christ as a passover sacrifice may also have contributed to seeing this last supper as a passover meal. (1 Corinthians 5:7) The Jewish passover feast of God's liberation is replaced by the passover of Jesus which leads God's people to a new freedom.

As the meal begins Jesus declares his awareness of being betrayed. (Mark 14:18) While in Matthew and John Judas is revealed as the betrayer, in Mark there is simply a general statement. Judas is not identified. Judas does not leave. The fourth gospel, by contrast, has Judas leave the company. The evangelist then declares: 'It was night.' (John 13:30) For Mark the identity of the traitor is less important than the fact that trusted disciples can turn traitor. The early Christians knew this from their own experience.

The New Testament contains four accounts of Jesus' giving bread and wine at the supper. (Mark 14:22-24; Matthew 26:26-28; Luke 22:19-20; 1 Corinthians 11:23-25) As happens frequently in the passion narrative, Matthew's text is very similar to that of Mark. The text given by Luke's gospel shows remarkable similarity with Paul's account of the supper in 1 Corinthians chapter 11. The interpretation of the words of Jesus has always been of immense importance to Christians. It seems clear that in two acts of giving, Jesus hands over the totality of himself in two ways. As regards the first of these, while Mark has Jesus state simply 'this is my body', Luke adds 'which is given for you', and Paul 'which is for you'. The gift of the bread is the gift of himself, of his life for his friends. Jesus confirms his readiness to give his life for others. The words over the cup express the same giving in a different way. All the synoptic writers speak of blood 'which is poured out'. Matthew and Mark say it is 'for many', while Luke prefers 'for you'. The life of Jesus is once again seen as a gift for others. His life's blood is shed for others. With the words over the cup the concept of covenant is evoked. Mark and Matthew have Jesus say: 'This is my blood of the covenant.' Luke and Paul record: 'This cup is the new covenant in my blood.' The covenant idea recalled here is the ancient one of the relationship between God and the people, traditionally ratified after the liberation from Egypt with the sprinkling of blood from sacrificed animals at Mount Sinai. (Exodus 24:8) Jeremiah had announced the future arrival of a new covenant. (Jeremiah 31:31) The giving of Jesus' life is understood as a new beginning. It is a covenant to replace the old. This blood is not animal blood sprinkled on a crowd, but blood drunk in to give new life to the disciple. Matthew adds that the blood is shed 'for the forgiveness of sins'. He thus evokes the biblical idea that the blood of a sacrifice brings about forgiveness of human sins, and he applies the idea to the death of Jesus.

It can be seen that the accounts of the Lord's supper in the four New Testament writings provide mutually enriching insights into the meaning of Jesus' actions in giving the bread and cup. On the night before he dies Jesus anticipates his self-giving in these gifts. He does this during the last meal he will share with his friends. Once he is no longer with them they will do the same. They are bound together by sharing one bread and drinking the cup of the new covenant. These gifts bring new life and the forgiveness of sins. Jesus is aware that he will lay down his life for the benefit of others. Earlier in the ministry, in an allusion to the death of the servant in the book of Isaiah, Jesus had said that he would give his life as 'a ransom for many'. (Mark 10:45 Isaiah 53:10-12)

The instruction to 'do this in memory of me' is a fundamental element of Christian understanding of the passover of Jesus. Both Luke and Paul give this instruction. (Luke 22:19; 1 Corinthians 11:24-25) It tells us that what Jesus did at his final meal was to be repeated in his memory. Writing in about 57 AD Paul shows that this was the understanding of Christian groups from the early years. The concept of 'memory', expressed by the important Greek term *anamnesis,* is crucial. To understand it fully we may recall the Hebrew idea, found in the instructions for the celebration of the passover feast, that the rite was to serve as a 'remembrance' (Hebrew *zikkaron*). (Exodus 12:14) This 're- membrance' is a bringing into the present of the beneficial events of the past. In the words of Jesus in Paul's and Luke's ac- counts, Christians see the command of Christ to share the meal once he has gone. Just as Judaism celebrates the passover as the making present of the gift of God's liberation to generations of Jews, so the celebration of the Lord's supper, the passover of Jesus, continues to make present to Christians the gift of Christ. The difference between the two lies in the fact that in the Christian eucharist a person is present, the person around whom the community of disciples once gathered and gathers still. In the eucharist the church renews its contact with Jesus and receives again the food of life he offers.

Jesus concludes the meal with a reference to the coming king- dom: 'I shall not drink again of the fruit of the vine until that day when I drink it new in the kingdom of God.' (Mark 14:25) Jesus relates this last meal with his disciples to the coming of the king- dom which he has proclaimed and to which he has witnessed in his mighty works. For Christians each eucharist recalls the last earthly meal of Jesus and looks forward to the feast of the king- dom of God. Matthew and Luke have Jesus express the same link with the kingdom. (Matthew 26:29; Luke 22:16,18) Paul re- places hope in the coming of the kingdom of God with expect- ation of the return of the Lord: 'Each time you eat this bread and

drink this cup, you are proclaiming the death of the Lord until
he comes.' (1 Corinthians 11:26)

An extraordinary omission must now be mentioned. John's
gospel has no reference to Jesus' gift of bread and wine at the
last supper. John gives ample consideration to eating the flesh
and drinking the blood of the Lord in chapter 6 of his gospel. At
the supper, by contrast, he reports the washing of the feet of the
disciples by Jesus. At the end of this action Jesus instructs the
disciples to 'do to each other what I have done to you'. (John
13:15) Christians will remember Jesus not only in sharing the
body and blood of the Lord, but also in works of loving service.
The remembering in prayer and worship must be accompanied
by a remembering in service of others.

The last supper may be understood as the passover of Jesus,
the meal in which Jesus adapts the Jewish passover into a new
rite. But it is equally a farewell meal. The evangelists Luke and
John have emphasised this dimension by providing substantial
teachings of Jesus in the context of the last supper. They are the
farewell words of Jesus to his disciples. We shall return to the
material in John chapters 13-17 later. The additional teachings of
Jesus in Luke chapter 22 focus on discipleship, its glories and its
trials.

Jesus in the garden
We have lingered long in consideration of Jesus with the disciples in a final melancholy meal. Events will now accelerate. The
Jesus who is about to be handed over leads his disciples to the
garden of Gethsemane. Luke suggests it was Jesus' custom to
visit the Mount of Olives. (Luke 22:39) Mark and Matthew will
give the more specific location of Gethsemane, the 'garden of the
oil press'. Luke avoids the Semitic term. The coming betrayal on
the slopes of the Mount of Olives recalls king David's desperate
escape from Jerusalem due to the plotting of his son Absalom in
chapter 15 of the second book of Samuel. As David was betrayed
by his trusted counsellor Ahithophel, so will Jesus be betrayed
by a trusted friend. (2 Samuel 15:31)

In Mark's version and in that of Matthew, close as ever, Jesus then declares that all will abandon him. (Mark 14:27) Luke does not report these words, for he has just had Jesus commend the fidelity of the disciples. (Luke 22:28) Jesus, as in the passion predictions earlier in the synoptic gospels, speaks not only of being struck down but also of being raised. Such trust goes almost unnoticed as Peter proclaims his undying fidelity. In all four gospels Jesus foresees Peter's three-fold denial 'before the cock crows'. (Mark 14:30)

The major and most powerful focus of Gethsemane is on Jesus himself as he faces abandonment, torture and death. In Mark and Matthew Jesus takes Peter, James and John with him away from the others. Is it significant that precisely these three disciples had forthrightly declared their willingness to die with Jesus? (Mark 10:39, 14:31) In Luke's gospel there is no separation of the three. The disciples remain together in solidarity. Mark describes Jesus as 'being distraught and anguished'. There is an echo of the lament in Psalm 42 in his words: 'My soul is very sorrowful, even to death.' (Mark 14:34) Mark does not hesitate to speak of Jesus' terror and unspeakable sorrow. Matthew softens the picture by describing Jesus as being 'sorrowful and anguished'. (Matthew 26:37) Mark's realistic portrayal seems to be omitted totally by Luke. The anguish of Jesus, toned down or omitted in the other gospels, is echoed in the words of the Letter to the Hebrews, which describes Jesus' 'strong cries and tears'. (Hebrews 5:7) Mark's text can be translated in such a way as to lessen its impact by speaking of 'fear and distress'. But Mark seems to suggest to us something much stronger, profound human terror and anguish. It is a phrase which readers of this gospel will value for it speaks most powerfully of Jesus' sharing in human pain.

The insight into the human predicament of Jesus continues with the words of Jesus' prayer. Only here in the four gospels does an evangelist record Jesus' use of the Aramaic term *abba*. (Mark 14:36) It is an intimate and respectful term of address. In his terror he is still able to address his God and father. The prayer of Jesus in the synoptic gospels is an honest human cry in the face of suffering that the cup of pain should be removed. But Jesus' words echo the Lord's Prayer not only in his cry to the Father but also in the concluding words that God's will be done. In John's gospel Jesus will not make this plea to his Father. John stresses that the Son of God has come into the world to face the hour. He already knows what God's will is and there is no suggestion of human fear impeding him. (John 12:27)

At this point there is considerable uncertainty about the genuine text of Luke. Some ancient copies of the text tell of the presence of an 'angel from heaven' bringing Jesus strength. (Luke 22:43) The following verse speaks of Jesus' sweat 'like great drops of blood'. The absence of these verses from many ancient copies of the gospel of Luke might be explained by attributing these two verses to an editor who sought to remedy the evangelist's lack of reference to the anguish of Jesus. We will see elsewhere that Luke tends to avoid significant reference to the pain of Jesus.

The three synoptic evangelists deal differently with the sleeping disciples. Mark and Matthew stress their weakness by reporting that on the three occasions that he turns to them Jesus finds them asleep. Luke, by contrast, narrates that Jesus finds them asleep once. He exonerates them, for they were sleeping 'for sorrow'. (Luke 22:45) Luke, as is his custom, sees no reason to emphasise the disciples' faults. At heart they are Jesus' faithful ones. This private scene ends with Jesus gathering his strength. His anguished prayer has given him courage to face the expected ordeal.

For the synoptic evangelists Judas arrives with an armed crowd, sent by the chief priests, the scribes and the elders. In unison the three gospel writers restate that Judas was 'one of the twelve'. The Judas who plotted with the religious authorities now brings them to their prey. Is this to be understood as the arrival of an official group, or are we dealing with a less organised crowd? John suggests that Roman soldiers too were in the crowd. (John 18:3) Judas is to identify Jesus by the sign of a kiss.

Both Mark and Matthew spell out the deed of betrayal, a deed of love misused in order to betray, but Luke's version avoids the pain of the betrayer's kiss. Jesus stops Judas in his tracks by his question: 'Judas, are you betraying the Son of Man with a kiss?' (Luke 22:48) Matthew adds to the pathos with Jesus' words to Judas: 'Friend, why are you here?' (Matthew 26:50) In Mark Jesus is silent.

The fracas which follows when one of those present draws his sword and attacks the high priest's slave, cutting off his ear, is more directly confronted in Matthew and Luke. In Luke's version Jesus the healer heals the slave. In all three synoptic gospels Jesus challenges the crowd for using such force against one who taught daily in the temple. The scene ends with the flight of the disciples. Mark and Matthew record that 'they all abandoned him and fled'. (Mark 14:50; Matthew 26:56) Luke characteristically omits this detail. The curious reference to the naked young man who loses his linen cloth suggests the oral stage of the handing on of Mark's story. Such a detail, omitted by later evangelists as unimportant and perhaps unsuitable, is recorded only by Mark. In Mark's portrayal Jesus is now abandoned both by those who were closest and, as seems the case with the naked young man, by those who followed out of curiosity. (Mark 14:51-52)

Jesus and the high priest

All four gospels agree that Jesus is taken to the high priest Caiaphas. It should be remembered that the high priest was both the religious and political leader of the Jewish nation. Throughout the centuries since the return from exile, under various foreign rulers, the high priest had this position. Caiaphas was high priest for nearly twenty years. He was a successful and shrewd politician. John's gospel displays his ruthlessness when he declares that 'it is better for one man to die for the people'. (John 18:14) The account of the interrogation of Jesus by Caiaphas and the Sanhedrin in the synoptic gospels reveals the deliberate intention of Caiaphas to eliminate Jesus as a threat to public order. It is John's gospel which spells out most clearly Caiaphas' reason for his decision to do away with Jesus. (John 11:49-50) To preserve order and avoid endangering the political situation, it was better to eliminate any potential source of unrest.

When dealing with the processes against Jesus it is important to bear in mind that each evangelist provides his own colouring of the events. Who was responsible for the killing of Jesus? As the gospel tradition progresses it is more and more emphasised that the Jews brought about his death. It will also be implied that the people joined the religious leadership in clamouring for Jesus' death. This growing emphasis is fuelled by the divisions and antagonisms developing between the early Christian communities and Jewish groups. Meanwhile the gospels tend to exonerate the Romans, demonstrating that the Roman authorities from the outset saw no real danger in Jesus or his followers. As we seek to discover the truth about the death of Jesus it is crucial to acknowledge the human prejudice of those who developed the gospel traditions. Some Jews, for political reasons, did decide to have Jesus killed. This was achieved with the collusion of the Roman authorities. Responsibility for the death of Jesus was limited to these people. One of the greatest injustices in the history of Christianity, with unspeakable consequences over the centuries, has been the assigning of guilt for the death of Jesus to the whole Jewish people.

We cannot really know what went on during the session with the high priest. Mark and Matthew present a trial of Jesus by night. Luke has an interrogation of Jesus once morning comes. Some have used later Jewish regulations recorded in the Mishnah, the rabbinic law-code put in writing about 200 AD, to try to evaluate the plausibility of the gospel accounts, but this has obvious problems. Were such regulations already in operation in Jesus' day? Were they adhered to in the procedures against Jesus?

The account of the trial of Jesus in Mark's gospel is in fact a caricature of a legal process. False witnesses are brought in.

They do not agree. The high priest asks an exasperated question. Jesus gives his reply. The high priest pronounces his verdict that Jesus should die. Mark suggests that a proper legal process was not followed. An innocent man suffers what is an obvious travesty of justice. The decision to have Jesus killed was taken before his arrest. His disturbance in the temple and his prophetic preaching about the kingdom had sealed his fate. The trial before the Sanhedrin is a formality.

But what of the charges? It seems that the Sanhedrin would have had only limited powers to execute, perhaps in the case of religious offences. John 18:31 has the Jews declare that they have no power to execute anyone. The strategy of the high priest and Sanhedrin is to present Jesus as a political agitator who threatens the stability of this Roman province. It is easy to misrepresent the actions of religious leaders as political crimes which threaten national security. History is littered with such instances. Oscar Romero is only one of a long line.

The first of the two charges concerns Jesus' perceived threats against the temple. Mark and Matthew both report the accusation of false witnesses who say that Jesus threatened to destroy the temple and build another in three days, (Mark 14:58; Matthew 26:61) Luke omits the accusation but in the Acts of the Apostles he narrates how Stephen is accused of saying that Jesus would destroy the temple. (Acts 6:14) In the synoptic gospels the disturbance caused by Jesus in the temple might be considered a threat and the religious authorities view it most seriously. (Mark 11:18) The reported words of Jesus about the temple's destruction, in his speech about the end-time, might have given rise to the accusation that he would destroy it. (Mark 13:2) Jesus in fact seems to be using the theme of Jerusalem's destruction much as the prophet Jeremiah used it. (Jeremiah 7:14, 26:6) God's displeasure might one day be seen again, as it had been centuries earlier, in the fall of Jerusalem and the destruction of God's temple. Later Christians would understand Jesus' words as an inspired prediction of the Roman destruction of Jerusalem at the end of the Jewish War in 70 AD.

Jesus is silent in the face of these confused and unconvincing accusations. Christian description of the silent Jesus seems to be modelled on the figure of the unjustly condemned servant, who is 'like a lamb silent before its shearers'. (Isaiah 53:7) The same passage is being read by the Ethiopian eunuch when Philip encounters him in Acts chapter 8. The high priest, determined to incriminate Jesus despite his silence, asks: 'Are you the Messiah, the son of the Blessed One?' (Mark 14:61)

In all four gospels, in the synoptic gospels both during the Sanhedrin interrogation and during the interrogation by Pilate, and in John's gospel in the latter, Jesus is asked such a question. Are you the Messiah? Are you the king of the Jews? In all cases but one his reply is evasive: 'it is you who say this'. As is so often the case in the ministry, Jesus challenges the person asking to take responsibility for the question. Christian memory and tradition have recorded this as his way of responding to any suggestion that he should accept the role of a messiah, or of a king. The questions are simplistic. To answer affirmatively to these questions would be to invite misunderstanding. Was Jesus interested in earthly power? Would he collude with political agendas? In keeping with his attitude throughout the ministry, as shown in Mark chapter 8 when he treats with great reserve Peter's statement that he is the Messiah, Jesus in the interrogations consistently answers: 'it is you who say this'.

The text of Mark 14:62 alone gives a different answer. The evidence of the ancient copies of Mark's gospel is almost unanimous in having Jesus reply 'I am'. (Mark 14:62) This stands in contradiction of Matthew's version, with its more normal 'it is you who say this'. If Matthew, as is generally accepted, used Mark's passion narrative to compose his own version, and if he had before him the unequivocal reply 'I am', there is no doubt that he would have recorded it in his gospel too. The most likely explanation of the difference between Mark and Matthew is that the text of Mark originally read 'it is you who say this'. The text was edited subsequently in order to have Jesus proclaim unequivocally for Christians: 'I am the Christ'. Jesus, who had remained silent on the issue of the temple, would surely not be presented as falling easily into Caiaphas' trap on the second point of interrogation. It is Matthew's gospel which hands down the more likely answer of Jesus.

The second part of Jesus' reply quotes the text of Daniel 7:13 that the Son of Man will come on the clouds, the text already on Jesus' lips in Mark chapter 13. But Jesus also says that this individual will sit at the right hand of God. We might recall that James and John had coveted such high positions, and that Psalm 110 declares that the Messiah should sit at God's right hand. The high priest uses this declaration by Jesus of his own vindication to claim that Jesus has blasphemed. The passion narrative in the synoptic gospels thus affirms that it was due to making claims of a special rapport with God that Jesus was judged a blasphemer. Having gone through a travesty of an interrogation, Caiaphas can be confident that he can present this troublesome prophet as a threat to stability. He trusts that the Roman prefect, Pontius Pilate, a man not noted for sensitivity, will back up his judgement and have Jesus executed for reasons of security. The prophet who claims to be establishing his God's kingdom and who is an obvious threat to the peace of the Roman province of Judaea will be crucified due to a collusion of injustice.

The Sanhedrin scene ends in Mark and Matthew with physical abuse of Jesus. (Mark 14:65; Matthew 26:67) He is spat upon and receives the blows of Sanhedrin members and guards. Even Luke records this ill-treatment though he omits the spittle. (Luke 22:63-65) There are echoes here of the ill-treatment of the servant in Isaiah chapter 50.

Closely related to the Sanhedrin scene is the denial of Jesus by Peter. It follows the night interrogation in Mark and Matthew, but comes before Luke's setting of the same interrogation on the morning of the next day. Again we are aware of Luke's sensitivity. Under pressure from repeated questions the Peter of Mark and Matthew begins to curse and swear. (Mark 14:71; Matthew 26:74) Luke reduces this to 'and Peter said'. (Luke 22:60) Luke's final touch in the scene of Peter's denials has

Jesus in custody turn to look at Peter. In Luke's gospel it is his Lord's look which provokes Peter's tears. (Luke 22:61-62) Luke is surely suggesting that Jesus' look is sufficient to convey his forgiveness.

Before he narrates Jesus' trial by Pilate, Matthew inserts an extra tradition. Matthew must complete the story of Judas. We have already recalled how king David, as he flees from Jerusalem and makes his way up the Mount of Olives in 2 Samuel chapter 15, learns of the betrayal of Ahithophel, a trusted advisor. The same Ahithophel hangs himself, seemingly out of remorse. (2 Samuel 17:23) Matthew has Judas return the money he had been paid by the chief priests. He too goes off and hangs himself. (Matthew 27:5) Luke will report the death of Judas in a different way in the Acts of the Apostles before the election of Matthias to take his place as an apostle. (Acts 1:18) Since Matthew emphasises Jewish responsibility for Jesus' death, it is no surprise that he informs us about the sad end of the Jew who plotted it and betrayed Jesus.

Jesus and Pilate

The reputation of Pontius Pilate, who was prefect of the Roman province of Judaea from AD 26-36, has always been tied up with his association with Jesus of Nazareth. In early Christianity, legends grew up about the later life of Pilate once Jesus had been killed. In some of these he becomes a Christian saint. We have reliable historical evidence that Pilate's style of governing in Judaea was problematic. He was lacking in sensitivity to Jewish religious concerns. He caused major problems by having Roman soldiers bring the emperor's standards, offensive to the Jews due to their religious use, into Jerusalem by night. Luke's gospel alludes to an incident when Pilate mingled the blood of certain Galileans with that of their sacrifices. (Luke 13:1) Pilate was eventually removed from office due to misrule.

The accusation laid before Pilate that Jesus intended to proclaim himself 'king of the Jews' was designed to mislead Pilate by making Jesus a political threat. Pilate's question to Jesus, 'Are you the king of the Jews?' elicits in all four gospels the expected reply, 'It is you who say this'. These are the only words of Jesus to Pilate during the trial in the synoptic gospels. The fact that the reply of Jesus to Pilate is identical in all four gospels and matches Jesus' reply to the high priest in Matthew and Luke is another strong indication that the tradition of 'I am' in Mark 14:62 is a later change. We are dealing, in the trial by Pilate as in the Sanhedrin interrogation, with a traditional account which makes up for the lack of eye-witness reports. The essence of the brief exchange, that Jesus is on trial for claiming to be a king, makes clear the real reason for the condemnation of Jesus. Pilate seems to have been willing to eliminate any potential trouble-maker. His limited efforts to release Jesus may be historical and due to a sense that Jesus had done nothing deserving the death penalty. But the evangelists, and Luke in particular with three statements from Pilate declaring Jesus' innocence, are keen to show that the representative of Roman rule established that Jesus had done nothing deserving death. It is quite plausible that Pilate made no such attempts to determine Jesus' innocence.

Luke inserts into the account of the trial by Pilate the sending off of Jesus to Herod, the tetrarch of the Galilee region, who according to Luke's information happened to be visiting Jerusalem. (Luke 23:7) Herod's interest in Jesus and desire to see him was reported earlier in Luke chapter 9, rumoured plots by Herod to kill Jesus in Luke chapter 13. Herod is now delighted to see Jesus, but Herod's questions receive no reply. Herod and his soldiers mock Jesus. They have no interest in achieving justice and he is sent back to Pilate. Jesus emerges from the story as the healer of the enmity between Herod and Pilate. (Luke 23:12)

As the trial before Pilate continues, the gospels introduce Barabbas. There is no evidence outside the gospels for a regular release of prisoners at the time of the feast. Possibly the release of a man associated with riots in the city at the time of Jesus' arrest became the basis for the story. Pilate is portrayed as attempting to engineer Jesus' release by using this custom. He eventually condemns an innocent man and releases a guilty one.

Matthew's gospel at this point has some interesting features. A variant reading of the gospel, which is quite well supported, has a reference to 'Jesus Barabbas'. (Matthew 27:16) In this case Barabbas' personal name would be the same as that of Jesus. According to this reading Matthew records Pilate's question as 'Whom do you want me to release: Jesus Barabbas, or Jesus called Christ?' (Matthew 27:17) This reading was rejected, probably because of veneration for the name of Jesus. Pilate's attempt to obtain the freedom of Jesus called the Christ was further complicated by a message from his wife, telling him to steer clear of Jesus. (Matthew 27:19) It is a curious episode and suggests that this Gentile woman, who presumably was left in the governor's residence in Caesarea Marittima, has more intuition than the Jewish people who clamour for his execution. Matthew's gospel, which begins with the Gentile magi recognising Jesus as Messiah, introduces towards the end a Gentile woman who proclaims him to be righteous.

The clamour of the crowd that Jesus should be crucified increases. Such attempts to influence the governor's decision were by no means unusual. The Jewish historian Josephus reports how protesting crowds brought pressure on Pilate on several occasions. Pilate is portrayed as pleading with the crowds that the innocent Jesus be released. Matthew adds another new element. Pilate washes his hands of the blood of Jesus. (Matthew 27:24) The symbol of washing hands to indicate innocence is found memorably in Psalm 26:6: 'I will wash my hands in innocence.' Matthew's portrayal of Pilate washing his hands serves to prepare for the words he places on the lips of the crowd: 'His blood is on us and on our children.' (Matthew 27:25)

It is difficult to exaggerate the damage done by Matthew's dramatic licence. To emphasise Jewish guilt amid Pilate's weak attempts to save Jesus, he reports a cry which has had terrible and tragic consequences. This welcoming of responsibility for the death of Jesus has been used over the centuries to assign guilt to all Jewish people. The exaggerated enthusiasm of the crowd to do away with one whom the religious leaders perceived as a trouble-maker has inflamed Christian hatred of Jews and sanctioned persecution of the Jewish people. It is essential to make clear that such use of this gospel verse is quite unacceptable. Some Jews were indeed responsible for bringing about the death of Jesus with Roman connivance. They were among his contemporaries. Some without doubt acted wickedly. It is unjust to hold others than these responsible.

Pilate gives in to the pressure. Barabbas is released and Jesus handed over to be crucified. Mark and Matthew recall that Jesus was scourged at this point. (Mark 15:15; Matthew 27:26) Such flogging was a normal preliminary to crucifixion. It was intended to weaken the victim, add to his suffering, and ensure he would not survive long once crucified. Jesus has been handed over to the first stage of his torture and execution. Both Mark and Matthew recount further mocking of Jesus after the scourging. (Mark 15:16-20; Matthew 27:27-31)

The crucifixion

People are used to seeing images of Jesus nailed to a cross. We have lost the sense of horror about this atrocious method of execution. The condemned person would carry the cross-beam to the place of execution. The vertical part of the cross was left in the ground at that place. All the synoptic gospels report that a passer-by called Simon was constrained to carry the cross for Jesus. Perhaps Jesus had become too weak from the scourging to bear his own cross. No reference to Simon is found in John's gospel, with its portrayal of the strong Jesus going freely to the place of execution. Only Luke reports another incident on the way to Golgotha. A great crowd of people and of women lament Jesus' fate. (Luke 23:27-31) Luke shows that not all the people were hostile to Jesus. Jesus is followed, as he was in his ministry, even to the place of death.

This place, Golgotha, which was outside the city walls in Jesus' day, was a disused quarry transformed into a refuse dump. The name, as the evangelists tell us, signifies 'skull' and suggests the shape of a small hill. The name 'Calvary' is similarly

derived from the Latin word for 'skull'. The victim was fixed to
the cross with rope or nails. The references to the wounds of the
risen Jesus in Luke and John indicate that Jesus was fixed to the
cross with nails. (Luke 24:39-40; John 20:25) There is contemporary evidence that nails were driven through the wrists and feet.
Jesus' refusal of the wine mixed with myrrh, which might have
reduced the excruciating pain, is reported in Mark and seems to
underline his acceptance of a most painful death. (Mark 15:23)
Matthew suggests that the wine was mixed with gall in an act of
cruelty to increase Jesus' sensitivity. (Matthew 27:34) It is likely
that Matthew has taken the idea from Psalm 69, which speaks of
the dire suffering of the just man. Luke simply reports the crucifixion of Jesus and the two criminals. At this point Luke alone
has Jesus speak: 'Father, forgive them, for they do not know
what they are doing.' (Luke 23:34) The words are omitted in
some ancient copies of Luke. It seems likely that some early
Christians found the tradition that Jesus forgave those who
brought about his death too challenging. But these words of
Jesus fit perfectly with Luke's portrayal of Jesus in the story of
his death. He forgives his executioners. He will bring healing to
the repentant criminal. (Luke 23:43)

The sharing out of Jesus' clothes, reported in all the gospels,
raises the issue of whether Jesus was crucified naked. This
would have been normal Roman practice, though the Romans
may have made concessions due to Jewish sensitivities about
nudity. All the gospels report the official charge against Jesus
placed on the cross. He was crucified for claiming to be 'King of
the Jews'. Mark and Matthew are then closely similar in the insults hurled at Jesus by passers-by, chief priests and scribes, and
those crucified with him. Luke reduces the insults and is the
only evangelist to report the dialogue between Jesus and one of
the criminals who proclaims Jesus' innocence and seeks his help.
(Luke 23:40-43) Jesus replies: 'Today you will be with me in paradise.' (Luke 23:43)

Mark's account is punctuated by indications of the hour of
day. At the third hour (9 am) Jesus had been crucified. (Mark

15:25). At the sixth hour (12 noon) there was darkness over the whole earth until the ninth hour (3 pm). (Mark 15:33) The dramatic nature of the events is accentuated by the darkness. Some have speculated about storms or eclipses. Others see the evocation here of the symbolism of the end of the world used by some of the prophets. Amos had spoken of darkness at noon on the day of the Lord. (Amos 8:9) In ancient tales of the deaths of emperors and rabbis darkness was said to have descended over the earth.

The four gospels record that Jesus spoke seven times in all from the cross. These are the 'seven words' which have been the theme of preaching, meditation and musical settings over the centuries. In Mark and Matthew there is just one of these words. It is given first by the evangelists in Aramaic (Mark) and in Hebrew (Matthew). It is followed by the translation into Greek. This is the desperate, anguished cry of Jesus to the Father: 'My God, my God, why have you abandoned me?' (Mark 15:34; Matthew 27:46) It is the opening line of Psalm 22, a psalm in which an innocent man cries to God in his torment. We cannot know for certain what Jesus said on the cross. Each evangelist has written down what he considered was in Jesus' heart and mind as he approached death. Mark and Matthew have bravely recorded a disturbing tradition, that Jesus felt abandoned by God. It is true to say that Psalm 22 ends with words of trust in God and confidence about deliverance. It is possible that the evangelists want us to remember this. But this must not distract our attention from the words they actually set down. Jesus, abandoned by all, experiences abandonment by God. There is a powerful message here for all who, for whatever reason, feel God's total absence. The Son of God too has experienced the same sense of lostness. Luke does not record these disturbing words. He has already recorded two of the seven words of Jesus, words of forgiveness to his executioners, and words of promise to the repentant criminal. At the point of death Luke places on the lips of Jesus a verse from another psalm: 'Father, into your hands I commend my spirit.' (Luke 23:46; Psalm 31:5) A further three different words of Jesus are found in the fourth gospel.

Both Mark and Matthew record an offering to Jesus of sour wine after his anguished words. This useless gesture is hardly over when Jesus gives a loud cry and dies. Mark and Luke simply state that Jesus 'breathed out' (Greek *exepneusen*). (Mark 15:37; Luke 23:46) Matthew suggests the free surrender of his life by Jesus: 'he gave up the spirit' (Greek *apheken to pneuma*). (Matthew 27:50) People have often questioned what the cause of the death of Jesus might have been. The brevity of the gospel accounts does not provide a precise answer. Asphyxiation and shock due to dehydration and loss of blood have been suggested as causes of death in victims of crucifixion.

The evangelists report extraordinary reactions to the death of God's Son. Mark and Matthew tell of the tearing of the veil of the temple after Jesus has died, while Luke records it before his death. (Mark 15:38; Matthew 27:51; Luke 23:45) The death of Jesus points to the end of the need for the temple. As will be fully explored by Christian reflection on the death of Jesus, most particularly in the Letter to the Hebrews, the end is announced here of the blood sacrifices which lay at the heart of temple worship. Matthew alone adds the details of the earth quaking, the rocks splitting, tombs being opened and the dead being raised. (Matthew 27:51-53) Matthew elaborates his story of Jesus' death with these significant elements of Christian catechesis. The death of Jesus leads to resurrection and triumph over death for all.

The three synoptic gospels then present the declaration of the centurion. In Mark and Matthew, he says: 'This was the Son of God!' (Mark 15:39; Matthew 27:54) It is the Gentile who has overseen the execution of Jesus who declares the fulness of Christian faith. Mark and Matthew clearly suggest that in his death on the cross the fulness of the divine sonship of Jesus is revealed, and revealed to a Gentile. Luke has the Roman officer simply reiterate the Roman view, already repeatedly affirmed by Pilate, that Jesus is an innocent man. (Luke 23:47) Rome has no cause against him. For Luke the friends of Jesus have not abandoned him. While the crowds returned home beating their breasts, faithful men and women 'stood at a distance and saw these things'. (Luke 23:48-49)

Mark and Matthew are keen to record the names of the women who stood near at Jesus' death. Their record, with its discrepancies, seems to give a more reliable picture of who remained to watch the end. The male disciples had all fled. It was the women who had assisted Jesus during his work in Galilee who stayed with him throughout. (Mark 15:40-41; Matthew 27:55-56) John will record the presence of the mother of Jesus and the disciple Jesus loved. (John 19:26-27)

The sudden appearance of a hitherto unknown disciple, Joseph of Arimathea, shows all the signs of a genuine historical element. He appears at this point in all four gospels. Mark stresses the considerable courage of Joseph in asking for the body of Jesus. (Mark 15:43) Jesus' body is laid in a new tomb hewn from the rock. Matthew says it was Joseph's own. (Matthew 27:60) There are many rock-hewn tombs in the vicinity of the traditional site of Golgotha. There is no cleaning or anointing of the wounded body. In the synoptic tradition the body is simply wrapped in a shroud. Luke explains that the sabbath was beginning and ointments would be prepared later. (Luke 23:54-56) The evangelists stress that the women were well aware exactly where the tomb was. Joseph rolls a large stone against the door of the tomb. Matthew alone mentions the posting of a guard. (Matthew 27:62-66)

CHAPTER 7

The Empty Tomb and the Risen Jesus

The empty tomb

Moving through the gospel story as told by the synoptic evangelists, we have become aware that the gospel material gives
answers to the deeper questions about Jesus. An overlay of
christological catechesis is built upon a foundation of historical
reports. Throughout the accounts of Jesus' life and of his suffering and death we have seen how the story is a vehicle for proclaiming the faith of believers concerning Jesus. This faith, always
limited and hesitant before the death of Jesus, was enlivened
and deepened by the experience of the risen Jesus and of the
Spirit he gave. Through these vital events of the resurrection and
the gift of the Spirit, Christian faith was born. This faith proclaimed Jesus as the Christ who had been killed but raised by
God. This faith gave new insights about the life of Jesus and his
work, and was expressed in preaching which answered people's
questions about Jesus. The gospel writers, in their *euaggelia*, produced a new and unique form of writing, which was both the
history of Jesus and the proclamation of their faith in him, a faith
inspired by the Spirit he gave.

Having seen how the synoptic writers record their accounts
of Jesus' ministry and death, we finally reach their accounts of
the risen Jesus. We should expect a similar blend of historical
record and faith statements. We might indeed expect the latter
to outweigh the former in these parts of the gospels, as the
evangelists struggle to express the totally unexpected and
unique experiences of the followers of Jesus.

All four gospels begin with the discovery of the empty tomb.
As in the previous chapter on the passion narratives, we shall at

this point look in detail at the material in the synoptic gospels, with passing reference where appropriate to John. The material in the fourth gospel will be considered fully in a later chapter.

The gospels concur that the tomb in which the body of Jesus had been laid in the late afternoon before the sabbath began was found on the Sunday morning to be empty. The gospels tell us of the discovery made by a group of women. The gospel of John presents only Mary Magdalene but there is a suggestion she is not alone. (John 20:2) There are some discrepancies between the gospel accounts in relation to the time of morning. Mark states quite clearly that the sun had risen, while John says it was still dark. (Mark 16:2; John 20:1) Such lack of agreement testifies to the spontaneous and unplanned way in which the accounts arose. The discovery of the empty tomb was unexpected. It produced confusion and consternation. Whatever did it mean?

The synoptic gospels show similar disagreement about who exactly came to the tomb. The confusion suggests several visits once news of the empty tomb spread. The evangelists agree in placing Mary Magdalene first. Mary is remembered as the one who discovered the empty tomb. In the differing empty tomb accounts she is among the women who said nothing due to fear (Mark 16:8), and among those who reported the mystery of the empty tomb to the eleven. (Matthew 28:8; Luke 24:9-10) In John she meets the risen Jesus. Mary, healed by Jesus during the ministry, is the first recipient of the good news of the resurrection. (Luke 8:2) Other women, who had come from Galilee with Jesus and had witnessed his death from a distance, accompanied Mary to the tomb.

The gospels give different reasons for the women's visit to the tomb. Mark and Luke report that they came to anoint the body. (Mark 16:1; Luke 24:1) There had been no time to honour the dead body of Jesus on the day of his death. Anxiety about burying the body safely and observance of sabbath rules had meant this task had to be delayed. But one needs to ask whether an anointing of the body would have been performed on the second day after death. Matthew tells us that the women came simply 'to see the tomb'. (Matthew 28:1) John's gospel reports that the body of Jesus was embalmed at burial. (John 19:40) The Bethany anointing recorded by Mark and Matthew had been explicitly understood as an anointing in preparation for death. (Mark 14:8; Matthew 26:12)

The issue of the removal of the stone closing the tomb is a puzzling one. The gospels report that the stone had been rolled back. Only Matthew states how. At the death of Jesus Matthew alone had reported earthquakes and other apocalyptic events. Matthew celebrates the resurrection in like manner. As the women approached there was an earthquake, an angel of the Lord descended, removed the stone and sat on it. (Matthew 28:2) In this verse we witness a filling out of the empty tomb story. Matthew implies that God has opened the tomb, and that these are the events of the end-time. Later Christian writers, such as the writer of the apocryphal gospel of Peter, will develop the scene further, even to the extent of describing the emergence of Jesus from the tomb. The stone was quite possibly rolled back from the tomb in no extraordinary way. The enthusiastic elaboration of the tale attributes the deed to an intervention of God. Matthew's previous account of tombs opening at the death of Jesus prepared for the more dramatic opening of the tomb of Jesus. Matthew's angel is a dazzling sight. The guards at the tomb, only mentioned by Matthew, are frightened to death. (Matthew 28:4)

The discovery that the tomb was empty led to confusion and raised an obvious question. It is Mary Magdalene's implied question in John's gospel: 'They have taken the Lord out of the tomb and we do not know where they have put him.' (John 20:2, 20:13) A similar question obviously arises for all those who see the tomb is empty. John's gospel records the visit of Peter and the beloved disciple to the tomb. Peter's reaction is contrasted with that of the beloved disciple, who sees and believes. (John 20:8) But there is a similar intriguing reference to Peter in the synoptic tradition. Luke 24:12 states that when Peter learnt that the tomb was empty, he ran to the tomb. Having seen the empty tomb and the linen cloths he went home 'wondering about what had happened'. The absence of this brief reference to Peter in some ancient manuscripts of Luke's gospel suggests some embarrassment that Peter was slow to believe. The empty tomb by itself simply raises a question. Peter and the disciples were not expecting an intervention of God. They had had their hopes, but such hopes had collapsed with the death of Jesus. (Luke 24:21)

The answer to their question about the tomb will be provided when they encounter Jesus alive. Then they will know why the tomb is empty. But the story of the empty tomb anticipates this answer with the words of the angel-messengers. The messenger explains all: Jesus has been raised. The young man in Mark, the angel of the Lord in Matthew, and the two men in Luke are there to voice what John makes clear with the meeting of Jesus and Mary Magdalene at the tomb. (Mark 16:5; Matthew 28:5; Luke 24:4) The messengers proclaim the understanding which will only come when the risen Jesus is seen: 'He has been raised!'

The expression used by the angels to refer to Jesus' resurrection echoes the preaching of the early Christians. The essence of the message recorded in the Acts of the Apostles is: 'You crucified him, but God raised him.' The angels at the tomb use similar language. They use the Greek word *egerthe*, which means 'he has been raised'. (Mark 16:6; Matthew 28:6; Luke 24:6) God is the one who has raised Jesus. Other gospel texts use the less precise term *aneste*, and convey simply that 'he rose', with no reference to the power by which he did so. (Luke 24:7) It will be important to John's christology to affirm that Jesus rose by his own power. He freely lays down his life, and takes it up again. (John 10:17-18)

The reaction of the women to the discovery of the empty tomb varies with the different accounts. Mark records that they ran from the tomb and said nothing to anyone because they were afraid. (Mark 16:8) We may well have another case here of Mark's honesty in recording an embarrassing truth. Luke, by contrast, has the women behave as faithful disciples, passing on the news to sceptical listeners .(Luke 24:9-11) Matthew records the women's intention to tell the disciples. But, just as the gospel of John has Mary Magdalene meet Jesus near the tomb, so in Matthew Jesus comes to meet the women as they leave. They are the first to worship the risen Jesus. (Matthew 28:9) It is the encounter with the risen Jesus which explains the mystery of the empty tomb. Sooner or later in each of the gospels the truth that he is alive is confirmed by meeting him.

Only Matthew reports the stationing of guards at the tomb and their being traumatised by the arrival of the angel of the Lord. Matthew's purpose becomes clear when he continues the story of the guards by saying that it was from their false testimony that the story arose that the body of Jesus had been stolen from the tomb by the disciples as the guards slept. (Matthew 28:11-15) The whole incident of the placing of a Roman guard at the tomb seems most unlikely, and was probably added to the story to counter the false claims that the disciples had stolen the body from the tomb.

The empty tomb of itself proves nothing. If this is so, might it not be fictitious, a catechetical story to assist belief in the resurrection of Jesus? This is most unlikely. We should recall that there were various types of belief in life after death in Jesus' day. Jesus himself uses the language of resurrection when he foresees his own death. (Mark 8:31) But he also shows awareness of another understanding of how human beings might survive death. In the discourse to the disciples in Matthew chapter 10 Jesus says: 'Do not be afraid of those who kill the body but cannot kill the soul.' (Matthew 10:28)

There was in fact a wide variety of beliefs about the after-life among the contemporaries of Jesus. The Greek idea of the survival of the person to immortality without a body, what we commonly refer to as the 'immortality of the soul', is found alongside the Hebrew idea that the person would live after death as before with a living body. Among those who adopted this second belief, belief in the resurrection of the body, there was speculation about the nature of the risen body. The Jewish historian Josephus testifies to this variety of beliefs concerning the afterlife. He maintains that the Essenes considered that the spirit would escape once and for all from the prison of matter. As regards the Pharisees, Josephus informs us that they believed people would be given a 'different body' for life after death. None of the options for understanding the after-life involved the body which lay in the tomb.

The disciples of Jesus did not expect him to return to life, despite Jesus' statements about his future. The experience of meeting Jesus alive amazed them, and also explained the puzzling discovery of the empty tomb. Even if they had expected Jesus to rise from the dead, they would still not have expected the tomb to be empty.

The empty tomb tradition speaks of continuity. The one who was nailed to the cross and hurriedly laid in a stranger's tomb is the one who is raised to new life. It speaks also of the dignity of the human body, even a body which is tortured, broken and blood-stained. A similar focus on the glorified body of the risen Jesus will be found in the resurrection encounters in the gospels of Luke and of John.

Luke and the risen Jesus

Luke's gospel, which says nothing of meetings with Jesus at the tomb, reports in some detail two encounters: the meeting of Jesus with the two disciples on the road to Emmaus, and the appearance to the eleven disciples in Jerusalem. (Luke 24:13-35; 24:36-53)

The story of the disciples journeying to Emmaus is a stylistic masterpiece as well as a precious and well-loved catechetical story. At its heart there lies the personal encounter of two disciples, one named Cleopas, the other unnamed, with the risen Jesus. It is extraordinary that Luke should record in such detail a tradition in which the eleven disciples do not even appear except for a brief moment at the end. Luke shows that all disciples are to encounter the risen Jesus. He shows too how they may encounter him: in the scriptures and in the breaking of bread.

The story has an elaborate structure. It begins in Jerusalem. It tells of a journey in the company of a stranger to a village where

the identity of the stranger is revealed. It tells of a return journey
to Jerusalem. The journey out is a journey in despondency with
closed eyes. (Luke 24:16) The journey back is a journey in
enthusiasm, their eyes opened. (Luke 24:31) Their talk of their
disappointed hopes and present confusion dominates the journey out. The memory of his words, when their hearts burned
within them as he explained the scriptures, animates the journey
back. The road to Emmaus and back is a journey to full faith in
the risen Jesus. The confusing report of the empty tomb did not
raise their spirits. The teaching of Jesus that it was necessary that
the Messiah should suffer and so enter his glory removed their
confusion. (Luke 24:26) This is the good news they finally understand when Jesus breaks the bread, the action which renews his
self-giving, and the good news they hear the eleven confirm:
'The Lord has really been raised.' (Luke 24:34)

Luke teaches that Christians discover Jesus in the scriptures
and in the breaking of bread. Luke's second work, the Acts of
the Apostles, will illustrate this in the work of evangelisation,
from Jerusalem to the ends of the earth. (Acts 1:8) People like the
Ethiopian eunuch and the centurion Cornelius will reach faith in
the risen Jesus when the scriptures are explained, and they are
baptised in the name of the Lord Jesus. (Acts 8:35-38, 10:34-48)

Luke in his gospel gathers all the traditions of the risen Jesus
into one day. This contrasts with the report in the Acts that he
showed himself during a period of forty days. (Acts 1:3) The
issue is further complicated by the references to Jesus' ascension
in Luke 24:51, after the meeting with the eleven disciples, and in
Acts 1:9, at the end of the period of forty days. The forty day period
is surely a later addition to the preaching which allows for all
the reported appearances of the risen Jesus. The ascension
marks the end of this period, of whatever length it was, and declares that the risen Jesus is now with God. We might consider
whether the Acts of the Apostles was once one work with the
gospel of Luke. If so, the separation into two works may have
led to the addition of a conclusion to the gospel in the report of
the ascension in Luke 24:50-53, and to a further addition of a
prologue to the Acts in Acts 1:1-5.

The climax of Luke chapter 24 is Jesus' appearance to the eleven, as the Emmaus disciples are still giving their good news. (Luke 24:36) The disciples are afraid they are seeing a spirit. Luke's account goes to great lengths to stress that Jesus is not a spirit. The good news was not simply that Jesus was alive, not that he lived now as a disembodied spirit, not simply that he had received immortality. The good news proclaimed that he had been raised and that he had a body. Jesus shows his hands and feet, clearly to demonstrate that his body bears the wounds suffered in crucifixion. (Luke 24:39) The disciples are portrayed as slow to believe. This is a consistent feature of the resurrection tradition. They did not expect Jesus to rise from the dead. They took some convincing of the reality before their eyes. Luke's account again underlines that Jesus has a body by having him eat in their presence. (Luke 24:42-43) The features of eating and teaching are present as in the Emmaus story.

Jesus had told the disciples on the road that the Christ had to suffer. Here, as there, the evangelist uses the Greek word *dei*, 'it is necessary', to stress that the plans of God had to be fulfilled. (Luke 24:26, 24:44) The law, the prophets and the psalms had to come to fulfilment. As is stressed constantly in the gospel of Matthew, there is a continuity between what God does and reveals in the Son and what God did and revealed in the scriptures. All the evangelists bind their gospels to the scriptures. Luke has the risen Jesus make the connection as he explains to the disciples that the scriptures are fulfilled in him, above all in his suffering and death.

It becomes obvious that this story has major catechetical uses. For Gentile Christians sceptical of the resurrection of the body, Luke underlines the bodily features of the risen Jesus. For those who began to doubt that the Son had really become man, Luke points to Jesus' wounds and his ability to share a meal. For those who still struggled, as the disciples had, with the very idea of a crucified messiah, Luke has Jesus explain the scriptures, which speak of suffering and of resurrection. One has only to recall how Paul's preaching of the resurrection was ridiculed in

Athens to see the catechetical value of this resurrection appearance. (Acts 17:32) One has only to recall Paul's difficulties with the people in Corinth, both Jew and Gentile, to appreciate the scriptural explanation of the fate of the Messiah. (1 Corinthians 1:23) The fundamental historical account of the meeting of the risen Jesus with the eleven is the basis for a catechesis which explores the nature of the resurrection and the reason for the death of the Messiah. Peter will explain to the centurion Cornelius that Jesus had sent the disciples as witnesses of his death and resurrection, and that he had eaten and drunk with them after his resurrection. (Acts 10:40-41)

The eleven disciples are to proclaim forgiveness to all nations. (Luke 24:47) There is a profound accord here with Jesus' commission in Matthew chapter 28. Jesus himself calls them 'witnesses' (Greek *martyres*). (Luke 24:48) He will send upon them the 'promise of the Father'. They will be clothed in 'power' (Greek *dynamis*). (Luke 24:49) The power which Jesus has demonstrated in the ministry will be extended to the disciples. (Luke 4:14) It is a power which Jesus will send from the Father. Jesus explains in Acts chapter 1 that they will receive this power when the Holy Spirit comes. (Acts 1:8)

Luke's gospel ends with a brief reference to the ascension: 'as he blessed them he went away from them and was carried to the heavens'. (Luke 24:51) Acts chapter 1 will give a somewhat fuller account. It is perhaps worth recalling here the tradition of the ascension of Elijah. (2 Kings chapter 2) Once the prophet has completed his task he is taken up to heaven. The disciples worship Jesus and return to Jerusalem, praising God in the temple. (Luke 24:52-53)

The risen Jesus in Matthew

The picture of the risen Jesus in Matthew is somewhat different. No Jesus with wounds who shares a meal, but a majestic, exalted figure. The catechetical thrust of the appearance in Matthew chapter 28 is different, but the fundamentals are similar. Jesus has triumphed over death and sends out the disciples to proclaim the good news.

The first question we might ask is how Matthew reports an appearance of Jesus in Galilee and seems to know nothing of the tradition in Luke of an appearance to the disciples in Jerusalem. The tradition of a Galilee appearance is firmly established in the synoptic stories of Jesus' death. Jesus declares that after his resurrection he will precede the disciples to Galilee. (Mark 14:28; Matthew 26:32) The same expectation is given in the angels' words at the empty tomb in Mark and Matthew. Luke does not record these traditions. John's gospel likewise records none of this but does have a different Galilee appearance in chapter 21. It would seem that there is no easy solution to this discrepancy. The disciples in Luke are told to remain in Jerusalem. (Luke 24:49) The disciples in Matthew return home to the place where they had first encountered Jesus. The most plausible solution may be to maintain a dispersal of the disciples, and that the two traditions of appearances of Jesus have both been expressed as commissions to the whole group of the eleven.

Matthew states that Jesus had directed the disciples to a mountain. (Matthew 28:16) One might recall Jesus ascending a mountain to teach in Matthew chapter 5. The mountain location is clearly symbolic of his authority. The Son appears on the mountain as God had spoken from the mountain to Moses. As in Luke's final scene the disciples worship Jesus. As in Luke's final scene there is some hesitation. The gospel concludes with a magisterial sending out of the disciples to the nations. The short speech is punctuated by different forms of the Greek word for 'all'. 'All' authority is given to Jesus. They are to go to 'all' nations and teach 'all' Jesus has commanded. He is with them 'all' the days. (Matthew 28:18-20)

The fundamental command of Jesus is to 'make disciples' of all the nations. In Matthew's gospel the mission of Jesus, and of the disciples, has been to Jews alone. The disciples were warned not to go to the pagans but to the 'lost sheep of the house of Israel'. (Matthew 10:5-6) But the final command of Jesus reverses these instructions. Matthew, like Luke, has understood the universality of the mission. For Matthew the Jewish people have

rejected the Messiah. A new people will be born who will produce the fruit required by God. (Matthew 21:43) The further
command to baptise 'in the name of the Father, and of the Son,
and of the Holy Spirit' is quite clearly a catechetical addition.
(Matthew 28:19) Baptism is the sign of belief for the earliest
Christians. It is understood as the command of the risen Lord
that new disciples from all nations should be baptised in this
way. The threefold formula surely reflects the liturgical practice
in the church of Matthew.

The Jesus who had taught on the mountain in his ministry
commands his disciples from the mountain to teach others to observe what he taught them. There is a clear awareness in this
gospel of the mission to evangelise not only by proclaiming the
death and resurrection of Jesus but also by giving instructions
for a new way of living based on the teaching of Jesus. The
gospel ends with the words: 'I am with you all the days until the
end of the age.' (Matthew 28:20) While Luke's Jesus had
promised the power of the Spirit, Matthew's Jesus promises his
own continuing presence. It is in Matthew's gospel alone that
Jesus had promised to be where two or three are gathered.
(Matthew 18:20) It is in Matthew's gospel alone that Jesus is described as 'Immanuel', 'God with us'. (Matthew 1:23) Jesus who
is 'God with us' sends out his disciples to the ends of the earth.

The ending of Mark
It is a puzzling aspect of the synoptic tradition that the original
gospel of Mark contains no accounts of meetings with the risen
Jesus. The final chapter of the gospel contains twenty verses but
shows remarkable changes after verse 8. The remaining verses
present a summary of the resurrection appearances found in
other later gospels. There is a reference to the meeting with
Mary Magdalene, to the two disciples on the road into the country, to the gathering of the eleven at supper, to the sending out to
the world, and to the ascension. Furthermore, many important
ancient copies of the text of Mark's gospel do not include these
verses. They were clearly added to provide a summary of the

meetings with the risen Jesus and to bring this gospel to an end in the way a gospel was expected to end.

But what was the intention of the evangelist? He did not write these extra verses. Nor did he write the other even less convincing attempts to provide an ending for Mark's gospel which are preserved in other ancient copies. What remains is a gospel which ends as the women leave the tomb. The final verse reads: 'they said nothing to anyone, for they were afraid'. (Mark 16:8) The ending is remarkable. Some consider it quite implausible that the evangelist should have intended to end the gospel in this way. One might argue, however, that Mark has never hesitated to portray the disciples in an honest way. He reports their constant slowness to understand, and their desertion of Jesus. Now he reports that the women disciples who have discovered the empty tomb are too frightened and confused to tell anyone. One can imagine that a fear of being blamed for the loss of the body, combined with the general fear of arrest of all the followers of Jesus, might have led initially to panic when the strange discovery was made. Mark's gospel constantly reports that those who had been healed by Jesus were told not to spread the news, but that they in fact spoke out openly. Mark ends the gospel by describing how those who are now told to speak out are too afraid even to tell their friends. Silence is now kept when silence should be broken.

The gospel of Mark nevertheless proclaims the resurrection of Jesus. The angel at the tomb declares: 'He has been raised.' (Mark 16:6) The disciples will see him in Galilee. For the first evangelist, this proclamation at the empty tomb seems to have brought the gospel story to an end. God's triumph is declared amid constant human failure.

CHAPTER 8

Matthew and the Teaching Jesus

Matthew's gospel

In the preceding chapters, we have moved through the synoptic record of the ministry of Jesus using the gospel of Mark as our guide. Whenever the material in Mark was also found in Matthew or in Luke we have noted the most significant differences introduced by the later evangelists. We have thus already gained some insights into important features of Matthew's gospel. We saw, for example, how Matthew added to the story of Jesus' baptism a short dialogue between John and Jesus in which John expresses his misgivings about baptising Jesus. (Matthew 3:14-15) We saw how Matthew added to the tradition of the temptation of Jesus a detailed account of three attempts by the devil to lead Jesus away from his chosen path. Throughout the story of the ministry we noted significant contributions of Matthew to an evolving portrayal of Jesus. In the story of Jesus' suffering and death we became aware again of a developing christology and of additions to the core tradition.

Matthew's gospel is considerably longer than Mark's. While Mark contains sixteen chapters, Matthew has twenty-eight. All but a very small amount of Mark's gospel is adopted by Matthew. But Matthew brings to the gospel tradition new perspectives and a great deal of new material. This material will be considered in this chapter, which will complete our survey of the gospel according to Matthew, with the exception of the birth stories in chapters 1-2. Some of the new material, such as the beatitudes and the 'Our Father', is found also in Luke. We will consider in this chapter how such material is presented in both gospels. Other pieces of new material, such as the drama of the last judgement, are only found in Matthew. Such traditions are described as Matthew's special material.

The material found in the synoptic gospels comes from several sources. Mark, as we have seen, provides the basic story of Jesus. Matthew and Luke have access to considerable amounts of new material, particularly the teaching of Jesus. Some of this is found in both gospels, sometimes in different contexts and presentations. All these traditions, found in Mark, Matthew and Luke, and any combination of them, have developed from the experience of Jesus, healer and teacher, the prophet who died and rose again. All these traditions are edited in order to give coherent and relevant presentations of Jesus. All these traditions are vehicles for an evolving picture of Jesus.

The first thing to be aware of as we turn to Matthew's gospel is its overall structure. Mark's gospel has a simple basic story: an initial ministry of Jesus in and around Galilee is followed by one journey of the adult Jesus to Jerusalem, where after a brief public ministry Jesus is apprehended and executed. This clear structure is adopted by Matthew too. Matthew even accentuates the contrast between the initial ministry in the north and the journey to the cross by using solemn formulae to emphasise new stages in the story. After his initial two chapters concerning the birth of Jesus, and his expanded presentation of the baptism and temptation of Jesus, Matthew signals the beginning of the ministry. His rather ponderous introduction reads: 'From that time onwards Jesus began to preach and to say: Repent, for the kingdom of heaven is near.' (Matthew 4:17) We saw how Mark's account of Jesus' work began with a similar manifesto. (Mark 1:15) Matthew accentuates further the beginning of Jesus' proclamation of the kingdom. Later in the gospel he will use a similar introductory technique. The formula this time reads: 'From that time onwards Jesus began to show his disciples that he had to go to Jerusalem, and suffer many things from the elders and chief priests and scribes, to be killed, and to be raised on the third day.' (Matthew 16:21) Matthew has adopted Mark's fundamental story line, but accentuates the different stages of the story.

But Matthew does not simply edit the material he found in the gospel of Mark. He has, as we have already noted, other material about Jesus to insert into the basic gospel structure derived from Mark. Much of this material is teaching of Jesus. Matthew superimposes on the basic gospel five major speeches of Jesus. Much of the material in these speeches is new, and some of it is borrowed from Mark. There is good reason to consider that Matthew's composition of five speeches of Jesus is a deliberate reflection of the five books of the Pentateuch. The five books attributed to Moses give way to the five discourses of Jesus.

Each of these speeches begins in solemn fashion. At the beginning of the first of them, the Sermon on the Mount, Jesus goes up a hill, sits, gathers his disciples, and solemnly begins his teaching. (Matthew 5:1-2) The second discourse is introduced by the naming of twelve apostles. (Matthew 10:1-5) The central discourse, which contains seven parables, also begins in solemn fashion as Jesus sits in the boat and addresses the crowd. (Matthew 13:1-3) The fourth discourse is located during the journey to Jerusalem and is triggered by the disciples' question about who is the greatest. (Matthew 18:1) The fifth and final collection of teachings is Jesus' speech about the time of the end, to which Matthew has joined other relevant material. It begins as Jesus and the disciples leave the temple and go to the Mount of Olives. Once again Jesus is seated to deliver his teaching. (Matthew 24:1-3)

The five speeches all begin in a deliberate fashion, but Matthew shows they form a group above all by his use of a concluding formula in Matthew 7:28, 11:1, 13:53, 19:1, 26:1. At the end of the Sermon on the Mount a literal translation of the original Greek gives: 'and it happened that when Jesus had finished these words.' (Matthew 7:28) The same formula is adapted to the content of each speech. The parable discourse ends: 'and it happened that when Jesus had finished these parables'. (Matthew 13:53) The fifth and final discourse leads into the passion narrative and reads: 'and it happened that when Jesus had finished all these words'. (Matthew 26:1) All these formulas are significant markers, by which Matthew indicates new stages in his gospel account.

The five speeches suggest Matthew's concern to present Jesus as a new and greater Moses. In fact this evangelist is constantly concerned to show that the coming of Jesus and the events surrounding him are the fulfilment of the Jewish scriptures. The God who spoke and acted throughout the history of the Jewish people, the God whose acts and words are recorded in the Jewish scriptures, this same God has acted decisively in Jesus to bring Jewish hopes and expectations to their fulfilment. All the evangelists quote and allude to texts of the Old Testament to demonstrate a similar sense of fulfilment. Matthew does this more frequently and more deliberately than the others. Throughout the gospel we will come upon quotations from books of the Old Testament introduced with a formula such as: 'all this happened in order to fulfil what was spoken by the Lord through the prophet'. (Matthew 1:22)

This survey of some general features of Matthew's gospel illustrates how this evangelist brings a strong editorial mind to the gospel tradition. He has a systematic and orderly approach. He assembles and demarcates. This is combined with his general activity of improving Mark's Greek, both grammar and style. All these features show a developing tradition. But more crucial than the literary improvements is the fact that Matthew presents a new vision of Jesus, who brings the hopes and expectations of Judaism to fulfilment, a teacher greater than Moses, one sent by God who can be acclaimed by his disciples even during the ministry as 'Son of God'. (Matthew 14:33) Matthew's gospel, both in its editing of Mark and in the new material it presents, provides a different but complementary portrait of Jesus. We can become more aware now of the developing rich variety of the gospel tradition.

The beatitudes

Matthew's gospel begins with two chapters related to the birth of Jesus. To these chapters we will turn our attention later. He follows these with his expanded presentation of the preaching of John the Baptist, the baptism of Jesus and the temptations. Before we reach his solemn introduction to the preaching of the kingdom, we hear that John was arrested and that Jesus left Nazareth and settled in Capernaum. (Matthew 4:12-13) Matthew makes explicit something only implied in Mark. Jesus leaves his own quiet village to move to a place which is a centre of trade and travel. Capernaum is by the Sea of Galilee and near the major trade routes. Matthew uses an Old Testament citation at this point to emphasise the significance of the move. (Matthew 4:14-16) He quotes words from the book of Isaiah that light will shine for the land of darkness. This land, he implies, is that of the tribes of Zebulon and Naphtali, tribes on the edge of Israel. The light comes to Israel but also shines for the nations beyond. Matthew emphasises again, as he does in the story of the magi, that the light of the Messiah shines out beyond the confines of Israel and Judaism for the nations of the world.

The lengthy quotation from the prophet Isaiah signals again the fulfilment of Jewish hopes and dreams as Matthew heralds the beginning of Jesus' preaching that the 'kingdom of heaven' has come. (Matthew 4:17) We can recall here that Matthew substitutes 'kingdom of heaven' for 'kingdom of God' out of respect for the name of God. Matthew then shows Jesus calling the first four disciples and gives a summary of Jesus' activity in his ministry. We reach the end of chapter 4 and all is ready for the Sermon on the Mount.

We could safely argue that the Sermon on the Mount in the gospel according to Matthew is the most well-known, loved and revered collection of the teaching of Jesus. The gospel of Matthew achieved its place of pre-eminence among the synoptic gospels largely due to the teachings of Jesus it contains, among which this first discourse is the most distinctive. Within the discourse it is the opening piece of teaching, the beatitudes, which attracts listeners and readers more than anything else. (Matthew 5:1-12)

It may seem inappropriate to deal with these sublime and treasured words in a somewhat academic way. In fact intensive study of the beatitudes has assisted awareness of their extraordinary depth. Beatitudes are found in both Old and New Testaments. One example from the book of Proverbs reads: 'Blessed is the person who finds wisdom, the one who gains understanding'. (Proverbs 3:13) This simple example gives us the essence of the beatitude form of speech, a form found frequently in the wisdom books of the Old Testament. A person in a particular situation or with specific qualities is declared to be the recipient of God's favour.

We must recall again here that Jesus spoke Aramaic, and that all the records of his teaching in the New Testament are in Greek. It is always difficult to establish the exact form of words Jesus used in his teaching. When considering the beatitudes we must note that Matthew lists nine of them at the beginning of the Sermon on the Mount, while Luke sets down four of these in different wording at the beginning of a sermon 'on the plain' in Luke chapter 6. Luke follows the beatitudes with a series of 'woe-speeches'. The poor, the hungry, those in sorrow and those who are persecuted are declared blessed. The rich, the satisfied, those who laugh and those who are praised are cursed. There is a further more subtle difference between Matthew and Luke. Matthew refers to each category of people indirectly, in the third person. Luke generally begins in the same way, but then addresses the listeners directly. Rather than Matthew's 'Blessed are the poor in spirit, for theirs is the kingdom of heaven', Luke has 'Blessed are the poor, for yours is the kingdom of God'. The resulting pattern in the first three beatitudes in Luke seems somewhat disjointed. Translations often read: 'Blessed are you who are poor, for yours is the kingdom of God.' Luke seems to have attempted to make them more immediate for his hearers. Matthew's way of expressing the beatitudes is closer to that found in the wisdom books of the Old Testament.

If we scrutinise Matthew's list and compare it to Luke's, another interesting feature emerges. Luke declares blessings on people in unavoidable situations, which they have not sought, but which have been thrust upon them: the poor, the hungry, those in sorrow, and those who are persecuted. If we compare this list with Matthew's we observe two things. Firstly, Matthew tends to spiritualise the situations: he speaks of the 'poor in spirit' and 'those who hunger and thirst for justice'. Secondly, Matthew's additional beatitudes focus not on unavoidable situations, but on qualities which people develop. He speaks of the gentle, the merciful, the pure in heart and the peacemakers.

Two different types of beatitude thus emerge. Blessings are declared on those in unavoidable situations of need. For these a reversal of situation is proclaimed. The kingdom will come for them. For those who show the virtuous qualities rewards are promised. Reversal of situations of loss, and reward for virtuous action, are the keys to interpreting the beatitudes.

We may now explore something of the qualities and situations considered to be channels of God's blessing. Matthew begins with the 'poor in spirit', his apparent broadening of Luke's simple 'poor'. This group recalls the Old Testament believers referred to as the *anawim*. The original sense of this Hebrew term is 'the poor', those who are lacking the bare necessities of life. The term encompasses also those who, due to their situation, know their need of God. They depend on God, and on those who, faithful to the laws of God's covenant, show kindness to them. The term has a fundamental material sense which attracts spiritual connotations too. Luke's 'poor' (Luke 6:20) and Matthew's 'poor in spirit' (Matthew 5:3) are not so different. Matthew broadens Luke's wording. In declaring that the poor are the heirs of God's kingdom Jesus reaffirms the place of the poor as God's chosen ones.

Matthew's second beatitude, also found in Luke's short list, concerns those who mourn. (Matthew 5:4; Luke 6:21) Matthew's Jesus announces comfort for them. This is the Jesus who, elsewhere in Matthew's gospel, summons those who labour and are burdened. (Matthew 11:28) Luke again uses more concrete terms: those who weep will one day laugh. Both Matthew and Luke also record the beatitude on those who hunger. (Matthew 5:6; Luke 6:21) Matthew expands it to speak of those who hunger and thirst for justice (Greek *dikaiosyne*). We shall return to this most important concept later in the Sermon. Once again Luke refers tersely to a concrete situation, while Matthew points to a broader meaning.

Only Matthew has beatitudes for those who display particular moral qualities: meekness, mercy, purity of heart, a passion for peace, and a passion for justice. There are rich rewards for each of those groups. While the meek will inherit the earth, those who show mercy will have mercy shown them. The pure in heart will have the clarity of vision to see God. Peacemakers will be named children of God. Those whose passion for justice has brought persecution will, like the poor, inherit the kingdom. There is an extraordinary variety of imagery here, as Jesus speaks of life in God's kingdom. The explicit reward of having a share in the kingdom begins and ends the first eight beatitudes in Matthew. The final beatitude in both Matthew and Luke is longer: those who suffer hatred and persecution for their following of Jesus are declared blessed. (Matthew 5:11-12; Luke 6:22-23) This final beatitude is directed to the listeners: your reward will be great. It was quite possibly added to the list after persecution of the early Christians.

The beatitudes of Jesus do not present an esoteric and remote wisdom, but relate profoundly to the everyday experience of believers. With the exception of the final beatitude, they often echo sayings from the prophets and psalms. The comfort and support of God is available for the needy. For Jesus the kingdom is the gift now offered by God to all, but particularly to those who suffer. The way to life for Jesus and for the Christian is amid and through human suffering. God's blessings come abundantly to the needy and the suffering. It is not surprising that Christians have always had an instinctive reverence for the beatitudes, recognising that they reflect the cross and the resurrection. They know the beatitudes to be supremely simple and unfathomably deep. These teachings of Jesus are treasured well beyond the confines of Christianity.

A more abundant justice

Matthew's collection of the teachings of Jesus in the Sermon on the Mount has many more treasures to offer. With the exception of the Lord's Prayer, we shall consider most of the other teachings more briefly. Jesus next addresses the disciples as 'salt of the earth' and 'light of the world'. (Matthew 5:13-16) While the image of salt is used to proclaim a warning lest the salt become tasteless, the image of light brings encouragement to let the light of discipleship shine out for all.

Jesus' next words are a declaration of his purpose. We might reflect that there are few such 'I statements' of Jesus in Mark's gospel. The later evangelists, by contrast, use them with increasing frequency to have Jesus himself declare the purpose of his coming. Matthew's Jesus says: 'I have not come to abolish (the law and the prophets), but to fulfil them.' (Matthew 5:17) This saying is of fundamental importance in showing us Matthew's view of Jesus and his mission. Jesus comes to bring to fulfilment what went before. At the time of Jesus Jews would refer to their scriptures as the law (Hebrew *torah*), the prophets, and the other writings. Jesus is thus suggesting that his mission brings to fulfilment whatever God has revealed in the scriptures of Judaism. Matthew, as we have seen, frequently quotes verses of scripture and declares them to have been fulfilled. This citation of specific texts is another way of asserting that Jesus has brought the past hopes and expectations of Judaism to fulfilment. As in the beatitudes Matthew here shows that the preaching of Jesus is deeply rooted in Judaism. The teaching Jesus in Matthew emphasises for Jews that acceptance of Jesus and the Christian good news is logical and natural to Jewish faith.

And yet Jesus takes things further and goes deeper. Jesus declares: 'If your justice (Greek *dikaiosyne*) is not more abundant than that of the scribes and Pharisees, you shall not enter the kingdom of heaven.' (Matthew 5:20) The Greek word *dikaiosyne* occurs repeatedly in the Sermon on the Mount. Its fundamental meaning is 'justice', but in its various uses in the New Testament different senses emerge. Paul refers to 'the justice of God' in his

Letter to the Romans to declare God's fidelity and solidarity. Jesus here speaks of the justice of faithful discipleship. Different translators have sought to render the concept more precisely. They speak of 'virtue', 'uprightness' and 'righteousness'. The essential meaning conveyed by 'your justice' is the disciple's response to God's fidelity in faithfully doing God's will. This justice can be more or less abundant. Jesus shows continuity with the faithful response of Judaism to God but suggests a fuller justice, a more abundant virtue. In this way Matthew prepares for some teachings of Jesus which relate to specific points of the law.

This section contains the six 'antitheses', in which Jesus quotes an accepted opinion of Judaism and challenges it with the words: 'But I say this to you.' (Matthew 5:21-48) These teachings of Jesus go beyond the law, and deeper than the law. In so doing they may even abrogate an instruction of the law. They illustrate the statement that Jesus comes to fulfil and not to abolish the law and the prophets. (Matthew 5:17) The command not to kill is deepened with the ruling out of any unworthy treatment of a neighbour. The command forbidding adultery is enriched by the exclusion of any kind of lustful abuse. As Jesus limits the allowance of divorce he takes a stand for the respect of marriage partners, and particularly of the wife. Oaths are excluded, for the disciple should have no need of them in order to speak with openness and truth. The law of retaliation expressed in the phrase 'an eye for an eye and a tooth for a tooth' set limits to the punishments which could be inflicted. Jesus replaces this with his counsel of forgiveness and submissiveness. Love of neighbour had been understood to imply hatred of enemies and there was much debate about the definition of neighbour. Jesus by contrast presents the radical challenge of loving enemies. In all these topics Jesus joins the debate about true virtue and living according to the law which was vibrant in the Judaism of his day. In every case Jesus goes to the heart of the customary command and, with his own authority, makes it more radical and more generous. He challenges disciples to live a more abundant justice.

The antitheses are concluded by Jesus' statement: 'You will be perfect (Greek *teleioi*) as your heavenly Father is perfect.' (Matthew 5:48) Jesus invites disciples to go beyond the law. The Greek word for 'perfection' has connotations of 'completeness' and of 'wholeness'. For Christian disciples morality is no longer a question of doing good or evil, but of striving for perfection. By the exercise of justice, virtue and fidelity the Christian comes to perfection, completeness and wholeness.

The exploration of how such justice is to be lived continues in Matthew chapter 6. Jesus considers three fundamental acts of virtue in Judaism: almsgiving, prayer and fasting. Jesus begins by saying: 'Take care not to parade your justice (Greek *dikaiosyne*) before others in order to be seen by them.' (Matthew 6:1) The issue here is the ostentatious performance of good actions. Jesus contrasts the behaviour he counsels with that of the 'hypocrites who have had their reward'. (Matthew 6:2, 6:5, 6:16) The three sections on these three acts of virtue use similar phrases: do not be like the hypocrites; let your justice be in secret; the Father who sees in secret will reward you. The literal sense of 'hypocrite' (Greek *hypokrites*) points to one who wears a mask, who covers up the true self, who puts on a good show, one who is acting in a play. Jesus does not find fault with virtuous actions. He criticises the display of such actions and the way they may be misused to cover up the true self. Actions such as these are to be performed in secret in order to avoid the pretence of having already reached perfection. Truth and honesty are once again fundamental to Jesus' teaching. In striving for the more abundant justice there is no room for self-satisfied and deceptive parades.

The section is extended by the insertion of extra teaching about prayer. Having said that prayer should not be ostentatious, but in secret, Jesus goes on to tell the disciples not to babble (Greek *battalogein*) like the pagans. (Matthew 6:7) Interestingly here the comparison is not with Jewish custom but with pagan styles of prayer. The prayer of the disciples of Jesus is to be simple. At this point Jesus teaches them the Lord's Prayer.

As with the beatitudes, there are two versions of the Lord's

Prayer in the synoptic gospels, one in Matthew's Sermon on the Mount (Matthew 6:9-13) and the other in Luke at the beginning of the journey to Jerusalem. (Luke 11:2-4) Luke's version is considerably shorter, consisting of two petitions in the third person which concern the name of God and the kingdom, and three requests in the second person asking for bread, forgiveness and avoidance of the trial. Matthew's prayer adds the petition that God's will be done, and the extra request for deliverance from evil. It seems logical to assume that Matthew added these new petitions. And yet Luke's form of the prayer also shows signs of development.

Luke's simple opening 'Father' is made more formal and solemn with Matthew's 'Our Father in heaven'. Paul also mentions Christian use in prayer of *abba*, the Aramaic word for 'father'. It is the Spirit who moves Christians to cry out *abba*. (Romans 8:15; Galatians 4:6) The 'Our Father' is the prayer of the kingdom. The two initial petitions in Luke, and the three in Matthew, pray for the coming of the kingdom. The name of God will be held holy with the full coming of the kingdom. Matthew adds the petition that the will of God be done on earth as in heaven. The ultimate fulfilment of the will of God will be the full coming of the kingdom. The ancient Aramaic Christian prayer *maranatha*, the prayer that the Lord Jesus may come (1 Corinthains 16:22; Revelation 22:20), is comparable to these first petitions of the Lord's Prayer. Jesus instructs the disciples to pray for the coming of the kingdom of God. Christian prayer has an added focus on the role of Jesus in the coming of that kingdom. The ancient Jewish Aramaic prayer known as the 'Kaddish', which may date to Jesus' time, has a similar juxtaposition of the concepts of hallowing God's name and the coming of the kingdom. Once again the profound Jewish roots of Jesus' teaching are apparent.

These initial petitions of the prayer focus on the end, on the complete establishment of God's kingdom. The petitions which follow have something of this emphasis too, though requests for bread, forgiveness, avoidance of the trial and freedom from evil are also understood to refer to the continuing life of Christians.

The most difficult of these petitions to understand precisely is the request for bread. Matthew's text reads: 'Give us today our daily (Greek *epiousios*) bread.' (Matthew 6:11) Luke has 'Give us day by day our daily bread.' (Luke 11:3) The sense of the Greek word *epiousios* is much debated, and the term is impossible to translate back into the Aramaic words Jesus used. The sense of 'future bread' or 'bread for tomorrow' which is often suggested points to the bread shared when the kingdom comes. The Latin Vulgate translation discovers here a reference to the eucharist and calls the bread *supersubstantialis*. The customary English translation as 'our daily bread' conveys the idea of relying on God for the needs of each day. Luke emphasises this meaning by requesting daily bread for each day. (Luke 11:3) Both the present sense and the future sense are suggested in the prayer.

The request for forgiveness is more straightforward. The acknowledgement of 'sins' in Luke is the acknowledgement of 'debts' in Matthew. Luke's word would perhaps be more understandable for Gentile readers. Human forgiveness of others is furthermore to reflect divine forgiveness. The same idea is in Matthew's beatitude: those merciful to others have mercy shown them by God. (Matthew 5:7) The theme of forgiveness is taken up again by Matthew in verses he appended to the Lord's Prayer. (Matthew 6:14-15)

Matthew's next request, which ends the prayer in Luke, seeks avoidance of the 'trial' (Greek *peirasmos*). This seems to refer to the end-time trial, which precedes the final establishment of God's kingdom. But *peirasmos* can also mean 'testing' or 'temptation'. It has a sense also for everyday Christian life. Christians seek God's protection in the testing of daily life. Matthew's final request is also ambiguous. 'Free us from evil' may be understood in two ways. The Greek form of the word *poneros* used here may mean either 'the evil one' or 'evil'.

Jesus who proclaimed the kingdom in word and deed gives the disciples a prayer for the kingdom. It focuses on the coming of God's kingdom and their needs in the light of that coming. It is a prayer which suggests the imminent coming of the king-

dom. But its ambiguities give it meaning for the daily commitment of Christians too. Trusting that God's kingdom will come,
that God's name will be held holy, that God's will will be fully
done, Christians pray for the bread, the forgiveness, the protection they need on the way.

The early Christian document known as the *Didache* continues the process Matthew seems to have begun by adding clauses
to the Lord's Prayer. The ending found in the *Didache* is used by
many Christians to conclude the prayer. It reads: 'For the kingdom, the power and the glory are yours now and for ever.' This
addition is not found in the most reliable ancient copies of
Matthew's gospel.

Up to this point the Sermon on the Mount has shown signs of
deliberate structuring. The beatitudes led on to six antitheses
and advice on three acts of virtue. The remaining verses in chapter six and the whole of chapter seven contain a collection of further sayings of Jesus in no particular order. Jesus' words on
providence, on the Father's care for the birds of the air and the
lilies in the field, have become proverbial. (Matthew 6:26-29) In
chapter seven Jesus pronounces the 'golden rule' as the meaning
of the law and the prophets: 'Always do to others what you
would like them to do to you, for this is the law and the
prophets.' (Matthew 7:12) This rule was commonly quoted in
ancient times. Its presence in the teaching of Jesus suggests a
continuing debate of Christians with ancient ideas of morality.
As the Sermon ends Jesus describes those who base their lives
on his teaching as building their homes on rock. (Matthew 7:24)
The Sermon provides enduring reliable guidance for Christian
discipleship, and a challenge which goes well beyond questions
of right and wrong.

Further teaching of Jesus

Concluding the Sermon on the Mount with the first use of his
customary formula (Matthew 7:28), Matthew turns his attention
to the miracles of Jesus. In chapters 8 and 9 he gathers together
accounts of ten miracles of Jesus, interspersed with some teaching.

As yet he has only given a cursory reference to Jesus' miracles in the summary statement in 4:23. Virtually the same statement is repeated in 9:35. This literary technique of repetition of the same material at the beginning and end of a section is known as an inclusion. The Sermon on the Mount and the collection of ten miracles are framed by summary statements about Jesus' teaching and healing. Many of the miracles stories are edited versions of accounts found in Mark's gospel. The story of the healing of a leper is placed first, and the leper in Matthew's version addresses Jesus as 'Lord'. (Matthew 8:2) Matthew will frequently have those who request help from Jesus address him in this way, reflecting how his Christian community addressed Jesus in prayer. Matthew follows this story with the healing of the centurion's servant, a story found in Matthew and Luke, and uses it to illustrate how Gentiles will replace Jews in the kingdom. (Matthew 8:11-12) Referring to the healing of many sick people, Matthew inserts a citation from the book of Isaiah: 'He took away our infirmities and carried our diseases.' (Matthew 8:17) The words are from the fourth servant song in the second part of the book of Isaiah. Once again the evangelist illustrates how Jesus fulfils Old Testament ideals.

We have already seen in an earlier chapter how Matthew edits the story of the stilling of the storm. Perhaps more perplexing is his replacing of the Gerasene demoniac with two possessed men. (Matthew 8:28) Matthew will also retell Mark's healing of blind Bartimaeus as a story of two blind men. (Matthew 20:29-34) A similar story is found in this collection. (Matthew 9:27-31) Matthew has assembled here a substantial collection of miracle stories to match the impact of the Sermon on the Mount. Jesus is both a great teacher and a great healer.

The second major discourse of Jesus, the discourse about mission, comes in chapter 10. It is considerably briefer, as are the subsequent discourses, than the Sermon on the Mount. Matthew places the call of the twelve, whom he names 'apostles', at the beginning of the discourse. Their mission, it is emphasised, is not to go to pagan nations. Jesus says: 'Do not go the way of the nations, and do not enter a Samaritan town. Go rather to the lost sheep of the house of Israel.' (Matthew 10:5-6) These verses pick up the compassion of Jesus for the lost, expressed at the end of the previous chapter. (Matthew 9:36) It is a basic tenet of Matthew that Jesus' mission was primarily to Judaism. A similar emphasis will be inserted by Matthew into Mark's story of the healing of the daughter of the Canaanite woman. Jesus will say: 'I was sent only to the lost sheep of the house of Israel.' (Matthew 15:24)

Matthew's discourse shows that the disciples imitate their master. They preach the good news of the kingdom. They heal the sick. Above all, they should expect persecution. The speech shows awareness of the difficulties of the early Christian mission and would seem to have been elaborated on the basis of these experiences. Jesus comes to bring not peace, but a sword. The preaching of the kingdom brings inevitable divisions. A quotation from the prophet Micah is used to illustrate this. (Matthew 10:34-36; Micah 7:6) The discourse gathers together diverse material relating to mission.

The third major discourse is Matthew's collection of the parables of Jesus in chapter 13. Much of the material here is Matthew's editing of parables from Mark chapter 4. But Matthew includes several parables only found in his gospel. Matthew does not record Mark's parable of the secret growth of the seed of the kingdom. Instead he tells of the secret sowing by night of bad seed among the good. This parable of the weeds and the wheat is also known as the parable of the darnel in the field, or the tares. Darnel and tares are types of virulent weed difficult to distinguish from wheat. The parable proclaims the patience of God who allows good and bad to flourish together until harvest. (Matthew 13:24-30) The parable of the dragnet speaks of the judgement by describing the fishermen sorting their catch. (Matthew 13:47-50) Both these parables prepare for the parables of judgement which are part of Matthew's fifth and final discourse in chapter 25. Matthew is also the only evangelist to record the short parables of the treasure hidden in the field and

the pearl of great price. (Matthew 13:44-46) The memorable imagery from daily life recalls similar imagery in the teaching on
providence in the Sermon on the Mount. Matthew has collected
together many parables of Jesus which no doubt were preached
on different occasions. He concludes the discourse with praise of
discipleship of the kingdom of heaven. (Matthew 13:52) Disciples
will bring forth treasures new and old. Jesus brings the old to
fulfilment.

As we move towards the fourth discourse we reach the point
where preaching of the kingdom gives way to Jesus' foreseeing
of his death. (Matthew 16:21) Matthew's fourth discourse is in
fact inserted in the journey to Jerusalem. It is the teaching of
Jesus about the community. It is built on some of the teaching on
discipleship which Mark recorded during the journey narrative.
The greatest is to be like a child. (Matthew 18:4) The members of
the community are not to lead others astray. (Matthew 18:6) The
lost are to be sought out. (Matthew 18:12-14) Believers are to
speak the truth to each other and challenge scandalous behaviour, first in private and then in the presence of the community
(Greek *ekklesia*). (Matthew 18:15-17) The community is to be one
of prayer and forgiveness. In this context Matthew places the
powerful parable of the unforgiving debtor. (Matthew 18:23-35)
Jesus' short speech contains a constantly relevant challenge to
the life of communities.

The journey to Jerusalem continues once the speech has
ended. Matthew edits the material found during the journey
narrative in Mark. In chapter 20 he inserts the parable of the
labourers in the vineyard. Those who work the whole day are
indignant that those who came late receive equal reward. They
grumble (Greek *goggyzo*) at the landowner, who represents God
in the parable. (Matthew 20:11) But God does not work by the
laws of human justice. The generosity of God to the lost, to those
found at the last moment, teaches that no worker, however long
their service, can earn the limitless gifts of God.

The final discourse

The fifth and final discourse is set in Matthew's account of the Jerusalem ministry. We have already seen how Matthew edits Mark's material in the Jerusalem ministry. But Matthew also has some major insertions before the final discourse begins. After his version of the parable of the wicked tenants Matthew introduces the parable of the wedding feast. (Matthew 22:1-14) Luke has a rather different version earlier in his gospel. (Luke 14:16-24)

The king provides a wedding feast and invitations are sent. Those invited refuse to come. They are replaced by people found at random, good and bad alike. (Matthew 22:10) Like the parable of the wicked tenants this parable too speaks of the unwillingness of Israel to respond to God's call. The invitation to good and bad has triggered an addition to the story. The man with no wedding garment is thrown out. (Matthew 22:11-13) The message of the parable that all are welcome to the wedding feast is qualified by this addition. The extended parable holds in tension two truths. The good news of the kingdom is preached to all. The presence of all at the wedding is desired. And yet the message of the kingdom contains a challenge to a change of life, to repentance.

We have already noted how Matthew adds to the account of the Jerusalem ministry of Jesus a lengthy speech directed against the scribes and Pharisees. (Matthew 23:1-39) Mark reported a very short speech of Jesus against the ostentatious behaviour of the scribes. (Mark 12:38-40) Matthew's expansion of this material is no doubt due to worsening relations between Christian believers and the Jewish religious leadership. It is of some importance that Christians realise how Matthew has exaggerated the negative aspects of the behaviour of the scribes and Pharisees. A more balanced impression of Jesus' relationships with contemporary religious leaders was given in Mark's account of the Jerusalem ministry.

The fifth and final discourse of Jesus is to be found in chapters 24 and 25. Chapter 24 is Matthew's editing of the end-time speech, the apocalyptic discourse, found in Mark chapter 13. But the fifth discourse of Jesus continues with the three sections of chapter 25: the parable of the ten virgins, the parable of the talents and the drama of the last judgement. All three take up and develop aspects of the apocalyptic discourse. It is with these elements that Matthew's Jesus will conclude his teaching.

The parable of the ten virgins takes up the theme of readiness for the Lord's coming. The Greek term *kyrios* means both 'Lord' and 'master'. The coming of this Lord and master was the theme of the last sections of chapter 24. (Matthew 24:42-51) The ten virgins display two ways of waiting for the Lord, who in this parable, as earlier in Matthew 9:15, is symbolised by the bridegroom. Some are prepared for his coming, while others are not. The delay of the bridegroom clearly picks up the delay of the return of Christ. The statement of the bad servant in the apocalyptic discourse that the master 'delays' or 'takes his time' (Greek *chronizei*) is echoed in the delay of the groom. (Matthew 24:48, 25:5) Those who are not ready are not admitted. Their plea 'Lord, Lord, open to us' receives the response 'I do not know you'. (Matthew 25:12) The urgent encouragement to watch brings the parable to an end and echoes the apocalyptic discourse once again. (Matthew 24:42, 25:13)

The parable of the talents is also closely related to the apocalyptic discourse. It is a lengthy parable which develops the theme of the master who departs and leaves his servants behind, a theme found in the concluding verses of chapter 24. In the parable of the talents the servants are rewarded for using their talents wisely. The unproductive servant is thrown out into the darkness, where there is 'weeping and grinding of teeth'. (Matthew 25:30) This phrase is frequently used in Matthew's gospel to speak of the situation of those who are condemned. He used it of the man with no wedding garment and of the wicked servant in the apocalyptic discourse. (Matthew 22:13, 24:51) The 'grinding of teeth' is an expression used in the book of Psalms to illustrate the anger and envy of the wicked towards the just. (Psalms 37:12, 112:10) In the Acts of the Apostles Stephen's accusers 'grind their teeth' at him. (Acts 7:54)

The final section of the teaching of Jesus in Matthew's gospel is the drama of the last judgment, which takes up and develops the image of the son of man in glory. (Matthew 24:30) Who are the 'chosen ones' gathered by the angels? (Matthew 24:31) Who are those who will inherit the kingdom? By what criterion will they be judged? 'All the nations' are gathered. (Matthew 25:32) Clearly there are no more distinctions of Jew and Gentile. The whole human race is judged by the same criterion. The son of man is likened to a king. The assembled nations are separated as a shepherd separates sheep and goats.

The criterion of judgement is the treatment afforded to those in need. Six opportunities for acts of kindness are listed: feeding the hungry, giving drink to the thirsty, welcoming the stranger, clothing the naked, visiting the sick, and going to those in prison. What is remarkable is the king's assertion that these deeds had been done to him. (Matthew 25:40) It recalls some of Jesus' earlier statements. In the missionary discourse he said: 'Anyone who receives you, receives me, and anyone who receives me, receives the one who sent me.' (Matthew 10:40) In the discourse on community he said: 'Whoever receives one of these little ones in my name, receives me.' (Matthew 18:5) Discipleship is expressed in service. Service of those in need is service of the Lord. The one who sees life as a call to serve is a disciple of Jesus. That person discovers God in others. There is a profound challenge here to some misunderstandings of the life of the disciple. To enhance and defend the lives of others is the heart of discipleship. To neglect to do this is to fail in discipleship. Those who enhance and defend the lives of others do the work of the kingdom, the work exemplified in Jesus' deeds of healing as he preached the kingdom. It is they who inherit the kingdom.

But what happens to the others? Those who fail to serve are sent away 'to the everlasting fire'. (Matthew 25:41) The synoptic gospels report that Jesus spoke of the 'eternal fire' and the 'gehenna of fire' as the place of condemnation. (Matthew 5:22; Mark 9:43-48) The valley of Hinnom (Hebrew *ge-hinnom*) on the south side of Jerusalem had been a place of child sacrifice to pagan gods. (2 Kings 23:10) It had later become a rubbish dump. This place of cremations and burning became an image of the place of punishment. The apocalyptic image of consuming fire is used as a parallel image to the darkness, with weeping and grinding of teeth, to which the unproductive servant was delivered. (Matthew 25:30) The powerful and terrifying image of eternal fire should not to be taken literally. The image speaks of the awful pain of losing God, losing the kingdom, losing the light. The last judgement scene is a challenge to recognise life as a call to service and community. For Jesus, love of God and love of neighbour are the greatest commandment. (Matthew 22:34-40) The last judgement again demonstrates that they are inseparable: whatever you do to the least, you do to me.

CHAPTER 9

Luke and the Compassionate Jesus

Luke's gospel

We have already had the opportunity to gain some impressions of the gospel of Luke. As we went through the story of the ministry, using Mark as our guide, we noted how Luke had adapted and added to the traditions. In dealing with the gospel of Matthew in the previous chapter we noted Luke's variant presentations of texts such as the beatitudes and the Lord's Prayer. We took time in the chapter on the resurrection of Jesus to examine Luke's special traditions. But it is important to note that almost half the material in Luke's gospel is unique to him. This is often described as Luke's special material. Luke obviously had a separate source of traditions about Jesus which makes a major contribution to our knowledge of Jesus. In considering this material in this chapter we will complete our survey of the gospel according to Luke, with the one exception of the birth stories in chapters 1-2, to which we will turn our attention in the next chapter.

Luke has his own characteristic portrayal of Jesus, a portrayal which has been cherished by Christians over the centuries. It is characterised by compassion. The compassionate Jesus demonstrates the compassion of God in reaching out above all to those who are lost. Luke also gives his particular account of the disciples. They are examples for believers to follow. Luke plays down their failings and infidelities.

It is of fundamental importance to remember that this gospel is the first part of a two-volume work. Luke's gospel and the Acts of the Apostles belong together. It is difficult to keep this in mind, particularly since the canonical ordering of the books of

the New Testament has placed the gospel of John between the
two volumes of Luke in order to keep the four gospels together.
There is an obvious continuity between the gospel and the Acts.
The gospel repeatedly underlines the presence of the Spirit in
the life of Jesus and in discipleship, preparing the reader for the
constant guidance of the Spirit in Acts. Jesus is filled with the
holy Spirit. (Luke 4:1) The Spirit of the Lord is upon him. (Luke
4:18) The heavenly Father will give the holy Spirit to those who
ask. (Luke 11:13) When the time comes the holy Spirit will teach
the disciples what to say. (Luke 12:12) This foreshadows how
the Spirit is always present in Acts. The prayer of Jesus repeatedly mentioned in the gospel likewise lays the foundation for
the prayer of the community in Acts. Luke's Jesus shows a particular concern for the poor and for the sharing of riches. In Acts
the community is seen to pool its resources, (Acts 2:44, 4:32) The
Jesus of Luke comes to look for the lost, to proclaim forgiveness
to both Jew and Gentile. Acts tells of the preaching of the gospel
of forgiveness from Jerusalem to the ends of the earth. (Acts 1:8)

There are also more specific parallels to be observed. The
particular way in which the call of Peter is presented in the
gospel, with Peter declaring himself to be a sinful man (Luke
5:8), may well be designed to prepare for the conversion of Paul.
Luke illustrates that all disciples, even the greatest, are granted
forgiveness and called to a new life by Jesus. The death of
Stephen has similarities with the death of Jesus. Stephen forgives his killers and, while Jesus commended his life into the
hands of the Father, Stephen offers his life to Jesus. (Acts 7:59-60)
Luke shows that Christians are to follow Jesus in trusting surrender of their lives. Pilate's sending of Jesus for questioning to
Herod Antipas is recalled when Paul's case is put before
Agrippa II by the Roman governor Festus in Acts chapters 25-26.
In the accounts of the trials of Jesus and of Paul, Roman tolerance
of Christianity is affirmed. The concerns and emphases of Luke
in the gospel are carried over into the Acts of the Apostles.

Luke, like Matthew, adopts the basic structure of Mark. The
initial ministry in Galilee is followed by the journey to

Jerusalem, the place of death and resurrection. Like Matthew, Luke adapts Mark's structure in order to accommodate the great quantity of material he adds to the written gospel tradition. This is most obvious in his expansion of the chapters covering the journey to Jerusalem. Luke's journey of Jesus begins in chapter 9 and he reaches Jerusalem in chapter 19. As Matthew inserted the discourse about the community during the journey narrative, so Luke inserts quantities of teaching of Jesus during the journey. The instruction given to the disciples in Mark's gospel in the context of the journey to Jerusalem, teaching about the cross and about service, is the foundation on which both Matthew and Luke build further teaching of Jesus.

The gospel of Luke begins with four remarkable verses. One extended sentence solemnly prefaces the gospel and provides what is unique in the synoptic gospels, a statement of the intention and goal of the evangelist. These words, addressed to 'most excellent Theophilus', provide another connection with the Acts of the Apostles, which also begins with such a preface. Neither Mark nor Matthew has included similar statements. Only John comes close to Luke with the concluding words of his gospel, when he affirms that it was written so that believers might have life in Jesus' name. (John 20:31)

Luke begins by affirming that many other writers have set down a record of the events concerning Jesus. (Luke 1:1) Luke's assertion that many have already written may be an exaggeration. On the other hand, there may well have been written material about Jesus which circulated freely and either found its way into a written gospel or was eventually lost. Luke confirms the impression given by study of the three synoptic gospels that he made use of earlier material. One of the others who had already written was surely the evangelist Mark. The events recorded are referred to as 'events which have been brought to fulfilment among us'. (Luke 1:1) Luke's use of the concept of fulfilment will be echoed later in the gospel. It underlines that all these events are guided by God and that ancient expectations are to be realised.

Luke declares that the written material had come from 'eye-witnesses', those who had been with Jesus, and from 'servants of the word', those who had preached the good news of Jesus. (Luke 1:2) The evangelist thus confirms modern insights about the development of the gospel tradition, illustrating how the gospel material originated in the experience of the living Jesus, was passed on in the preaching and eventually written down.

In the third verse of this long and carefully constructed sentence he addresses 'most excellent Theophilus'. Theophilus may well have been a historical individual, perhaps some kind of official, who had become a Christian, or intended to do so. The preface in Acts is similarly addressed to Theophilus. It has been suggested that the name Theophilus, which means 'lover of God', could be fictitious and represent all those lovers of God who seek fuller knowledge of the gospel. Luke intends to write 'in an orderly fashion' (Greek *kathexes*). (Luke 1:3) The order intended is not chronological. As with the other evangelists, there is a logical and catechetical ordering of the story of Jesus. Luke emphasises that he sets about his task after examining all things carefully. Finally he describes the goal of this written work: that Theophilus should come to know the reliability (Greek *asphaleia*) of the things about which he has been informed (Greek *katechethes*). (Luke 1:4) Luke uses the same Greek term (*katechein*) to refer to the instruction given to the Alexandrian Jew Apollos. (Acts 18:25) Luke's carefully researched and carefully compiled new gospel will confirm those who have been catechised in their new faith. His gospel will build on the preached message and the earlier written traditions as he elaborates his own distinctive presentation of Jesus.

Jesus at Nazareth
Luke reorganises the narrative of Jesus' early ministry. After the account in chapters 3 and 4 of John the Baptist, the baptism of Jesus and the temptations, into which Luke also inserts his genealogy of Jesus, Luke begins the story of the ministry. He summarises Jesus' activity: 'Jesus returned to Galilee in the

power of the Spirit. And news of him spread throughout the surrounding region. He taught in their synagogues and was praised by all.' (Luke 4:14-15) This summary statement leads immediately into Luke's account of Jesus' visit to Nazareth.

Luke begins Jesus' ministry with a dramatic story of the acceptance and rejection of Jesus by his own people. (Luke 4:16-30) Mark and Matthew record an account of his visit and his rejection at Nazareth later in their story of the Galilee ministry. (Mark 6:1-6; Matthew 13:54-58) Luke uses this tradition of the Nazareth visit to provide what amounts to a foretaste of the ministry as a whole. The content of Jesus' speech, the quotation from the scriptures followed by the briefest of commentaries, prepares for the speeches of the apostles in Acts. Though much longer, they use Old Testament texts as the basis for preaching.

The Old Testament quotation, which is based on the first verses of chapter 61 of the book of Isaiah, is a declaration by an anonymous prophet about his mission. It should be remembered that the final chapters of the book of Isaiah gather material from various sources. Jesus reads: 'The Spirit of the Lord is upon me, for he has anointed me. He has sent me to bring good news to the poor, to proclaim liberty to captives, and sight to the blind, to set the downtrodden free, to proclaim the Lord's year of favour.' (Luke 4:18-19) There is no mention of the kingdom. The focus is on Jesus and the deeds he will perform. We can observe here the transition which takes place in the gospel tradition as the preaching of Jesus about the kingdom gives way to the preaching of believers about Jesus. This preaching about Jesus is placed on the lips of Jesus himself. Luke proclaims once more what was implied at Jesus' baptism. Jesus is filled with the Spirit. Jesus is the anointed one of God, the Messiah.

The text continues by listing the activities of this anointed one. He brings good news to the poor. In the beatitudes of both Luke and Matthew the poor are the first to whom the kingdom is promised. (Luke 6:20; Matthew 5:3) The poor of the Old Testament (Hebrew *anawim*), who looked to God as the mainstay of their lives, are the first to receive the good news. Luke's

choice of this particular Old Testament text as the manifesto of
Jesus establishes Jesus' particular concern for the poor. It is a
concern for all those in need, all the marginalised, all those who
depend on God, all those listed as the prophetic text continues,
the captives, the blind, the downtrodden. For them Jesus shows
God's compassion. The free citation concludes with reference to
the year of jubilee. Each fiftieth year was the occasion for the re-
mission of debt, the freeing of slaves and the return of property
to the original owner. (Leviticus 25) The prophet's reference to a
'year of favour' means that God's healing is extended to remedy
the ills of all those in need. This text spells out the implications of
the preaching about the kingdom. God's power is available, as
the words and healing acts of Jesus make clear, to challenge evil
and pain, sickness and death. The reign of God is to be established. Jesus announces God's year of favour as God's constant
compassion.

Having read the text Jesus declares: 'Today this scripture has
been fulfilled as you listen.' (Luke 4:21) The concept of fulfilment has already been encountered in Mark, and particularly in
Matthew's gospel. Jesus' statement here at the beginning of the
ministry that a particular text of scripture has been fulfilled prepares for the statement of the risen Jesus at the very end of the
gospel that everything about him in the scriptures has been fulfilled. (Luke 24:44) The implications of Jesus' words here are
momentous for those who listen. Luke proclaims the presence of
healing, here and now, the presence of salvation today. At other
significant moments Jesus will proclaim again the today of salvation. To Zacchaeus Jesus says: 'Today salvation has come to
this house.' (Luke 19:9) To the good thief Jesus says: 'Today you
will be with me in paradise.' (Luke 23:43) The reaction of the audience in the synagogue at Nazareth is positive. They marvel at
his 'words of grace'. (Luke 4:22)

The initial verses of this summary of Jesus' ministry proclaim
the mission of Jesus to bring the good news of the kingdom. They
record the enthusiasm of those who heard him. Quite abruptly
the mood turns sour. Luke condenses the hostile questioning of

the people of Nazareth found in Mark and Matthew. They challenge him with one question: 'Is not this the son of Joseph?' (Luke 4:22) Jesus picks up their resentment that he works no mighty deeds in their village, and angers them further by citing the miracles Elijah and Elisha worked for those who were not even Israelites, the Sidonian widow and the Syrian leper. The Jesus of Luke not only implicitly challenges their lack of faith, but also suggests that foreigners will be more receptive to his message. A parallel situation is worth noting in Acts chapter 13. Paul and Barnabas proclaim the good news to Jews. Some accept the teaching while others are hostile. Paul and Barnabas then announce their decision to bring the message to foreigners.

Luke concludes the Nazareth drama with the physical hostility of the crowd. (Luke 4:29) This evangelist, who often avoids brutality and violence, reports the manhandling of Jesus to give the fullest picture of reactions to Jesus. This dramatic scene presents the extremes of admiration of Jesus and violent rejection. As well as being made aware of the extremes, the reader is challenged to decide for or against Jesus at the outset. In the final verse there is the extraordinary statement that Jesus simply walked through the crowd and went on his way. (Luke 4:30) It suggests divine power and prepares us for a similar statement in John's gospel when the Jews intend to stone Jesus. (John 8:59) This is a clear example of christological development. In both these texts the vulnerable Jesus is being presented as the sovereign Son of God.

The Galilee ministry

The rearrangement by Luke of the traditions of Jesus' ministry in Galilee is apparent as he follows the visit to Nazareth with accounts of ministry in Capernaum. (Luke 4:31-44) These are Luke's reworking of material found in Mark's gospel. (Mark 1:21-39) Peter's miraculous catch of fish precedes the call of Peter. (Luke 5:1-11) Luke's 'sermon on the plain' (Luke 6:20-49) contains significant parallels with Matthew's Sermon on the Mount. The raising of the son of the widow at Nain is unique to Luke. (Luke 7:11-17)

Luke's emphasis on Jesus' outreach to sinners is particularly evident in the story of the 'woman who was a sinner'. (Luke 7:37) This unnamed woman anoints the feet of Jesus with her tears and with precious ointment. This act of tenderness causes scandal. The woman is known to be a sinner. Jesus reads the thoughts of Simon the Pharisee, who had invited him to the meal. He challenges him with a short parable, which makes the point that forgiveness of greater debt leads to greater love. Jesus declares: 'Her many sins have indeed been forgiven, for she has shown such great love.' (Luke 7:47) The woman does not gain forgiveness due to her love. The parable makes clear that forgiveness provokes love. The woman is somehow aware of God's forgiveness and expresses her gratitude in an act of tender service to Jesus. Jesus' declaration to the woman that her sins are forgiven is public confirmation of what she already knew in her heart. (Luke 7:48) Forgiveness is not earned. It can only be gratefully received. Forgiveness engenders love. Jesus is the compassionate prophet of the forgiveness of God.

Luke follows this story with reference to the many women disciples who accompanied Jesus and the twelve and provided for them out of their own resources. (Luke 8:1-3) Luke stresses that they were many, and gives the names of three: Mary called the Magdalene, Joanna the wife of Chuza, and Susanna. The evangelist states that these women had been healed by Jesus 'from evil spirits and sicknesses'. (Luke 8:2) Mary Magdalene is mentioned first and it is emphasised that she had been healed of seven demons. This description suggests a particularly severe illness of some sort. We should recall that both physical and mental illnesses were attributed to unclean spirits or demons. There is no justification whatsoever for identifying Mary with the woman who was a sinner in chapter 7. There is no evidence at all in the gospels that Mary was a sinner. Healed by Jesus Mary had become a disciple. She will be the first to encounter the risen Lord. (Mark 16:9)

It is appropriate to recall here Luke's reference in chapter 10 to another Mary and her sister Martha. Luke is unaware that

they lived in Bethany, not far from Jerusalem, and inappropri-
ately places the story about them at the beginning of the journey
narrative. Luke introduces the story with the simple statement:
'as they journeyed he came to a village'. (Luke 10:38) Luke is
also seemingly unaware of their brother Lazarus and of the tradition of the raising of Lazarus in John chapter 11. In this short
scene Martha serves Jesus. In this she is like the women who accompanied Jesus and the twelve. Mary, by contrast, listens to his
word. Jesus teaches her. She has chosen 'the good portion'. (Luke
10:42) The image here of the woman who becomes a student of
the gospel recalls the Mary of Luke chapter 2, who ponders
everything in her heart. Luke's gospel testifies to the significant
presence of women among the disciples and to their various
gifts. In the Acts of the Apostles there is a somewhat diminished
involvement of women and an emphasis on the leadership role
of men. Luke's account of the involvement of women in the ministry of Jesus challenges us to consider whether the discipleship
of women has been adequately recognised and encouraged by
the leadership of men.

As a last word on Luke's account of the Galilee ministry, we
may note that Luke omits some parts of Mark's record, notably
the walking on the water and the second bread miracle. Luke
also alters the impact of the journey to Jerusalem as reported in
Mark. In Mark's gospel it is punctuated by three passion predictions and the challenges of discipleship. In Luke's gospel two
passion predictions and the story of the transfiguration, which is
profoundly related to them, occur before the journey begins in
chapter 9. For Luke the journey is the context for extensive
teaching, and above all for many parables found only in the
gospel of Luke.

Parables and the poor
The parables in this part of Luke's gospel are artistic masterpieces which have enriched the faith and reflection of generations of Christians and non-Christians. They illustrate the compassion of God to those in any kind of need. This compassion is

seen in the activities of Jesus. The same compassion is taught to the disciples. It is exemplified in the actions of the 'good Samaritan'.

The accounts of the Jerusalem ministry in Mark and Matthew included the question of a scribe: 'Which is the greatest commandment of the law?' Luke presents a similar dialogue at the beginning of the journey narrative and transforms it from an intellectual discussion to practical teaching. An expert on the Jewish law asks: 'What must I do to inherit eternal life?' (Luke 10:25) Love of God and love of neighbour are required. Jesus and the lawyer are in agreement but the lawyer pursues the debate and asks a question which various groups debated in Jesus' day: 'Who is my neighbour?' (Luke 10:29) Jesus replies with a famous parable.

'A man went down from Jerusalem to Jericho.' (Luke 10:30) The man is not named, and not described. It is not known whether he is a Jew or a Gentile. He is any man, any woman. The priest and the Levite disregard the presence of this beaten, half-dead individual. One might speculate that they were anxious not to be defiled by contact with what seemed a corpse. The good Samaritan is driven not by legalistic rules but by love. Jesus' choice of the Samaritan as the hero in this story is deliberate. Samaritans were Israelites who had intermarried with the Assyrians. They had lived apart from the Jews for centuries. They were considered heretical. They did not recognise the Jerusalem religious authorities and did not go to the temple. It happens often in Luke's gospel, both in parables and in the general narrative, that those generally despised become models of virtue. The woman who was a sinner is an example of love. The heretic Samaritan shows what it means to be a neighbour.

The parable shows that no qualifications are needed for being a neighbour. Every person is a neighbour. The parable focuses on how to act towards a neighbour. Generous and ready assistance to those in need is the challenge of Jesus. Is it a priority of those with power in our time to bring assistance to those in need? Is it our own priority? Self-congratulation, selfish pride and reckless waste are often preferred to providing for the poor, the sick, the hungry, the traumatised, and the half-dead.

The key to the parable lies in the statement that the Samaritan 'was moved to compassion' (Greek *esplagchnisthe*). (Luke 10:33) The Greek expression is based on the word for entrails or bowels. The entrails of Judas are poured out at his death. (Acts 1:18) But it has the metaphorical sense of the deepest emotions. Jesus is frequently described in the synoptic gospels as being 'moved with compassion' for the crowd. (Mark 6:34; Matthew 9:36) He was similarly moved by the widow of Nain. (Luke 7:13) The Samaritan is moved by the plight of the beaten man. His compassion is the compassion of Jesus. It reflects the 'compassion of mercy' (Greek *splagchna eleos*) of God. (Luke 1:78) Luke has Jesus conclude the parable 'Go and do the same yourself!' (Luke 10:37)

Outreach to those in need is the theme of several other parables. The rich man who stores up his riches for himself is described by God as a 'fool'. (Luke 12:20) The alternative behaviour, to be 'rich towards God' (Luke 12:21), suggests the disposal of possessions and the giving of alms encouraged by Jesus later in the chapter (Luke 12:33), and so prevalent in the opening chapters of the Acts of the Apostles. Luke's version of Matthew's parable of the wedding feast (Matthew 22:1-14) is the parable of the banquet in chapter 14. While Matthew made the point that those first invited, the Jewish people, were to be replaced by foreigners, Luke's new arrivals are all those in need. The servants are sent out to summon 'the poor, the crippled, the blind, and the lame'. (Luke 14:21) God's call through Jesus is to all those in need. The poor are the first to receive the good news of the kingdom. God's special concern for those in need is to be reflected in the behaviour of the disciples.

The most severe warning concerning love of the poor neighbour comes in the parable of the rich man and Lazarus. (Luke 16:19-31) Luke's version of the first beatitude, 'Blessed are the poor, for yours is the kingdom of God' (Luke 6:20), and his first woe-speech, 'Woe to you who are rich, for you are receiving your consolation' (Luke 6:24), are dramatised in this parable.

Two lessons are taught in the parable, that the poor are to be cared for, and that the word of God is to be heeded.

The rich man is not named. He is anyone who closes his heart to the poor. The poor man is introduced as Lazarus. The name means 'God helps' and is ideally suited to express the trust of the *anawim*. The parable gives a lavish description of the rich man's lifestyle, and a desperate picture of the plight of Lazarus. Familiarity with the parable should not lessen the impact of the outrageous behaviour of the rich man. Death comes to both and they go their separate ways, the rich man to torment, and Lazarus to the bosom of Abraham.

The obstinate blindness of the rich man is stressed in the dialogue which follows. The rich man still considers Lazarus his slave. Abraham should send Lazarus with some water. He should send Lazarus to the rich man's brothers. Despite his torment, he still regards the poor as his inferiors. The widespread view that the poor were sinners and the rich God's favoured ones is deeply rooted in his heart. His concern for his like-minded brothers betrays the beginning of awareness, but it is a selfish awareness. Moses and the prophets, the faith and social conscience of Israel, should have been enough to make them see their error. The parable makes the point that the word of God is sufficient incentive for right action. If people are not open to the voice of God they will not be convinced even by the return of a dead man. God speaks in the everyday. People need to have attuned their ears to the words God speaks in the heart of each individual. The capacity to listen for God can, now as in Jesus' day, be smothered by fine linen and feasting, selfishness and self-indulgence.

Parables and the sinners

The concern of the compassionate Jesus of Luke's gospel is for the heart of the person. It is a concern for those in any kind of need, those who are poor in whatever way, but equally for those whose hearts have turned from God and need to turn back. The teaching in parables in the chapters covering the journey from

Galilee to Jerusalem offers various perspectives on God's attitude to the sinner. Jesus' association with sinners is emphasised
in all the gospels, but particularly in Luke.

Luke gives no account of the strange cursing of the fig tree,
which both Mark and Matthew report as part of the Jerusalem
ministry. This may be because a similar point is made in the
short parable of the barren fig tree in Luke chapter 13. A man
has sought figs from the fig tree in his vineyard for three years.
The gardener appeals to the man: 'Lord, leave it just this year.'
(Luke 13:8) The use of *kyrios* allows two interpretations. The plea
to the master brings with it a prayer to God. The parable surely
speaks of the patience of God. While the symbolic action of Jesus
of cursing the fig tree represented final punishment, Luke's
parable keeps open the possibility that the fig tree may yield
fruit, that sinners may turn back. The lack of explicit agreement
from the owner of the vineyard is a challenging feature of the
story. Will God's patience be exhausted?

While in this parable God waits for the sinner's heart to
change, in the first parable of Luke chapter 15 God seeks out the
sinner. Luke has placed together in this chapter two short parables, the lost sheep and the lost coin, and what is arguably the
finest of all the parables, the prodigal son. Luke's introduction to
this group of three parables reports the complaints of Pharisees
and scribes that Jesus associates with sinners. While 'all the tax
collectors and sinners' were coming to Jesus, the Pharisees and
the scribes were complaining (Greek *diegoggyzon*): 'This fellow
welcomes sinners and eats with them.' (Luke 15:1-2) The searching heart of the sinners who come to Jesus contrasts with the
closed heart of those who have their minds made up about the
mercy of God.

The focus of each of the three parables in chapter 15 is on
what is lost: the lost sheep, the lost coin, and the lost son.
Celebration of the finding of what is lost is the climax of each
parable. Celebration of the sinners' openness to the good news
of Jesus is the reality evoked in each story. The short parable of
the lost sheep presumes that anyone would seek out the lost one

when the ninety-nine were showing no sign of straying. (Luke 15:4) But it may seem somewhat foolish to leave the ninety-nine unprotected. This risk emphasises the concern of God for each individual, and God's primary concern is for the lost one. There is unrestrained rejoicing when the lost one is found.

The parable of the lost coin presents a somewhat different picture. There is no risk involved in the search. But the search requires commitment. The woman must light a lamp and sweep the house before she can even begin to search. (Luke 15:8) God does not treat all people equally. The full divine love offered to all is fuller for the lost. There is more rejoicing over the lost one who has been found.

The parable of the prodigal son has retained a place in the hearts of Christians since earliest times. The story is told in such a way that each of the three characters takes centre stage for a time. The primary emphasis is on the lost son. But it is also a parable about an anxious and loving father, and a parable about a resentful elder son.

It is the younger son who initiates the action. It is he who provokes the crisis and gets the drama started. After leaving home and squandering his share of the inheritance he ends up tending pigs in a far-off land. He comes to his senses with the classic words of change of heart: 'I will arise and go to my father and I will say to him: Father, I sinned against heaven and against you. I am no longer worthy to be called your son. Treat me as one of your hired servants.' (Luke 15:18-19) The younger son has made his mistakes. He chooses the way back to life. In his ministry Jesus always respects the free choice of the individual. Sinners come freely to hear him. The journey of the son back to life is now in no doubt.

The focus of the second part is on the father. This parable allows a more detailed exploration of the attitude of God. The owner of the fig tree waited for its fruit. The owner who is God was asked to delay destruction of the fruitless tree. The father who is God in the parable of the lost son also waits and shows patience. But he does more. He longs for the return of the son.

He sees him while he is still a long way off. He has not rejected him. His heart is with him.

Just as the actions of the younger son dominated the first section of the parable, the actions of the father accumulate now. He sees his son from a distance. He is moved with pity (Greek *esplagchnisthe*). (Luke 15:20) He runs to the boy. He hugs and kisses the boy. The father's love and forgiveness are such that the son's prepared speech is not completed. The father takes over the action with his instructions for celebration. There is a crescendo of preparations leading to the climax: 'We are going to rejoice.' (Luke 15:23) The father gives the reason: 'This son of mine was dead and came back to life. He was lost and is found.' (Luke 15:24)

The parable is not finished. There is still the elder son. He and his problem will dominate the third section of the parable and will remain once the sound of the rejoicing has died away. The complaints of the Pharisees and scribes are confronted. The elder son is their angry spokesman. Their complaints are heard. The father, guilty only of forgetfulness, goes to meet the elder son just as he went out to the younger son. (Luke 15:28) The elder son complains: 'All these years I have slaved for you.' (Luke 15:29) But the words of the father to the elder son are the most tender words spoken in the whole story: 'My son, you are with me always, and all that is mine is yours.' (Luke 15:31) It is remarkable that nowhere in the parable does the father speak to the younger son. When they meet on his return the words of the father are hurried commands to the servants to prepare the welcome feast. The elder son by contrast is called 'my son'. There is a tenderness in the words, but are they really heard? The father offers the explanation of the rejoicing, repeating words used earlier to the servants: 'He was dead and came back to life. He was lost and is found.' (Luke 15:32) They are the last words of the parable.

The reader is left with the unresolved question: did the elder son go in? Can the elder son rejoice that the younger son has been found? Can he accept him as 'my brother' rather than as 'this son of yours'? (Luke 15:30) This would involve a change in relationship with the father too. The elder son, unlike the younger, does not address him as 'father'. He considers himself his slave. (Luke 15:29) The challenge is to become a member of a family, in which faults are forgiven.

The challenge to Pharisees and scribes is the same: to become members of a community in which forgiveness is practised. Like the elder son, they have difficulty in accepting a God who not only forgives sinners, but goes in search of them. Their incomprehension recalls that of the labourers in the vineyard, who in similar fashion complain about God's equal treatment of those who began work at the end of the day. (Matthew 20:12) The message of both parables is similar. Nobody can earn God's tender love, the lavish robe, the ring and sandals, the feast of the kingdom. All need to be brought from death to life, all are lost and need to be found. The three parables of chapter 15 illustrate God's extraordinary concern that the lost one, that all lost ones, be found and be brought to the life of the kingdom.

There is an urgent decision to be made: either to accept the message of the kingdom and the forgiveness of a compassionate God, or to remain outside. Luke follows these parables with a difficult parable concerning the need for decision. The parable of the dishonest steward is perhaps the most obscure of the longer parables of Jesus. The steward is found out. He has been defrauding his master. He is to be sacked. 'What am I to do?' he asks. (Luke 16:3) He does what he is best at and plans a last act of dishonesty. He reduces the amounts owed by his master's debtors. In this way he provides himself with friends who owe him favours and who can be called upon in time of need. The key to the parable lies in verse 8: 'The master (Greek *kyrios*) praised the dishonest steward for he had acted astutely (Greek *phronimos*).' Once again Jesus chooses an unlikely individual as a model for others. The dishonest steward grasps his situation. He is aware of his dire need to make friends. He takes action in the way he knows best, by further swindling.

The parable challenges the reader to take action. The offer of the kingdom is available now. The elder son has but moments to decide whether to enter the feast. The dishonest steward needs to take urgent action. It is the astuteness, not the dishonesty, of the steward which is to be emulated. The evangelist has collected various sayings about the honest use of money and placed them after the parable in order to ensure no reader gets the wrong idea about the meaning of the parable. (Luke 16:9-13) It is an invitation to timely action, not to dishonesty.

The approach of the sinner to God is the theme of another popular parable unique to Luke, the parable of the Pharisee and the tax collector. It is a parable for those who trust in their own justice. (Luke 18:9) The Pharisee stands and 'prays to himself'. (Luke 18:11) He thanks God that he has performed so many righteous actions. The tax collector remains a long way off and shows by his actions and his prayer that he knows his need of the forgiveness of God. The second went home justified. (Luke 18:14) The two are like the elder and younger sons. The Pharisee is convinced he will earn his salvation. The tax collector knows he cannot. In the use of the word 'justified' (Greek *dedikaiomenos*) we can hear Paul's concept of justification. Christians are justified, they come to the life of the kingdom, not by righteous actions, but by faith in Jesus Christ. The tax collector knows his need of God's forgiveness. The Pharisee does not.

As the journey section approaches its end we come upon the endearing story of a real-life tax collector, the short man in the sycamore tree. The life of Zacchaeus is transformed by the attention Jesus shows him. As chief tax collector (Greek *architelones*) (Luke 19:2) he would have been unpopular. He had no doubt cheated many of those he had taxed. Jesus takes the initiative. As the Father ran out to meet the younger son, so Jesus calls Zacchaeus down from the tree and invites himself to his home. Jesus again has a meal in the company of sinners. The Greek term *diegoggyzon* appears again as 'they all complained'. (Luke 19:7) Zacchaeus, however, declares he will give half his money to the poor and pay back double whatever he has defrauded. There follows a significant statement of Jesus about his ministry.

At the end of the journey narrative, in which the outreach of God to sinners has been repeatedly illustrated, Jesus says: 'The Son of Man has come to seek out and save what was lost.' (Luke 19:10) Zacchaeus, like the younger son, was dead and came back to life. He was lost and is found.

The gospel of Luke is the gospel of God's compassion, shown by Jesus in words and actions. He welcomes sinners and eats with them. Jesus calls not the virtuous but sinners. The lives of sinners are changed. The sinner woman shows great love because she knows forgiveness. Zacchaeus gives generously to the poor and to those he has cheated. Those who feel resentful that Jesus reaches out to the poor and the sinners have a more difficult time. They too are invited to the feast, but will they go in? They need to be part of the community in which forgiveness is available. They need to recognise their own poverty and their own lostness. Jesus, who brings good news to the poor and seeks out and saves what is lost, has a welcome for them too.

The disciples of Jesus must be faithful to Jesus' outreach to the poor and sinners. They are called to welcome sinners and eat with them. They are called to reach out to the poor, whatever their situation. This they have done, often heroically, through the centuries. But the disciples of Jesus have also failed. They have often shunned the sinners and the poor. The gospel of Luke remains a powerful challenge to live in a new way.

CHAPTER 10

Conception and Birth

The infancy narratives

It may appear strange that we are dealing with the conception and birth of Jesus in the last chapter dedicated to the synoptic accounts of Jesus. The material in Matthew chapters 1-2 and Luke chapters 1-2 is popularly referred to as the 'infancy narratives'. The chapters consider the conception, birth and some parts of the early life of Jesus. In addition, the conception and birth of John the Baptist are dealt with by Luke, who draws a parallel between John and Jesus and makes this the foundation of his two chapters.

The fundamental gospel message concerned the death and resurrection of Jesus. This was the good news proclaimed by the disciples after the resurrection. As the preaching continued, details of the public activity of Jesus were also remembered, elaborated and written down. It is significant that the earliest gospel begins the story of Jesus with his meeting with John the Baptist and his baptism. There is no mention of his earlier life. There is a fleeting glimpse of his mother Mary anxiously seeking him out. (Mark 3:31) Mark, however, either knows nothing or chooses not to write about the conception and birth of Jesus.

It is only in the later gospels of Matthew and Luke that we read of these things. Matthew provides a story in which Joseph, Mary's husband, is the focus. It involves Joseph's willingness to take the pregnant Mary and care for her and her child. It involves the visit of magi from the East seeking a new-born king. It involves further actions of Joseph who is warned to flee to Egypt and eventually returns not to Bethlehem but to Nazareth. Luke, on the other hand, provides stories both of John the Baptist and of Jesus. Their respective conceptions are announced to Zechariah and Mary. Their births are recounted. Shepherds are the first to visit the baby Jesus. The piety of Joseph and Mary is recorded as they offer the child in the temple, and as they make pilgrimage to Jerusalem year by year. The two sets of stories in Matthew and Luke have little in common but the basics. Jesus was conceived virginally and born of Mary, who was betrothed to Joseph, in the time of Herod the Great, in the city of Bethlehem, and brought up in Nazareth.

We have seen throughout the synoptic accounts that the fundamental historical basis of words and actions of Jesus is elaborated with christological explanations. Jesus' identity and his role are thus explored. The historical core of the baptism scene, for example, is embellished with God's declarations concerning the chosen Son. Jesus' questioning of the disciples, 'Who do people say I am?', becomes a lesson in Christian catechesis about Jesus as Messiah. The narrative of the death of Jesus is the vehicle for teaching about salvation, about forgiveness, about the resurrection of the dead. Examining the infancy stories we would expect to find a similar blend of historical elements and catechetical overlay. The gospels of the infancy, just like the rest of the gospel record, are a blend of historical and catechetical elements.

The infancy narratives present particular problems when it comes to identifying the historical elements in the traditions. As far as the records of the public ministry of Jesus, his death and resurrection are concerned, we can safely assume continuity between the witnesses of these things and those who preached about Jesus. The witnesses passed on their experiences of Jesus, which were then preached by others. The events of the conception and birth of Jesus lie further back in time. The link with witnesses is more difficult to establish. The suggestion is made that Joseph might have been a source of the information found in Matthew's gospel, but Joseph never appears in the gospel record after the infancy narratives. He may well have died before Jesus began his ministry. The suggestion that Mary, the mother of

Jesus, could have given information to the disciples is much more plausible. She is associated with the apostles at the beginning of the Acts of the Apostles. (Acts 1:14) Contributions from eye-witnesses may make up some part of the infancy narratives.

More significantly, we need to return to the issue of the blending of historical and catechetical material. Given the length of time between the birth of Jesus and the writing of the gospels, it is to be expected that there will be a more substantial amount of catechetical elaboration. Where factual information was scarce, catechetical ingenuity would fill in the gaps. Most importantly, we need to be aware of the type of material found in these chapters, the nature of the stories found here, the imagery used, the allusions to Old Testament prophetic material, the mirroring of Old Testament figures and events, and the insertion into the infancy narratives of insights from the later life of Jesus and from the developing faith of the church. The infancy narratives are an incredibly rich collection of christological and theological reflection presented in the form of stories. They provide summaries of the essential message of each gospel. In both Matthew and Luke the opening chapters not only prepare for the rest of the gospel but also reflect it.

Matthew's gospel is written for those who had come from Judaism to faith in Christ. The whole gospel provides reassurance that Jesus is indeed the fulfilment of the hopes and dreams of the Old Testament. It also portrays the tragic rejection of Jesus by Judaism and emphasises the antagonism between Jesus and his opponents. The gospel goes on to proclaim the mission to all the nations. All peoples are to hear the good news. The infancy narratives, in their stories of Joseph, Herod and the magi, give a foretaste of all this. They are frequently interrupted by quotations to demonstrate the fulfilment of the Old Testament. Herod the Great with the chief priests and scribes plots the downfall of Jesus. Judaism rejects Jesus, but the magi from foreign lands adore the Messiah. They seek out the light which the Jewish leaders have spurned. The gospel of Matthew in miniature is found in chapters 1-2.

Luke's infancy stories in their own way reflect Luke's whole gospel. The exemplary conduct of the two mothers, Elizabeth and Mary, and the presence of Anna in the temple, prepare for the significant role of women in this gospel. These women listen for God, as Mary, the sister of Martha, will listen to the words of Jesus later in the gospel. They do the will of God as an example to all disciples. The angels proclaim to Zechariah, Mary and the shepherds the fulfilment of the hopes of Judaism. The gospel which emphasises the outreach of Jesus to the poor and marginalized shows the good news of the birth of the Messiah being proclaimed first of all to the shepherds: 'Today is born for you a saviour, who is Messiah and Lord, in the city of David.' (Luke 2:11) The today of salvation will be proclaimed by Jesus in the synagogue at Nazareth, it will be welcomed by Zacchaeus whose life is transformed, and it will be grabbed by the good thief in his death throes. The good news of God's compassion preached to sinners and the poor, to the marginalised and the humble, is the theme of the infancy narratives just as it is of the whole of the gospel of Luke, and indeed of the Acts of the Apostles. In the words of Simeon, there is a foretaste of the fate of the Messiah. Yes, he will be a light for the nations, but he will also be a 'sign which is contradicted'. (Luke 2:34) A sword will pierce the soul of Mary. (Luke 2:35) Luke's infancy stories also reflect the division that will be brought about both by the work of Jesus and by the preaching of the church as many reject the Messiah.

Matthew's five scenes

The infancy traditions in Matthew's gospel are divided into five scenes in which Joseph, Herod and the magi are the principal actors. Before this the whole gospel opens with a title and a genealogy. Matthew's gospel begins: 'This is the record of the birth of Jesus Christ, son of David, son of Abraham.' (Matthew 1:1) The phrase 'record of the birth' (Greek *biblos geneseos*) reflects the titles given in the Old Testament when genealogical lists of descendants are provided. In Genesis chapter 5 we find the record of generations (Hebrew *sepher toledot*) of Adam.

Matthew's genealogy is an attempt to provide a list of the ancestors of Jesus beginning with Abraham. (Matthew 1:1-17) The coming of Jesus is presented as the climax of the history of his people. Genealogical lists are a frequent feature in the Old Testament. Luke also provides a genealogy but inserts it between the baptism and temptations of Jesus. (Luke 3:23-38) Luke's genealogy moves backwards from Jesus to Adam. It shows limited agreement with Matthew's list. This should alert us to the somewhat fictional nature of the lists. Matthew has constructed a genealogy which comprises three sections of fourteen generations each. The number of generations, three times fourteen, or six times seven, is deliberate. Apocalyptic speculation had asserted that the final age would be the seventh age. Matthew deliberately places the time of Jesus after six groups of seven generations. It is the time of fulfilment.

Matthew's genealogical construction is a list of men. But surprisingly Matthew inserts the occasional woman too: Tamar, Rahab, Ruth and Uriah's wife. The story of each of these women is one of difficulties overcome. Tamar had manipulated her father-in-law to conceive a son by him. Rahab, the prostitute of Jericho, is listed as mother of Boaz, which raises impossible chronological difficulties. Ruth, the Moabite woman who became ancestress of David, is the least problematic. Uriah's wife, Bathsheba, had committed adultery with David, who then had had Uriah killed. Jesus was born into human history with all its problems. The genealogical line comes down to Joseph. It is through Joseph, the legal father of Jesus, that Jesus is proclaimed son of David. He descends from the royal line. That the genealogy begins with Abraham shows Jesus to be a descendant of the man of faith through whom all nations would be blessed.

The first of Matthew's five scenes places the focus on Joseph, to whom Mary is betrothed. (Matthew 1:18-25) Betrothal, which lasted for a year, meant that they were already man and wife but had not yet come to live together. During this time, Mary was found to be with child. The tradition of the virginal conception of Jesus in the womb of Mary is reported in the gospels of

Matthew and of Luke. The evangelists introduce this explanation of the pregnancy of Mary in their annunciation stories. Matthew has the angel of the Lord declare to Joseph what the angel Gabriel will announce to Mary in Luke's gospel. (Matthew 1:20; Luke 1:35)

The human conception of the Son of God is a theme only dealt with in these two gospels. Mark did not consider the conception and birth of Jesus at all. John's gospel, while proclaiming the existence of the Word of God in the beginning, and the becoming flesh of that Word, does not give such details. Matthew and Luke alone assert a conception of Jesus without a human father. Some Christians consider this to be a theological assertion and doubt the historical truth of the statement. Catholic and Orthodox Christians have consistently maintained that the statement is to be understood literally. The Son of God became man in the womb of the virgin Mary through the power of the Spirit of God. No human male was involved.

The annunciation to Joseph in Matthew chapter 1 shows Joseph realising that his wife is with child and not knowing how. It is the angel of the Lord who explains the matter to him. Joseph, like Mary in Luke's gospel, is presented here as a person of faith, one who listens to God in his heart. He has a choice to make. He is inspired to accept the strange pregnancy and to be the protector of mother and child. Joseph, described as 'a just man', has to struggle with the issue. (Matthew 1:19) That Mary is guilty of adultery does not seem possible. God shows him the way forward. Furthermore, he is to name the child 'Jesus'. The evangelist explains the name by alluding to the popular interpretation, 'God saves' (Hebrew *yehoshua*, abbreviated as *yeshua*). (Matthew 1:21)

There are many annunciation scenes in the Old Testament. Hagar, mother of Ishmael, is told of the future achievements of her son before he is born. (Genesis 16:11-12) The mother of Samson is similarly addressed by an angel. (Judges 13:3-5) We will see the same technique used by Luke in annunciations to Zechariah and Mary. Annunciation stories celebrate the greatness and achievements of important individuals, and proclaim them as sent by God for a particular purpose. The essence of the annunciation to Joseph, the historical kernel of the story, is his decision, inspired by God, not to divorce Mary, but to care for her and the child to be born. It is a particular feature of the annunciation to Joseph that it is set in a dream. As the story progresses, Joseph will have further dreams in which God speaks to him through angels. The Joseph of Matthew is clearly modelled on the Joseph of the book of Genesis, 'the man of dreams'. (Genesis 37:19)

Each of the five scenes in Matthew's infancy narratives contains an Old Testament citation which, it is announced, has been fulfilled. As we have seen, this is a frequent feature of the whole gospel of Matthew. Matthew's first quotation towards the end of the annunciation scene is from Isaiah chapter 7. (Matthew 1:23) The promise of Isaiah made to Ahaz, king of Judah, is that a child will be born. The child, no doubt a son for the king and an heir to the throne of David, will be the sign of God's continuing solidarity with the people, and will accordingly be named 'Immanuel', 'God is with us'. The words of Isaiah do not in themselves suggest a virginal conception, but they lend themselves to Matthew's reinterpretation. A new meaning is read into Isaiah's words: the young woman will conceive by virginal conception. The birth of the son is reported without any elaboration as chapter 1 ends.

The second scene of the five in Matthew's stories of the birth of Jesus introduces new characters. (Matthew 2:1-12) Herod the Great, king of the Jews, and the magi from eastern lands are the main actors here. It is reported in passing that Jesus was born in Bethlehem. Matthew implies that Mary and Joseph had their home in Bethlehem, the city of David's birth. They migrate to Nazareth only at the end of the infancy stories. (Matthew 2:22-23) Herod, the father of a large dynasty of Herods, was king until 4 BC. A mistake made in the sixth century AD in calculating the year of the birth of Jesus led to the strange situation that Jesus was born earlier than 4 BC. Herod was universally disliked and ruled with cruelty and in arbitrary fashion. The slaughter of the innocents later in the chapter would match his character, though there are no reports of it from other sources, such as the Jewish historian Josephus. What does Matthew mean by 'magi' (Greek *magoi*)? Their reading of the heavens suggests they are astrologers, seekers after signs. It is only in later tradition that they become kings.

The travelling star has been a source of wonder and puzzlement. It is well known that great leaders and teachers were said to have their own stars, stars which first appeared at their births. This seems a more plausible explanation of the appearance of the star in the magi story than the failed efforts to track down some astrological phenomenon. There is also a connection with the book of Numbers. Balaam, a seer called from the east by the king of Moab in order to deliver a curse on the Israelites during their desert wandering, blesses them instead, and heralds the arrival of 'a star from Jacob'. (Numbers 24:17) This is a messianic text in which a future leader is described as a 'star'. It is noteworthy that a Jewish messiah after Jesus' time was known as Bar Kochba ('Son of a star').

Herod's consultation of the chief priests and the scribes concerning the birthplace of the Messiah is the opportunity for the evangelist to introduce the Old Testament text for this scene. Micah chapter 5 speaks of a ruler to be born in Bethlehem, a leader who will shepherd Israel. Matthew's freedom in quoting scriptural texts is demonstrated in his changing the sense of this text. The Micah text asserts that Bethlehem is the least of the leaders of Judah. The evangelist says that Bethlehem is 'by no means' (Greek *oudamos*) the least. (Matthew 2:6) This is a useful illustration that the evangelist uses scriptural texts to explain God's purpose in the events of Jesus and is not unduly bound by the precise wording. All quotations affirm that God is present now as God was present then.

The journey from Jerusalem to Bethlehem is a short one. The magi enter the house (Greek *oikia*) and worship the child. (Matthew 2:11) In Matthew's gospel there is no trace of a manger. In addition, the first to recognise Jesus as Lord, the first to worship him appropriately, are the seekers after truth who come from the ends of the earth. They offer to him gifts suitable for a king, gold, frankincense and myrrh. (Matthew 2:11)

This scene of the adoration of the child Jesus is an obvious fulfilment of Old Testament hopes. Psalm 72, which gives the fullest description of the hoped-for Messiah, speaks of kings coming from distant lands to offer him gifts. (Psalm 72:10-11) A poem in the post-exilic sections of the book of Isaiah proclaims that the nations will come to the light of Sion. They will bring gold and incense. (Isaiah 60:6) These texts have no doubt influenced the elaboration of the magi story. Suspicious of Herod, and warned in a dream, the magi return to their own land by a different route. (Matthew 2:12)

In this second scene Matthew has shown that Jesus is the fulfilment of Jewish hopes, as expressed in the prophecy of Micah, but more significantly that he is the Messiah of the nations. Herod attempts to deceive the magi that he too is a true worshipper, but it is only the wise men from afar who truly accept the Messiah. They recognise the light. They offer the gifts.

Joseph, who does not appear in the second scene, is the chief actor for the next three scenes. (Matthew 2:13-15, 2:16-18, 2:19-23) Joseph, as we have discovered, is modelled on the son of Jacob, the 'man of dreams'. This Joseph of the book of Genesis is above all the saviour of the lives of his people. Joseph, deported to Egypt, rose to a position of power and was able to save his people. Joseph says to his brothers, when they come to Egypt looking for food: 'God sent me before you to save your lives.' (Genesis 45:7) The story of the massacre of the innocents allows Matthew to develop Joseph's role as saviour. He is once again addressed by an angel in a dream. The story also shows that Jesus lives out episodes of the life of Moses. In Matthew's account of the public ministry Jesus is the new Moses, who delivers his five speeches and announces the fulfilment of the teaching of Moses. In the infancy narratives the child Jesus is under threat, as the child Moses was. In due time Jesus will be called out of

Egypt, as Moses was. The evangelist concludes the third scene with a suitable quotation from the prophet Hosea. Referring to the exodus God says: 'I called my son out of Egypt.' (Matthew 2:15) Jesus is the new Son, the new Israel, the new Moses.

Matthew's fourth scene, the massacre of the male children of two years or less in Bethlehem, recalls the massacre decreed by Pharaoh against all new-born Hebrew males. (Exodus 1:22) As Moses escaped the decree of genocide of Pharaoh, Jesus escapes the slaughter ordered by Herod. Matthew inserts a text from the prophet Jeremiah. The connection with the massacre at Bethlehem is loose, but Rachel's weeping for her children evokes the desperate sense of loss at the slaughter of the children of Bethlehem. (Matthew 2:18)

Joseph has his final dreams in the fifth scene of Matthew's story. He is told to return to Israel, for Herod is dead. But he is warned not to go to Judaea, the province now ruled by the eldest son of Herod, Archelaus. Archelaus was in fact removed from office due to his dictatorial ways after only ten years. Joseph takes his family to Galilee, which is part of the territory controlled by Herod Antipas. His settling in Nazareth allows Matthew to insert another scriptural text: 'He will be called a Nazarene.' (Matthew 2:23) It is uncertain which scriptural text he is quoting. It is possibly a recollection of Samson, who is to be a Nazirite, dedicated to God's service. (Judges 13:5-7)

There are significant connections between the main characters of Matthew's infancy stories and various Old Testament traditions. To what extent catechetical ingenuity has filled in the gaps which historical memory left must remain an open question. The value of the infancy stories lies in Matthew's significant presentation of Jesus as the one virginally conceived in his mother's womb, the one whose death is sought by Herod and the Jews, the one who is worshipped by those who come from afar. Matthew also provides a portrait of the just man Joseph, who by obedience to the instructions of God saves the lives of Jesus and Mary. The two chapters give a foretaste of the preaching of the gospel, good news rejected by Israel but accepted by the nations.

Luke's two annunciations

The opening two chapters of Luke contain quite different material from that found in Matthew's infancy stories. There is much more material packed into Luke's chapters, and there is a double focus. Luke tells of the conception and birth of both John the Baptist and of Jesus. His infancy material gives us two annunciation stories, the annunciation about John the Baptist to his father Zechariah, and the annunciation about Jesus to his mother Mary. The two annunciation stories are followed by two birth stories. Luke has also added to this basic structure the story of the visitation, which acts as a link between annunciations and birth stories, several canticles, and the stories of the presentation and the finding in the temple. There is no trace in Luke's first two chapters of the magi, the star and the flight into Egypt. Joseph's role is far less prominent.

Luke's interest in John the Baptist in the infancy narratives is designed both to show John as the last of the prophets and the one who prepares the way, and also to underline the superiority of Jesus over John. There is a deliberate parallel between the two annunciation stories. While John is conceived by a mother who is both old and barren, there is an even more wonderful divine intervention in the virginal conception of Jesus. Luke's account of the birth, circumcision and naming of John is eclipsed by the much more detailed narratives of Jesus' birth.

Luke's annunciation to Zechariah takes place in the temple. (Luke 1:5-25) The temple in Jerusalem is in fact where his infancy narratives begin and end. His final stories will show the infant Jesus presented in the temple and welcomed by Simeon and Anna, and Jesus as a young boy teaching in the temple at the age of twelve. For Luke the temple is the place of God and the place of worship. Fidelity to temple worship is demonstrated by the priest Zechariah, by Mary and Joseph, and by Simeon and Anna. The child Jesus too shows reverence for the temple. Luke ends the whole gospel with the twelve worshipping daily in the temple. (Luke 24:53)

Luke has obtained, from whatever source, information about

the priestly ancestry of John the Baptist. His subsequent description of Zechariah and Elizabeth as old and childless is reminiscent in particular of the Genesis description of Sarah and Abraham. (Genesis 18:11) Once again we must face the issue of how historical and catechetical material has been blended in these traditions. Is the evangelist emphasising that John the Baptist is a child who fulfils God's promise by drawing the parallel between his aged parents and Sarah and Abraham, the aged parents of Isaac, the child of the promise?

As the angel of the Lord had appeared to Joseph in a dream, so now the angel of the Lord appears to Zechariah as he performs his priestly duties in the temple. Luke will identify the angel of the Lord in both his annunciation scenes as Gabriel. (Luke 1:19, 1:26) In the final centuries of the Old Testament era reflection on angelic beings developed, and named angels, Michael and Gabriel, appear in the book of Daniel. Gabriel is particularly prominent in Daniel as a messenger who interprets God's secrets, a role he fulfils in Luke chapter 1. (Daniel 8:16-17, 9:20-22)

As is customary in annunciations of births, the angel reveals to Zechariah the future greatness of his son. He is to be called John, a name which may be interpreted as 'God has shown kindness'. The rejoicing at his birth prepares for the even greater joy for the whole people at the birth of Jesus. (Luke 2:10) The child is to drink no wine or strong drink. There is an echo here of the annunciation to his mother of the birth of Samson. She is to drink no wine or strong drink, for the boy is to be a Nazirite. (Judges 13:4-5) The book of Numbers lays down that Nazirites, men especially dedicated to God, should take no strong drink and leave their hair uncut. (Numbers 6:1-5) The allusion to the Nazirite vow here would seem to stress both John's dedication to God and his asceticism. The general prophetic role of John is indicated by the statement that he will be 'filled with the Holy Spirit from his mother's womb' (Luke 1:15), rather like the prophet Jeremiah who is consecrated before his birth. (Jeremiah 1:5) He is to 'bring people back' to God, the task of all the prophets. (Luke 1:16) All the synoptic gospels show John as a preacher of repentance.

More specifically, John inherits the mantle of Elijah. The portrayal of John as a new Elijah, even to his wearing similar clothing, is found in Mark's opening verses. (Mark 1:6) The expectation that Elijah would come before the Lord at the end-time expressed in the final verses of the book of the prophet Malachi is quoted here. (Luke 1:17) John is to be a preacher of repentance who prepares people for the time of the end and the coming of God.

It is common for those who receive annunciations to respond. Both Abraham and Sarah express their amazement at the news they are to have a son. (Genesis 17:17, 18:12) Zechariah replies in similar fashion: 'How can I know this is true?' (Luke 1:18) Old age surely rules out the birth of a child. Gabriel's response is to declare his identity and announce a sign. Zechariah is to be dumb until the birth occurs. This is surely not intended as a punishment. Mary will ask for clarifications at her annunciation. (Luke 1:34) The sign given to her is her own virginal conception, and the pregnancy of Elizabeth. Zechariah's dumbness is best understood as a sign, a guarantee that God who spoke these words has the power to fulfil them. A parallel may be seen in the dumbness of the prophet Ezekiel. Having proclaimed the fall of Jerusalem and its temple, this son of a priest is struck dumb until the event is reported to him as having taken place. (Ezekiel 33:21-22) Similarly, Zechariah remains dumb until after the birth of his son. This first annunciation story ends with the announcement that Elizabeth has indeed conceived. (Luke 1:24-25) The essence of the annunciation to Zechariah is a celebration of the coming birth of John and of his important role in preparing for Jesus.

The annunciation to Mary follows. (Luke 1:26-38) There is a deliberate link in the opening words, 'in the sixth month'. (Luke 1:26) Mary receives the message of an angel six months after Elizabeth became pregnant. Once again Luke is demonstrating the close connection between the two births. A shift in time is accompanied by a shift in location. Mary lives in the town of Nazareth in Galilee. She is betrothed to Joseph. There is a contrast here with Matthew's assertion that Joseph brought Mary and Jesus to settle in Nazareth only after the birth of Jesus. (Matthew 2:23)

Gabriel's opening words to Mary suggest the joy of salvation, and celebrate the role of Mary. She is described as 'one who has received grace' (Greek *kecharitomene*). The emphasis lies on the particular intervention of God in her life, the fact that she is especially chosen for the unique task of bringing the Messiah to birth. Mary is said to be disturbed by the angel's presence, just as Zechariah was. She, like Zechariah, is told: 'Do not be afraid!' (Luke 1:30)

The regular development of the annunciation story continues with the angel's announcement of the coming birth and future greatness of the child. As with the annunciation to Joseph in Matthew's gospel, so here the name Jesus is announced, but Luke does not explain its sense. His emphasis lies on the identity of the child as Son of God and son of David. The words given to the angel derive from Nathan's prophecy to David in 2 Samuel chapter 7. Nathan announces God's promise of solidarity to David and his line for ever. The hope of a Messiah which developed from this tradition is declared fulfilled in the birth of Jesus. Nathan's description of the descendants of David as sons of God is taken up by Luke in a unique sense. Jesus is not only a son of David, but also 'Son of the Most High'. (Luke 1:32)

The annunciation pattern continues with the question of Mary. It is at this point that the evangelist explains for the reader the virginal conception of Jesus. The question put on Mary's lips suggests its own answer, and the angel explains: 'The Holy Spirit will come upon you, and the power of the Most High will overshadow you.' (Luke 1:35) Luke affirms here what Matthew had explained in the annunciation to Joseph. It is through the Spirit of God that Mary will conceive. The angel also announces the wonderful pregnancy of Elizabeth, who is presented as a relative of Mary. (Luke 1:36-37) Luke thus shows that God

intervenes both in the conception of John and even more won-
derfully in the conception of Jesus. It has been the constant tradition of Catholic and Orthodox believers to understand the
virginal conception as literally true. God directly intervenes in
the conception of the Son as the life of his earthly body begins in
the womb. God will directly intervene again in the raising of
that earthly body from the tomb.

Given the nature of the annunciation story and its conformity
to the pattern of announcements of births repeatedly found in
biblical material, what can we say of the experience of Mary? Is
the story of the annunciation merely a catechetical construction?
The communication of the angel is a communication from God
in the heart of Mary. Description of the future greatness of Jesus
was surely not part of this. Mary shows no awareness of his
greatness later in the gospel story. Even in Luke's story of the
finding in the temple, his mother is unaware of his role. (Luke
2:50) The essence of the communication of God must surely
have been the invitation to do the will of God, the strange will of
God, in accepting her virginally conceived child. How such a
communication took place, how Mary came to hear God's voice
through the angel Gabriel, how she came to say her *Fiat,* to declare herself the 'slave of the Lord' (Greek *he doule kyriou*), to say
'yes' to God, remains hidden in the mystery of God's gracious
dialogue with human beings. (Luke 1:38) She is the first to hear
the word of God and do it. As a poor one of God, who had listened for God's word, she was ready to respond in obedience to
the call of God. Quite unique in her role, she is nevertheless the
model for all disciples of her son, who are, like her, called to hear
the word of God and do it. (Luke 11:28)

After the two annunciations Luke presents an extraordinary
encounter. The two women, each carrying her extraordinary
son, meet. (Luke 1:39-45) There is a dialogue at two levels. The
child in Elizabeth's womb leaps for joy. Already filled with the
Holy Spirit from his mother's womb, the child is aware of the
presence of the Messiah in the womb of Mary. The mother of
John declares the mother of Jesus blessed, more blessed than any

woman before her. She is aware too that Mary is carrying her 'Lord'. (Luke 1:43) This story of the visitation is the link which connects the two annunciations with the two births. It expresses the joy of salvation as the Messiah is encountered and acknowledged for the first time.

Luke inserts at this point the first extended canticle. The hymn, known as the *Magnificat*, from its first word in the Latin version, praises the saving actions of God. It is no surprise that the gospel narrative breaks off into a hymn of praise at this moment of the encounter of the Baptist and the Messiah. Close scrutiny reveals that the *Magnificat* is a general hymn of praise of God. It has considerable similarity with the canticle attributed to Hannah, mother of Samuel, in 1 Samuel chapter 2. Only the opening verses reflect Mary's special calling and her unique role. (Luke 1:46-49) God, says Mary, has looked upon the 'lowliness of his slave'. There is a deliberate recalling here of Mary's response to the angel earlier in the chapter. (Luke 1:38) It is quite possible that Luke has taken over a Jewish hymn of praise of God and adapted it for use here. A similar procedure seems to have been followed for the other extended canticle, the *Benedictus* of Zechariah. The God portrayed here, who reverses human situations, raising the lowly and filling the hungry with good things, will be reflected in the preaching of Jesus, particularly in the reversals announced in Luke's beatitudes and woes. (Luke 6:20-26) Mary likewise is raised from her lowliness to receive the greatest gifts of the Mighty One. (Luke 1:49)

Luke's two birth stories
The birth of John is briefly reported. (Luke 1:57) The joy of neighbours and relatives is stressed. (Luke 1:58) Extraordinary events occur, not at the birth, as is the case with Jesus, but at John's circumcision and naming. Elizabeth declares that the child is to be called John. (Luke 1:60) The evangelist implies here that the name was revealed to Elizabeth just as it had been to Zechariah. More remarkable is the return of speech to Zechariah. As Ezekiel's dumbness was healed on the fulfilment of God's

word, so Zechariah speaks again when he fulfils the angel's command and lays it down that the boy's name shall indeed be John. (Luke 1:64)

Zechariah speaks with the power of the Spirit. (Luke 1:67) The child was filled with the Spirit in his mother's womb. (Luke 1:15) The mother spoke in the Spirit when visited by the mother of the Messiah. (Luke 1:41) Now the father pronounces his hymn of praise, the *Benedictus*. (Luke 1:67-79) It is a traditional celebration of God's promises and deeds for Israel. The final verses connect what seems to be a general Jewish hymn to the birth of John. Zechariah addresses the child directly and points to his role of preparing the way for the Lord. (Luke 1:76) God will bring a new dawn (Greek *anatole*) to give light to those in darkness and in the shadow of death. (Luke 1:78-79) The rising star of the magi becomes the rising dawn of Zechariah. The section concerning John's birth ends with a statement about his growth: 'The child grew and became strong in spirit, and he was in desert places until the day of his manifestation to Israel.' (Luke 1:80) He will reappear as the adult John in Luke chapter 3.

The story of the birth of Jesus is understandably far more detailed. (Luke 2:1-20) Luke begins by reference to the Roman emperor, Caesar Augustus. He thus places the birth of the Messiah on the world scene. Luke tells us that the home of Mary and Joseph was Nazareth. To provide a reason for the Messiah's birth at Bethlehem, in accordance with messianic expectations, Luke speaks of the census of Quirinius. The infancy narrative is at variance with historical records here. The census of Quirinius, Roman governor of Syria, did not take place until the year 6 or 7 AD. It was the cause of the revolt of Judas the Galilean and led to the founding of the Zealot movement. It has no relevance to the birth of Jesus, for according to the gospel tradition Jesus was born before the death of Herod the Great, which occurred in 4 BC.

Mary gives birth to a son. She wraps the child in swaddling, strips of cloth used to support and restrain the child. (Luke 2:7) The book of Wisdom has king Solomon speak of being wrapped in swaddling as a baby. (Wisdom 7:4) Ezekiel's graphic description of the birth of the nation of Israel describes a child unswaddled, a child neglected. (Ezekiel 16:4) The exact meaning of the Greek word *phatne*, usually translated 'manger', is disputed. The child was laid in a manger, a trough used for feeding animals, or simply in an animal stable. Resort to a stable due to the coming birth when other accommodation could not be found seems the intended meaning. The swaddling clothes and manger are the signs announced to the shepherds for recognising the child. They are also simple signs of the love and nurturing shown by the mother to her child. Luke stresses the loving care given to the child. The curious words of the prophet Isaiah, that 'the ox knows its owner, and the donkey the manger of its master', may have contributed to further elaboration of the nativity scene among Christians. (Isaiah 1:3) In any case, the location of the birth in a stable suggests the presence of animals.

While Matthew's Jesus was worshipped by foreign wise men, the Jesus of Luke is visited by shepherds. It is the local ordinary people, not wise men from afar, who are involved here. Luke celebrates the birth with the arrival of the angel of the Lord accompanied by a host of angels. The angel proclaims to the shepherds the joy of the gospel: 'I announce (Greek *euaggelizomai*) to you a great joy which is for the whole people.' (Luke 2:10) The angel continues: 'Today is born for you a saviour, who is Messiah and Lord, in the city of David.' (Luke 2:11) The use of the term 'saviour' to refer to Roman emperors is implicitly challenged here. The Messiah, not Augustus, is the true saviour.

The short canticle sung by angels adds to the celebration of the birth. 'Glory to God in heaven, and on earth peace to those who enjoy favour!' (Luke 2:14) God is praised for the gift of the Messiah. Peace on earth comes from God and God's Messiah, not from Augustus. It is the birth of the Messiah which brings good news of peace to all. The concept of 'favour' (Greek *eudokia*) suggests God's goodness but also the grateful reception of that goodness. The good news is for all whose hearts welcome it. The presence of the shepherds watching their flocks at night in the vicinity of Bethlehem, the city of the shepherd David, is certainly plausible. Luke may also have in mind that shepherds were despised and considered dishonest. Such people are the first to visit Jesus.

Luke's story of the shepherds contains a further reference to Mary: 'She kept all these things, pondering them in her heart.' (Luke 2:19) Mary is the one who listened for God and was ready to be God's slave. She now ponders the events she has experienced. The circumcision of Jesus on the eighth day speaks of observance of Jewish religious rites, and prepares for the next scene, the presentation, in which Luke accentuates that all is done according to the law of the Lord. (Luke 2:21)

It is clear by now that both Luke and Matthew have utilised Old Testament narratives, their characters and their situations, to fill out the story of the birth of Jesus. Connections have been made between Joseph and the Joseph of Genesis, Jesus and Moses, John the Baptist and Elijah, Elisabeth and Sarah. We have noted in passing one connection with the story of the birth of Samuel. Mary's *Magnificat* uses material from the song of Hannah, the mother of Samuel, as she praises God for her son. A first implicit parallel was drawn there between Jesus and Samuel. We encounter more of these in Luke chapter 2. The early life of Jesus will reflect the early life of Samuel. Catechetical use of the Old Testament will fill the gaps where historical information is lacking.

The presentation and the finding in the temple

In his story of the presentation of the child Jesus in the temple Luke reports that the day came 'for them to be purified'. (Luke 2:22) The book of Leviticus chapter 12 clarifies that only the mother was to be purified. If she could not afford a lamb, she was to offer two young pigeons or doves. A rite of presentation of a child in the temple is not known, but a sum of five shekels had to be paid to 'redeem' or 'buy back' the first born child. (Numbers 18:15-16) The first born of certain animals were sacrificed. Luke quotes from the book of Exodus regarding sacrifice of the first born. (Luke 2:23; Exodus 13:11-16)

The presentation of Jesus in the temple reflects the bringing of the boy Samuel to the sanctuary of Shiloh. When the child was weaned he was left at the sanctuary, the place where the ark of the covenant was housed at that time, in the charge of Eli the priest. He is presented to the Lord. (1 Samuel 1:24-28) On the yearly visits of his mother Hannah and her husband Elkanah to the sanctuary Eli would bless them (1 Samuel 2:20), just as Simeon blessed Joseph and Mary. (Luke 2:34) Simeon is modelled on the old priest Eli. Luke stresses that the Spirit rests on Simeon. (Luke 1:25) He expected to see the Messiah.

Simeon delivers two speeches. The first is the *Nunc dimittis*, a short canticle which expresses Simeon's satisfied welcome of the Messiah. Simeon can now die, for he has 'seen salvation'. (Luke 2:29-30) Simeon uses phrases from the second part of Isaiah to illustrate that this is a saviour for all nations. Like the servant in the book of Isaiah, Jesus is to be a 'light of revelation for the nations'. (Luke 2:32; Isaiah 49:6) What was conveyed by Matthew in the story of the magi is expressed succinctly by Luke in the *Nunc dimittis*. Simeon continues with words which foresee future suffering. He tells Mary that her child is destined 'for the fall and the rising of many in Israel, a sign which is contradicted'. (Luke 2:34) Luke brings into the infancy narratives at this point the theme of rejection. Matthew had illustrated this through the story of king Herod's plot to kill the Messiah. Luke prepares us here for the first rejection of Jesus in Nazareth, and for the ministry as a whole. Jesus will bring division. (Luke 12:51) Simeon's final words to Mary, that a sword will pierce her soul so that the thoughts of many may be revealed, remain enigmatic. (Luke 2:35) The suffering of Mary is clearly envisaged. There is a choice to be made and painful division will result. Mary will face suffering on the road of discipleship. She stands as an example for all disciples. She is the first disciple in doing God's will and in her acceptance of suffering. The thoughts of others will be revealed as they accept or reject the sign of the child.

The presence of Anna, the elderly prophetess who lived in the temple, allows Luke to display the wisdom of a woman of great age. She too seems aware of the child's mission. (Luke 2:38) Her description has some similarities to the portrayal of Judith, the ideal Jewish woman, the heroine of the book of Judith. The return to Nazareth concludes the scene. Reference to the growing maturity of Jesus reflects similar statements about John the Baptist and about the prophet Samuel. (Luke 2:40, 1:80; 1 Samuel 2:21, 2:26)

After this conclusion Luke inserts a final tradition, not a tradition of the child but of the adolescent Jesus. (Luke 2:41-50) It is the only story in the canonical gospels which belongs to the period of the hidden life of Jesus at Nazareth. Certain apocryphal gospels, like the 'Infancy Gospel of Thomas', attempt to satisfy Christian curiosity with somewhat dubious stories. In the story of the finding in the temple in Luke there is possibly a loose parallel with the story of the boy Samuel responding to the voice of God in the sanctuary at Shiloh in 1 Samuel chapter 3. This final section allows Luke to show Jesus speaking for the first time, filled with wisdom and already aware of the Father's call. (Luke 2:49) Luke asserts again that Jesus is the Son of God. The assertion is on the lips of the boy Jesus. At the end of the story Luke refers again to Mary's keeping these events in her heart. (Luke 2:51) Luke also inserts another statement about Jesus' growth to maturity. (Luke 2:52) Nothing more will be told of Jesus now until his baptism and public ministry.

The infancy narratives of both Matthew and Luke have recorded some historical details concerning the birth of Jesus. On the basis of limited information about Jesus these evangelists have built narratives which express crucial truths about him. It is no surprise that Christian believers have always treasured these stories, pondered them in their hearts and drawn inspiration from them. They complete the synoptic panorama of the life of God's Son.

CHAPTER 11

John's Prologue and the First Signs

John's gospel

We have completed our examination of the traditions about Jesus in the synoptic gospels. We saw how the basic account of Mark was augmented and enriched by new material in the gospels of Matthew and Luke. We were aware that even in the earliest gospel there was a blend of historical material and preaching about Jesus. The fundamental aim of the evangelists, made explicit by Luke and John (Luke 1:4; John 20:31), was to encourage faith in Jesus and to facilitate the new life which such faith brings. The 'events which have been brought to fulfilment among us' (Luke 1:1) are the foundation on which teaching about Jesus and his significance is built.

The christological and catechetical preaching was often expressed through the narratives, even dramatically as in the stories of the walking on the water and the transfiguration. Jesus is the one who, like God, has power over nature. Jesus, the beloved Son of God, having surrendered himself to death, will be raised to transfigured glory. But understanding of Jesus' role and mission was also increasingly put on the lips of Jesus himself. Jesus declared that he had not come to abolish but to fulfil the law and the prophets. (Matthew 5:17) Jesus stated that he came to bring good news to the poor (Luke 4:18), and to seek out and save what was lost. (Luke 19:10) In both the narratives and the speeches of Jesus the evangelists assembled new material from the developing understanding of the Christian communities. Some narrative material may have quite limited historical basis and represent largely catechetical development. The stories of the infancy seem to fit this description. Some words of Jesus may be much more plausibly understood as words which Christian tradition gave to Jesus as believers grew in understanding of him. This process of development, this growth of catechetical explanation of Jesus and his role, is found most significantly in the fourth gospel, the gospel according to John. In this gospel the evangelist will elucidate in much greater detail the meaning of the divine sonship of Jesus.

The truth of the gospels lies not only in the truth of the historical core, but also and most significantly in the truth of faith statements about Jesus. To know the precise response of Jesus to Peter's profession of faith is a matter of less importance. To know Jesus as the one who comes from God and shows the way from death to eternal life is crucial. The evangelists write not simply to provide facts about Jesus but to lead people to life in his name. (John 20:31) But how can we be sure that such developments are trustworthy and true? John's gospel tackles this issue, for John's gospel more than the others testifies to this rich development of understanding. For John, Jesus is the incarnate Word, who 'was with God and was God' (John 1:1), and who now makes God known. (John 1:18) For John, Jesus is the divine Son who does the work of the Father. (John 5:19) For John, Jesus and the Father are one. (John 10:30) In John's gospel the Easter faith of Christians acclaims Jesus 'my Lord and my God'. (John 20:28)

John's gospel explains how such insights are achieved. For this evangelist the Spirit of Jesus leads believers to the complete truth. (John 16:13) John in fact provides the explanation of the whole process of development of the gospel material. The Spirit of Jesus guides the understanding of believers as they reflect on the work of Jesus and live in his name. The faith of the community of believers is expressed by the evangelists in their gospels. The gospels are the inspired expression of the truth about Jesus. The Spirit of Jesus leads the writer of the fourth gospel to explain more of the truth about Jesus, seeing him as the divine Son of God, who was with God in the beginning, became human and lived among us. It is no surprise then that John's gospel also testifies to the animosity of those who did not accept Jesus, who are presented as rejecting this developing faith of Christians, above all faith in the divinity of Jesus. As Matthew's gospel reflected increasing hostility between Matthew's Christians and the Jews who rejected Christian claims, so John's gospel shows signs of the hostility of contemporary Jews to claims made by John's believers about the divinity of Jesus.

John's gospel is quite different from the synoptic gospels in both content and structure. Clearly the gospel will culminate with the account of Jesus' death and resurrection. But John's account of the ministry has few parallels with that of the synoptic gospels. His account reports no baptism of Jesus and several visits of Jesus to Jerusalem. There is no extensive preaching of the kingdom. There are no exorcisms. The most significant features of the account of the ministry are the seven signs worked by Jesus. John does not speak of the miracles of Jesus as mighty works (Greek *dynameis*), as the synoptic writers did. He calls them signs (Greek *semeia*), thus following his general tendency to explain meaning rather than give bare historical detail. John takes further the synoptic gospels' tendency to treat the miracles as 'epiphanies', incidents which reveal. They are signs of the profound transforming work brought about by Jesus in the lives of believers. The initial two signs are worked in Cana. (John 2:1-12, 4:46-54) The miracle of the healing of the lame man (John 5:1-18) is followed by the miracle of the loaves and the walking on the water. (John 6:1-15, 6:16-21) These two miracles are found together in the synoptic tradition in Mark and Matthew. The final two signs of the healing of the man born blind in chapter 9 and the raising to life of Lazarus in chapter 11 are the occasion of elaborate portrayals of Jesus as light which overcomes darkness and life which conquers death.

The seven signs are contained in the first part of John (chapters 1-12). Several chapters are then dedicated to the meal before Jesus died. Jesus is at table with the disciples. John does not narrate his giving of the eucharistic bread and wine, but has Jesus wash the disciples' feet. (John 13:1-15) Most of this section of the gospel is dedicated to Jesus' last words to the disciples. (John 13-17) The gospel of John concludes with John's passion narrative (John 18-19), the account of the empty tomb and the appearances of the risen Jesus. (John 20-21)

The prologue

The synoptic account of Jesus saw him as the Son of God. He was acknowledged as such by the Father's voice at the baptism. Luke, in the words of angels to Mary and to the shepherds, declares that the child born is Son of the Most High. But these first evangelists go no further. They do not ask about the origins of the Son of God. It is John who raises this issue in the opening lines of his gospel.

The book of Genesis begins with the phrase 'in the beginning'. John's prologue relates the life of Jesus to this beginning. John states: 'In the beginning the Word was.' In his opening statement he affirms that this Word existed already in the beginning, when God created all things. The Word, who will become a human person as Jesus born of Mary, existed and was 'with God' (Greek *pros ton theon*). (John 1:1) This Greek expression suggests a dynamic relationship between God and the Word: the Word, who is the Son, relates to God. John also states: 'the Word was God.' John does not say here that God and the Word are identical. He states that whatever God was, the Word was. He affirms the divinity of the Word. For John, the one who becomes human in Jesus is the Word, who was with God before creation, who related to God, and who was God. The prologue will later clarify that this Word is the Son, who relates to God, who is Father. (John 1:14, 1:18)

We are suddenly floundering in a deep ocean of theological reflection. To put it at its simplest: the Son of God existed with God from before creation. But why does John call this Son 'the Word'? Again we must return to the first chapter of Genesis. The first action of God is to speak: 'And God said.' (Genesis 1:3) As God's commands come forth from God, so does the Word, who is the Son. The Son is God's Word to all creation. The Greek expression *Logos,* meaning 'word', was put to good use in Greek philosophical thought. People have asked whether the evang-elist is alluding to Greek concepts here, but it seems much more relevant to recognise the many parallels with the opening of the book of Genesis. God's first act is to speak. It is God who brings forth and sends forth the Word.

Quite naturally the evangelist then spells out how the Word worked with God at the creation. 'All things were made through him.' (John 1:3) God in Genesis chapter 1 creates the wholeness of the heavens and the earth with the assistance of the Word. 'Without him nothing was made.' (John 1:3) The involvement of the Word in creation brings life. As the Word brings life in creation, so the Son will bring life in salvation.

John stays with the first chapter of Genesis, where the first creating act of God is to create light, by affirming that the Word brought light to the world. Though the fundamental description of the Son in the prologue is as Word, the evangelist also intro-duces this most significant description of the Son as light. While reference to the Son as Word will disappear after the prologue, the Son as light will return. As in the opening verses of Genesis, this light comes into darkness, but the darkness of the world, the darkness where God is absent, the darkness of evil, cannot over-power the light. (John 1:5)

The prologue now interrupts its reflection on the Word to in-troduce John the Baptist, 'a man sent by God'. (John 1:6) The issue of John's role is immediately tackled. He comes 'in order to witness' (Greek *eis martyrian*). (John 1:7) He is not the focus. He is to point the way. (John 1:34) He is not the light. He is to speak for the light. (John 1:8)

The evangelist continues to reflect on the Word: 'he was the true light.' (John 1:9) He offers light to all people, like the star of the magi and the new dawn of Zechariah. (Matthew 2:2; Luke 1:78) The world (Greek *kosmos*) had been made through him, and yet the world did not recognise him. (John 1:10) We are in-troduced to the concept of *kosmos* as the world which does not accept the Son of God, those who collude with darkness and shun the light. He comes to his own (Greek *ta idia*) and his own (Greek *hoi idioi*) do not accept him. (John 1:11) The sense here is that he comes into the place where he belongs, for all was made by him, and his own people reject him. The rejection of the prophet in his own country, illustrated in Jesus' visit to Nazareth in the synoptic gospels, is here expressed in a more abstract way.

Not all who encounter the Word fail to receive him. For those who do receive the Word, for those who believe in his name, new possibilities of life are available. (John 1:12) They become children of God. This rebirth is not of a physical nature. They are born of God, as the Word is born of God. (John 1:13, 1:18) In these brief verses the whole drama of the human response to the Word is suggested. Acceptance of God's Word, belief in his name, faith in the Son of God, brings new birth and new life. What Jesus preached in the synoptic gospels as the urgent challenge of the kingdom is replaced by acceptance of the Word who is the Son.

The evangelist has already spoken of the coming of the Word into the world of belief and unbelief. He now expresses this coming in the most momentous terms: 'And the Word was made flesh and pitched his tent (Greek *eskenosen*) among us.' (John 1:14) The eternal Son, the Word, takes on our humanity. The one who is God with God from the beginning enters human history. The Son becomes flesh in incarnation. At this point we should explore a further parallel between John's prologue and the Old Testament. The existence of the Word with God and the co-operation of the Word in the work of creation recall the Old Testament description of Wisdom. For the book of Proverbs chapter 8 Wisdom was with God at the creation and delighted in the work of creation. Later reflection in the book of Sirach (Ecclesiasticus) chapter 24 has Wisdom, who has her tent in the heavens, make her tent in Jacob. The Wisdom of God, with God at the creation, lives among the people of Jacob, the people known as Israel. We become aware that it is not only the Word of God in Genesis but also the Wisdom of God in Proverbs and

Sirach which have fed into this Christian meditation on the eternal Son who enters human history. The statement that the Word, on becoming flesh, 'pitched his tent among us' is clearly a reflection of the settling of Wisdom among the people of Israel.

But there is more. The evangelist writes: 'The Word was made flesh, and pitched his tent among us, and we beheld his glory, the glory that is his as the only Son of the Father, full of grace and truth.' (John 1:14) The writer of the prologue utilises more momentous Old Testament concepts to explain the significance of this incarnation. The coming to humanity of the Son allows us among whom he pitches his tent to behold his glory (Greek *doxa*). In the priestly narratives of the book of Exodus the glory (Hebrew *kabod*) of God is present on Sinai. (Exodus 24:16) Moses requests to see God's glory and is not allowed to see God's face. (Exodus 33:18-23) The glory of God comes to dwell in the tabernacle constructed by the Israelites. (Exodus 40:34) The God of the covenant dwells among the people of the covenant. That glory which would come to dwell in the Jerusalem temple in later times (1 Kings 8:11), the presence of God with the people of Israel, now gives way to the human life of the only Son of the Father, the Word made flesh. The glory of God is now seen in the Son.

The Exodus connections continue with the phrase 'full of grace and truth'. When God passes Moses by, not allowing him to see God's face, God's self-description uses similar terms. God is 'rich in faithful love (Hebrew *hesed*) and constancy (Hebrew *'emet*)'. (Exodus 34:6) The two Hebrew terms are repeatedly used together in the Old Testament to describe God's dealings with Israel, characterised by love and constancy. They are rendered in the Greek of John's prologue with the terms *charis* and *aletheia*, 'grace and truth'. The shift from the Hebrew of the Old Testament to the Greek of the New brings with it the connotations of the terms as used in the Old Testament and opens up new possibilities of meaning from the Greek language. The merciful and faithful God of the book of Exodus is revealed in the only Son who is 'full of grace and truth'. The Son is the one who comes from the Father as Word and as Wisdom, full of those qualities of the God of Exodus, faithful love and constancy, grace and truth. The God of Israel is revealed in the life of the Word, the only Son.

The prologue changes gear again with reference to John the Baptist. As in the earlier references to him, John is the witness. John testifies to the superiority of the one who existed before him. (John 1:15) The prologue reconnects then with the theme of grace: 'Indeed from his fulness we all received, and grace upon grace.' (John 1:16) The faithful love of the God of Israel gives way to the faithful love shown in the Word made flesh. A new grace follows the old, and yet they are one and the same. The grace of the God of Israel is the grace shown in the life of the Word. There follows a suggestion that the new gift outweighs the old: 'Indeed the law was given through Moses, grace and truth came through Jesus Christ.' (John 1:17) But this evangelist seems to stress the continuity of God's gifts. What has changed is that God is now made visible. The prologue recalls that no-one, not even Moses, had seen God. The Son who comes from intimacy with the Father makes him known (Greek *exegesato*). (John 1:18) This Greek term, which gives us the word 'exegesis', has connotations of interpreting and explaining. The Word by incarnation reveals God to us. The prologue to the First Letter of John will reiterate that the Word, who is Life, was made visible, drawing us into the new life, the gift of the Father through the Son. (1 John 1:2)

The first days and the first sign
A curious feature of the verses following the prologue to John's gospel is that there is repeated reference to the passing days. The phrase 'on the next day' is found three times. (John 1:29, 1:35, 1:43) The section concerning the wedding at Cana is introduced by the phrase 'on the third day'. (John 2:1) The evangelist has deliberately bound together these verses, which introduce the disciples and the mother of Jesus, into a week of activities. It is a week of revelation, which reaches its climax in the showing of

the glory of Jesus. It is a journey for the disciples from tentative, inadequate statements about Jesus to full faith: 'He showed his glory and his disciples believed in him.' (John 2:11) But why the week? Many consider this is yet another allusion to creation and Genesis chapter 1. But there is a much stronger parallel, once again from the book of Exodus. Exodus chapter 24 tells how the glory of the Lord rests on Mount Sinai for six days. The cloud is the visible sign of God's glory. Moses is called by God: 'And on the seventh day he called to Moses from the midst of the cloud.' (Exodus 24:16) After six days of preparation Moses goes to be with God on Sinai. Similarly, after six days of preparation the Son shows his glory to the disciples at Cana.

During the week of revelation the focus moves from John the Baptist to Jesus. The Baptist assists the coming to faith of the disciples. The evangelist has condensed into this week the process of understanding Jesus which for the synoptic evangelists continues throughout the gospel story. In the synoptic story the disciples will struggle to reach that faith. In John's gospel various inadequate descriptions of Jesus will be given on the first days of this week of revelation. But at the end of the Cana story they will be believers, ready to accompany Jesus on his journeys to Jerusalem and elsewhere. (John 2:11-12)

The week begins with the focus on John the Baptist. There is a remarkable parallel here with the synoptic picture of Jesus. In Mark's story of Jesus there were two occasions when scribes had come up to Galilee from Jerusalem, seemingly an official delegation to investigate the work of Jesus. They challenge him about his exorcisms and about his disciples' laxity concerning ritual purity. (Mark 3:22, 7:1-2) On the first day of the week of revelation a delegation comes from Jerusalem to John to clarify his role. This time those sent are priests and Levites. The fourth gospel records a plausible historical tradition here, one which is not reported in the synoptic gospels. The Baptist would no doubt have attracted the attention of the religious authorities since he drew crowds to hear his preaching of repentance.

The initial part of the dialogue between John and the priestly group has the Baptist give a negative answer to any claims which might be made for him. The evangelist here spells out in detail what he has John say later on: 'He must grow greater, I must grow smaller.' (John 3:30) John is neither the Messiah, nor Elijah, nor the expected prophet. We may note that for the synoptic gospels John was indeed understood to be the new Elijah. For the fourth gospel, the Baptist is one who has freely responded to God's call. He is simply a voice. This evangelist agrees with the synoptic tradition in describing John in the words of Second Isaiah as the voice calling out in the desert to prepare the way for the Lord. (John 1:23) His baptism is to be understood in this light. John's gospel in reporting this meeting provides a clear catechesis about the Baptist. As in the synoptic gospels, so in this gospel, the Baptist's role and subordinate relationship to Jesus are made clear. The day ends with John's first declaration about Jesus, which reflects closely the Baptist's words in the synoptic accounts. (John 1:26-27)

John has more to say about Jesus on the second day. On this day Jesus appears for the first time. Jesus is described as 'coming towards him'. (John 1:29) On this second day the Baptist provides a much fuller catechesis about Jesus. He is in fact the voice for the christology of the fourth gospel. The developed insights of this evangelist's community are placed on the lips of John the Baptist, who in this scene strangely bears witness with no mention of an audience.

As Jesus approaches the Baptist says: 'Behold the lamb of God (Greek *ho amnos tou theou*) who takes away the sin of the world.' (John 1:29) In this evangelist's presentation Jesus' death takes place as the lambs are slaughtered in preparation for the passover feast. (John 19:14) The fourth gospel, with St Paul, offers us the understanding of Jesus as a paschal lamb. (1 Corinthians 5:7) As the passover lamb proclaimed freedom from slavery for the Israelites, the lamb provided by God brings forgiveness of sin for the world. The killing of the passover lambs in the temple reminds us too that animal sacrifices were offered regularly in the Jerusalem temple to seek forgiveness of sin. The

Baptist proclaims the evangelist's understanding of Jesus as the lamb whose death brings forgiveness. The use of the lamb image is the most striking part of the Baptist's testimony on the second day. But the evangelist also has him refer to Jesus as the one who existed before him, in an apparent allusion to the existence of the Son in the beginning. (John 1:30) The Baptist also testifies to seeing the Spirit descend on Jesus. This evangelist makes no mention of Jesus' baptism. Jesus' solidarity with sinners has already been expressed in his description as the lamb of God. The descent of the Spirit demonstrates Jesus' identity to John. John concludes: 'I have seen and I bear witness that he is the Son of God.' (John 1:34) The Baptist comes very close to expressing the fulness of faith of the fourth gospel that Jesus is the divine Son of God.

On the third day two of his disciples are with John. He points Jesus out to them as the 'lamb of God'. Their rapid process of learning the truth about Jesus begins. The disciples now replace the Baptist in teaching the readers of this gospel the truth about Jesus. Andrew and another disciple, and then Peter, Philip and Nathanael are drawn to Jesus. They initially call Jesus 'rabbi'. (John 1:38) Later on Andrew finds his brother Simon and declares to him: 'We have found the Messiah.' (John 1:41) It is at this moment in their rapid progress in discipleship that Simon is especially chosen by Jesus and given the new name of Cephas, the 'rock'. (John 1:41)

The fourth day has Jesus find Philip, who along with Andrew and Peter is described by this evangelist as being from Bethsaida. (John 1:44) Philip in turn finds Nathanael, a disciple known only from John's gospel. He tells him that Jesus of Nazareth is the Messiah. Nathanael is not impressed. (John 1:46)

The dialogue between Jesus and Nathanael is enigmatic. Attempts to explain it have often been unconvincing. As Nathanael approaches, Jesus says of him: 'Here indeed is a man of Israel in whom there is no deceit!' (John 1:47) This is quite obviously a compliment. Furthermore, Jesus' words suggest that he knows Nathanael instantly. In John's gospel Jesus has complete knowledge of people and events. The evangelist refers again later to Jesus' ability to know people's hearts (John 2:24-25), and will frequently have Jesus display extraordinary awareness. (John 4:17-18) Nathanael asks how Jesus knows him. The answer of Jesus is evasive: 'I saw you under the fig tree.' (John 1:48) Nathanael, who has been so warmly greeted by Jesus and is now impressed by him, proclaims faith in Jesus in words which summarise the disciples' growth in faith up to this point: 'Rabbi, you are the Son of God, you are the king of Israel!' (John 1:49) We should recall that the anointed kings and the expected Messiah are considered God's Son. It is possibly only at this level that Nathanael's declaration should be understood. But Jesus is clear that such faith in him is still inadequate. He says to Nathanael: 'You will see greater things than these.' (John 1:50) The disciples already have vision, but not the fulness of faith. It is only the fourth day.

The Nathanael episode ends with words of Jesus for the whole group of disciples: 'You will see heaven open and the angels of God ascending and descending upon the Son of Man.' (John 1:51) This curious saying recalls certain synoptic statements about the coming of the glorious Son of Man with his angels. (Mark 13:26-27; Matthew 25:31) The allusion is clearly to the final glory of the Son. We saw how the synoptic gospels used the phrase 'Son of Man' to speak of the risen glory of the Son. John's gospel uses the phrase in a similar fashion. There is a possible allusion to Jacob's vision of the stairway leading to heaven and of the angels ascending and descending. (Genesis 28:11-12) The Son of Man is the new way to God. This final statement of Jesus on the fourth day makes clear that the eyes of faith are to see yet more wonderful things. The week is not yet complete.

'On the third day there was a wedding at Cana in Galilee.' (John 2:1) The week reaches its climax. The story of the changing of water into wine at the wedding in Cana is rich in symbolism and allusion. We will explore what seem the major points intended by the evangelist. First and foremost, there is no doubt that the story should be seen as the conclusion of the week of revelation that began in chapter 1. The disciples will come to full faith on the basis of this 'beginning of the signs' which Jesus gives. (John 2:11)

The story acts as a link between Jesus' life in Nazareth, in contact with his mother and relatives, and his new life in company with the disciples. Both the mother of Jesus and the disciples attend the wedding. (John 2:1-2) We see here how Jesus moves from the family context into the context of public ministry. There are some similarities with the story of the adolescent Jesus engaging in dialogue with the teachers in the temple. (Luke 2:41-50)

The evangelist speaks of 'the mother of Jesus'. The name of Mary is not given either here or in John chapter 19, which is the only other occasion when the mother of Jesus appears in this gospel. The evangelist stresses relationships. The relationship of the Son to the Father dominated the prologue, and dominates the gospel. Here the evangelist considers Jesus' human ties. He speaks not of 'Mary', but of 'the mother of Jesus'. It is she who initiates the main action of the story: 'They have no wine.' (John 2:3)

The words of Jesus to his mother have been the object of much debate. His first words are a Greek rendering of a Hebrew expression found occasionally in the Old Testament. Jesus says literally: 'What is this to me and to you, woman?' (John 2:4) A similar question is found when the possessed man challenges Jesus in the synagogue at Capernaum. (Mark 1:24) But the aggression shown there is quite absent in Jesus' words to his mother. There is a closer parallel in words of king David as he flees from Jerusalem due to the revolt of his son Absalom. David is cursed and pelted with stones by Shimei, who belonged to the clan of Saul. David's companion Abishai suggests that the troublesome Shimei should be struck down. David's reply is 'what is this to me and to you?' (2 Samuel 16:10) Neither David nor Abishai should get involved. Similarly Jesus seems to be telling his mother that neither she nor he should be involved in the issue of the wine running out.

It is of more significance that Jesus addresses his mother as 'woman'. She who is introduced as the mother becomes the woman in the public context of Jesus' ministry. This feature of the story has given rise to abundant reflection on Mary as the woman who replaces Eve. She is at the beginning of Jesus' story, as Eve was at the beginning of creation. Others have seen here a preparation for the sign of the woman in Revelation chapter 12. We will explore a more obvious sense which has clear connections to Jesus' behaviour in the synoptic gospels. In Mark chapter 3 Jesus said: 'Who are my mother and my brothers?' (Mark 3:33) It is those who do God's will, those who follow in discipleship, who are Jesus' family. This does not exclude Mary, who heard God's word and heeded it, but her relationship to Jesus in the ministry is the relationship of a disciple. She is addressed as 'woman', just as the Samaritan woman and Mary Magdalene will be. (John 4:21, 20:15) As Jesus is dying on the cross she is again addressed by Jesus as 'woman'. (John 19:26) There she receives her role in discipleship. She is mother of the ideal disciple who stands with her as Jesus dies. Mary, acknowledged as 'mother of Jesus' on both occasions, becomes the mother of the community of disciples.

Jesus concludes by saying: 'My hour has not yet come.' (John 2:4) John constantly emphasises the freedom of Jesus. He has complete power over his life. (John 10:18) Jesus is never forced to act contrary to his will, which is the will of the Father. In the account of the second sign, also at Cana, Jesus again initially refuses an urgent plea. (John 4:48) The 'hour' of Jesus in John's gospel is the time of Jesus' death and resurrection. To begin moving towards that hour by working his first sign is something no-one can force. The Son acts with freedom. The evangelist's account of the dialogue between Jesus and his mother carries with it some significant theological truths.

The action will nevertheless proceed. The mother tells the servants to follow any instructions Jesus may give. (John 2:5) She is shown to have complete trust in the Son. Through her trusting attitude the disciples will come to full faith.

The sense of this first sign in John's gospel derives from the six huge water jars which suddenly contain an abundant quantity of remarkably fine wine. The fourth gospel stresses how Jesus comes to replace Judaism and its feasts and practices. The time of Moses is passed. This is the era of grace and truth. (John 1:17) The water for purposes of ritual purifications is replaced by the wine of the messianic banquet. Isaiah expected abundance of wines at the banquet of God. (Isaiah 25:6) For Amos and Joel the mountains would run with new wine. (Amos 9:13; Joel 4:18) Like the figure of Wisdom in the book of Proverbs, the Son who pitched his tent among us provides abundance of food and wine. (Proverbs 9:5) We might recall the similar abundance of bread provided in the miracle of the loaves so that the scraps left over filled twelve baskets. (John 6:13) The gospel tradition has already alluded to Jesus as bridegroom and to a wedding feast. (Mark 2:19; Matthew 25:6) The symbolism of the story is clear. Jesus brings the new wine of grace and truth. We might ask what the historical core of the tradition is. We can give no definite answer to such a question.

This first sign is the climax for John of the disciples' growth to full faith. The glory of the Son is revealed to them at Cana. (John 2:11) They know him as Son of God. In this way the evangelist completes the story of their coming to believe in Jesus. Their week of discovery is like a new week of creation. The mother of Jesus will fade into the background. Now Jesus relates to the disciples, and they to him. The gospel continues with the portrayal of other journeys towards faith in Jesus. John presents the coming to faith of the disciples as a model and a challenge to others. Many will not reach the fulness of belief in Jesus.

The story of the first sign illustrates very clearly how this gospel, like the others, presents the story of Jesus as a challenge to believe. The fourth gospel transforms the relationship of Jesus and the disciples so that from the outset they become models of discipleship. They understand quickly that it is not sufficient to herald Jesus as a great rabbi, nor even as the Messiah. There is some similarity here with the disciples' developing understanding of Jesus in the synoptic gospels. Jesus is the showing of the glory of God. (John 2:11) He is the divine Son. The time of

Judaism is at an end. Grace and truth are revealed in the glory of
the Son. John's gospel, like that of Matthew, will demonstrate on
many occasions that the Christian community from which this
gospel emerged had clarified their faith in Jesus as Son of God,
and had realised that the call of God to the Jewish people was to
accept Jesus as Messiah and Son of God. (John 20:31)

Jesus in Jerusalem

After the coming to faith of the initial followers of Jesus, who
witness how Jesus comes to replace Judaism and all its institu-
tions, the fourth gospel goes immediately to the heart of Judaism.
Jesus goes to Jerusalem and there challenges the temple itself.
(John 2:13-22) The tradition of Jesus' disturbance in the temple is
part of the final days of Jesus' public activity in the synoptic
gospels. The fourth gospel places the story here to clarify from
the start Jesus' relationship with Judaism. For this gospel it is the
raising of Lazarus, not the cleansing of the temple, which is the
immediate cause of plots to kill Jesus. (John 11:53)

John's gospel combines two stories found in the synoptic
tradition of the Jerusalem ministry of Jesus. In Mark's gospel the
disturbance in the temple (Mark 11:15-19) is followed by questions to Jesus regarding his authority to do such things. (Mark
11:27-28) In John the two stories are fused. John's account of
Jesus' attack on the temple has Jesus use considerable violence.
He even makes a whip. (John 2:15) By contrast with the synoptic
accounts Jesus does not quote scripture. It is the disciples who
recall Psalm 69. (John 2:17)

The second part of the scene presents the intervention of 'the
Jews'. For John's gospel this term almost always has negative
connotations. It speaks primarily of the religious leaders who
always oppose Jesus. By contrast with the synoptic gospels, the
term is extremely frequent in John. The Jews ask Jesus for a sign
to show his authority. (John 2:18) Jesus replies: 'Destroy this
sanctuary and in three days I will raise it up.' (John 2:19) This
reply must first be understood as a reference to the temple and
its sanctuary. Jesus speaks of the destruction of the temple in the

synoptic gospels. (Mark 13:2) He is accused in his trial of making threats against it. (Mark 14:58) The words of Jesus at this point in John's gospel are very similar. If the Jewish nation were to provoke the destruction of the temple, the Messiah of God would be able to raise it up in three days. This idea seems to have been part of speculation about the time of the end. The response of the Jews is one of misunderstanding. They understand his reply in a purely material sense. We might recall that in the account of the trial in Mark the new temple was to be 'not built with hands'. (Mark 14:58) The dialogue here makes sense with reference to the temple in Jerusalem in Jesus' day and the temple of the messianic age.

The final verses add a new insight. (John 2:21-22) Jesus is the sanctuary of God. His body replaces the temple as the place where God's glory dwells. As the wine replaced the water, Jesus replaces the temple. The evangelist intimates that the disciples understood this deeper sense of Jesus' words only after his resurrection.

The general picture of Judaism's conflict with Jesus is attenuated by comments added by the evangelist at the end of chapter two. Many in Jerusalem believed in Jesus but they believed due to the signs he gave. (John 2:23) One such individual is named Nicodemus.

Nicodemus and the Samaritan woman

In chapters three and four of the gospel the evangelist presents two encounters of Jesus which include lengthy dialogues. One is an encounter with a Jew who is attracted to Jesus by the signs he worked. Another is a chance meeting with a Samaritan woman. Both reach a certain level of faith in Jesus. In both dialogues Jesus spells out what believing in him means. In both chapters Jesus becomes the voice of the early Christian community teaching both Jew and Samaritan that he has come to replace the religion of their fathers, Moses and Jacob.

Nicodemus, who is described as 'a ruler of the Jews' and was probably a member of the Sanhedrin, comes to Jesus by night.

There is a clear symbolism here as Nicodemus comes from his darkness to seek the light. (John 1:5) He stands for those Jews who were attracted to Jesus but who did not have the courage to act openly. Nicodemus has the beginnings of faith. He knows of the signs Jesus works. They demonstrate he is from God. He calls Jesus a 'teacher' (John 3:2), echoing the opinion of the disciples on their first encounter with Jesus. (John 1:38)

Jesus solemnly begins his teaching to Nicodemus: 'Amen, amen, I say to you: unless a person is born from above, he cannot see the kingdom of God.' (John 3:3) It is significant that at the start of this first piece of teaching, and only here, Jesus introduces the concept of the kingdom so prominent in the synoptic gospels. But the emphasis here is quite different. In John Jesus is the bringer of new life. In John a person has to be born again from above to experience God's reign. The prologue has already referred to being born as children of God. (John 1:13)

The words of Jesus have a double meaning: the Greek term *anothen* means both 'again' and 'from above'. The word will occur on a second occasion later in the chapter in the phrase 'the one who comes from above'. (John 3:31) Nicodemus thinks Jesus is speaking about being born again and asks: 'How can a man be born when he is old?' (John 3:4) In a clear allusion to baptism as the way of entry into the Christian community Jesus replies that he has to be born 'of water and the Spirit'. (John 3:5) Jesus speaks of the freedom of the Spirit, which is like the freedom of the wind. The Greek term *pneuma* means both 'spirit' and 'wind'. Prophetic yearnings for renewed life for the people had spoken of the gift of a spirit from God which was associated with life-giving and cleansing waters. (Ezekiel 36:25-26; Isaiah 44:3)

Nicodemus is still confused: 'How can these things happen?' (John 3:9) He will not speak again. He fades away back into the darkness. At this point the words of Jesus clearly take on the status of a declaration of the community's faith: 'We speak about what we know and witness to what we have seen, but you people do not accept our witness.' (John 3:11) Jesus proceeds to tell Nicodemus how this new life is received. It is the gift of the

one who came down from heaven and has returned to heaven.
(John 3:13) Indeed this Son of Man, a term adopted by John for
the whole of the work of the Son, will be lifted up so that those
who believe in him will receive eternal life. (John 3:15) A parallel
is drawn with the story of the bronze serpent with which Moses
healed the Israelites in the book of Numbers. (Numbers 21:6-9)
The gift of eternal life from Jesus shows him to be greater than
Moses.

The fourth gospel speaks on three occasions of the lifting up
of the Son of Man (John 3:14, 8:28, 12:32-34), just as the synoptic
gospels contain three predictions by Jesus of his death and resurrection. Jesus is raised up, as the servant in Second Isaiah.
(Isaiah 52:13) It is through his being exalted in death and resurrection that Jesus gives the new life of the Spirit. God gave the
Son in love to the world so that those who believe in the Son
may have eternal life. (John 3:16-17; 1 John 4:9) They are born
from above as children of God. They come into the light. They
live by the truth. (John 3:21)

Nicodemus reappears later in the gospel as one who timidly
argues for Jesus with his colleagues. (John 7:50-52) He is among
those who bury Jesus. (John 19:39) He is a model of those who
believe in Jesus but who do not have sufficient courage to speak
openly in his favour. (John 12:42-43) As the chapter draws to an
end there is another scene involving John the Baptist. He gives
his final witness to Jesus. (John 3:27-30) The final verses of the
chapter take up again themes from the discourse of Jesus to
Nicodemus. (John 3:31-36)

The Samaritan woman in John chapter 4 provides a clear contrast with Nicodemus. After the planned encounter with
Nicodemus at dead of night this is a chance meeting in full day-
light in a town of Samaria. But the evangelist uses this story too
to illustrate what it means to receive new life from Jesus. Like
the disciples in the opening days, the Samaritan woman makes
progress in understanding the identity of Jesus. Nicodemus
seemed to have understood little of Jesus' teaching. The
Samaritan woman becomes an enthusiastic witness to Jesus with
the people of her town.

Only John's gospel gives details of a ministry of Jesus in Samaria. In Matthew's gospel Jesus explicitly forbids the disciples to preach in the towns of Samaria. (Matthew 10:5) Luke's gospel reports that a Samaritan village would not receive Jesus because he was going to Jerusalem. (Luke 9:52-53) Contact between Jesus and Samaritans cannot be ruled out. Indeed Luke tells of the grateful Samaritan healed of leprosy. (Luke 17:15-16) In the Acts of the Apostles we read of early evangelisation in Samaria by Philip. (Acts 8:1-25) The behaviour of Jesus in entering into conversation with an unknown Samaritan woman comes as no surprise.

The dialogue about water to drink opens up a new presentation of the gift of God brought by the Son. He offers 'living water' (Greek *hydor zon*). (John 4:10) In this he is indeed greater than Jacob, the father of Jews and Samaritans. (John 4:12) We have already noted the use of the image of water in association with prophetic utterances about the gift of the Spirit. Jesus will speak of this water as a life-giving spring inside a person. (John 4:14) Later in the gospel the evangelist will identify the living water with the Spirit of God. (John 7:37-39)

As Nicodemus had struggled to understand the concept of being born from above, so the Samaritan woman misunderstands 'living water'. (John 4:11, 4:15) It is Jesus who changes the subject to more mundane matters. The conversation about the woman's husbands displays again Jesus' insight into people's lives. (John 4:18) Just as Nathanael had made a leap of faith when he became aware of Jesus' extraordinary insight, so now the Samaritan woman makes a first step of faith. Jesus must be a prophet to know what he knows. (John 4:19) She rapidly changes the subject back to a more comfortable topic.

The question of the proper location for worshipping God is not unrelated to the issue of new life from living water. Samaritans, since their ancient break with the Jews, worshipped on mount Gerizim. The temple there had been attacked by the Jewish political and religious leader, John Hyrcanus, within recent memory. For Jesus the geographical location in Samaria or

in Jerusalem is of no importance. The hour will come when believers will worship 'in spirit and truth'. (John 4:23) The living
water given to believers in Jesus leads them to worship the God
who is Spirit in spirit and truth. (John 4:24)

The woman makes another tentative step of faith. She raises
the issue of the coming of a Messiah. (John 4:25) The raising of
this question might suggest the unlikely nature of this dialogue.
The Samaritans expected the coming of a prophet like Moses.
(Deuteronomy 18:18) Jesus' answer and claim to be the Messiah
(John 4:26) contrast strongly with the synoptic gospels' portrayal
of a Jesus reluctant to be heralded in such terms.

The evangelist has presented us with a chance encounter
from which the faith of the Samaritan woman grows. It grows to
such an extent that she becomes a preacher of Jesus. She tells her
friends: 'Come and see a man who told me all I ever did. He isn't
the Messiah, is he?' (John 4:29) The woman's departure and the
return of the disciples with provisions give the opportunity for
Jesus to speak of his mission. His 'food' is to do the Father's will.
(John 4:34) Indeed the fields are already ripe for harvest. (John
4:35) The story of the evangelisation of this Samaritan town and
the dialogue with the disciples about sowing and reaping a harvest may well have developed in the light of successful missionary preaching in Samaria. (John 4:36-38) The evangelist has offered us another presentation of a journey to faith. While the
Jewish teacher Nicodemus was confused and cautious, the
Samaritan woman is wholehearted and enthusiastic. With her
friends she reaches the conviction that Jesus is 'the saviour of the
world'. (John 4:42) In faith they are born from above. They receive the living water of the Spirit.

John's fourth chapter concludes with Jesus' return to Galilee
and the second sign at Cana. The evangelist stresses the link
with the first sign. (John 4:46) As he tested his mother, Jesus
again tests the faith of the one requesting help. (John 4:48) Jesus
restores health to the dying son of the royal official. He is indeed
the bringer of new life. As in the similar healing in Matthew and
Luke (Matthew 8:5-13; Luke 7:1-10), the miracle is worked from

a distance. It closes the first stage of John's accounts of the public ministry of Jesus.

The Jesus of John reveals the glory of God. Even in the earliest stages of the story there are those to whom the glory is revealed. Clearly the fourth gospel sets out to stress from the very beginning of the narrative the full truth about the Son. No-one has ever seen God. The Son comes to make God known. (John 1:18) The developed faith of the community which produced the fourth gospel is apparent throughout. What was alluded to occasionally in the synoptic gospels is proclaimed openly here: Jesus is the incarnate Son of God. In this gospel Jesus will make no secret of this truth. But the Jesus of John will also spell out throughout the gospel, in a variety of images, that Jesus offers to believers a share in the divine life.

CHAPTER 12

More Signs and Discourses

The sick man at the pool

The first substantial discourses of Jesus in John's gospel, his words to Nicodemus and the Samaritan woman, spoke of the gift of life brought by Jesus. In the discourses John's Christian community presents a catechesis on Christian faith. Jesus has also worked two signs at Cana in Galilee. As we reach chapter 5 of John's gospel we come to texts where the signs worked by Jesus become the basis for discourses of Jesus containing further catechesis. John presents the miracles of Jesus not as 'acts of power', as the synoptic gospels do, but as 'signs', for they point to the identity of Jesus. At the same time these new signs introduce individuals like the man at the pool and the man born blind, who may or may not come to full faith in Jesus.

The man at the pool in Jerusalem is a rather pathetic individual. Like so many gospel characters, he has no name. It will be Jesus who takes the initiative and heals him. Once again, as in chapter 2, Jesus is in Jerusalem. The evangelist tells us he is there for a feast (John 5:1), but does not say which feast. In fact it will be a feature of Jesus' visits to Jerusalem that he is there for pilgrimage feasts, for the feast of Tabernacles in chapter 7, for the feast of Dedication in chapter 10 and for the passover in chapter 12. This is historically very plausible but also has a theological dimension. Just as Jesus replaced the purification rites and temple worship, he will also replace the feasts of Judaism.

Excavations near the Lion Gate in old Jerusalem have uncovered what seems to be a pagan healing sanctuary with several pools, one of which with its five porticoes reflects the evangelist's description of the sheep pool at Bethzatha. (John 5:2)

Crowds of sick people would gather at the pool and healing was available when the waters were disturbed. (John 5:7) There may well be connections here with pagan healing practices. Some later copies of John's gospel include an explanation that this was the work of the 'angel of the Lord'. (John 5:4) This explanatory verse is not to be found in most of the oldest and most reliable copies of the gospel of John. The focus for the evangelist is not on the healing properties of the waters of the pool, but on the healing power of the word of Jesus. The man healed by Jesus had been ill for thirty-eight years. The evangelist points out that Jesus does not have to be told these details of the man's life. (John 5:6) It is Jesus who offers healing. The man's response is rather petulant.

The command which Jesus gives, 'Arise, take up your bed and walk!' (John 5:8), is similar to the command given to the paralytic in Mark chapter 2. The use of the Greek verb *egeirein*, which means 'to arise' and 'to raise', has connotations of resurrection. The discourse of Jesus which follows the sign will focus on the power of Jesus to raise people to life. (John 5:21) The command of Jesus is found three times in the story. The sick man repeats the words to the Jews, and they too repeat them. (John 5:11-12) Even those who do not believe lay stress on the life-giving words of the Son. This will also be a theme of the discourse. (John 5:25, 5:28)

The healing happened on a sabbath day. This healing and the cure of the man born blind in John chapter 9 both take place on the sabbath and, as in the synoptic gospels, provoke accusations that Jesus is breaking the sabbath. This leads to the focus on the work of God and the work of the Son in the discourse. (John 5:17) The healed man is challenged by the Jews for carrying his bed. He tells them of the man who told him to do so, but he does not know his name. A curious feature of the story is the brief second meeting of Jesus and the healed man. There is a touch of anger in Jesus' words to the man, who has totally failed to understand the sign. (John 5:14) The man tells the Jews it was Jesus who healed him.

Jesus replies to the accusation of breaking the sabbath by saying: 'My Father continues to work and I continue to work.' (John
5:17) The evangelist comments that the Jews pursued Jesus not
only for breaking the sabbath but also for making himself equal
to God. (John 5:18) Whereas the accusation of working on the
sabbath was surely made to Jesus by his contemporaries, the accusation that Jesus claimed equal status with God more probably
reflects complaints made to John's community by their Jewish
opponents concerning their faith in the divinity of Jesus. The
discourse which follows will explain Jesus' relationship to the
Father as understood in the developed faith of John's believers.
The sign of the healing of the man by the pool is the basis on
which a catechesis about the work of Jesus, the work of the Son
of the Father, is built.

Jesus clarifies that he can do nothing by himself but only
what he sees the Father doing. (John 5:19) As the Father raises
the dead and restores people to life, so indeed does the Son.
Furthermore, the Father has entrusted all acts of judgement to
the Son. Life is obtained by listening to the words of the Son. The
one who believes in the Father who sent the Son already has
eternal life. Such a person is not brought to judgement, but passes
from death to life. It is refusal to believe which brings judgement
on a person. (John 3:18) Just as in the synoptic gospels, the Son of
Man gathers believers into new life. (John 5:26-27; Mark 13:26-27)
The resurrection of the dead is announced in words which echo
the opening verses of Daniel chapter 12. Jesus does the will of
the Father by judging and by bringing people to the life of the
resurrection.

The theme of the final verses of the discourse is that of witness. (John 5:31-47) The Christian community defends Jesus by
listing the mighty witnesses which speak out in his support.
Jesus does not rely on his own testimony. (John 5:31) He mentions the witness of John the Baptist, fully elaborated earlier in
the gospel. The works Jesus has performed are a further and
greater witness to the truth of his claims. These works are the
way by which the Father too bears witness to the Son. Jesus then

delivers his attack on his listeners. They have no awareness of God. They do not believe the testimony which the scriptures bear to Jesus. (John 5:39-40) Indeed, they have no love of God in them. They are unwilling to accept the one who is loved by the Father and sent by the Father. They seek their glory from each other, and do not welcome the glory which comes from God, the incarnate Son. (John 5:44) The discourse following the healing of the sick man at the pool ends as a strong defence of the validity of Christian beliefs about Jesus.

The bread of life

In chapter 5 we saw how this evangelist attached a long discourse of Jesus to an account of an act of healing in order to point out its value as a sign. In chapter 6 he does the same, but on this occasion uses the story of the multiplication of the loaves, a story found repeatedly in the synoptic gospels. In considering the multiplication of the loaves in an earlier chapter, we realised that the story is an epiphany of Jesus. The basic story of the working of a miracle reveals that Jesus provides for the people, as Moses provided for the Israelites in the wilderness. The synoptic story also showed similarities with the last supper accounts. John's gospel will develop these connections, both in the narrative of the miracle and in the discourse. Following the sequence of events in Mark and Matthew, John also reports the walking on the water immediately after the multiplication of the loaves. The tradition behind John's gospel obviously received these two miracles together, just as the synoptic tradition did.

John's account of the feeding of the five thousand receives a particular presentation here. Jesus is again in Galilee and it is the time of the passover. (John 6:1-4) We should remember here the strange fact that in his account of the farewell meal of Jesus John does not mention Jesus' giving of the bread and wine of the eucharist. For John this sign in Galilee is the passover meal of Jesus. He gives a new passover, to be celebrated not in Jerusalem but in the place where the disciples gather. But those who gather are by no means all disciples. The evangelist stresses that a great crowd followed Jesus because they had seen the signs he had performed in healing the sick. (John 6:2) These people have, like Nicodemus, only an inadequate faith. They have an idea Jesus might come from God because he works such signs. (John 3:2) As the chapter unfolds they will not progress to full faith.

There are other elements in John's account which differ from the synoptic presentation. Philip and Andrew are involved in the initiative to get food for the crowd. (John 6:7-9) Philip and Andrew brought new disciples to Jesus in John chapter 1. They will be approached by certain Greeks who wish to see Jesus in John chapter 12. They are remembered in the fourth gospel as mediators and men of initiative. Another addition to the story comes when the evangelist affirms that, though Jesus asks Philip how sufficient bread can be obtained for the crowd, he knows precisely what he is going to do. (John 6:6) The reaction of the crowd is to move to a new stage of faith. Like the Samaritan woman, they declare that Jesus is the prophet to come. (John 6:14) The story concludes with an interesting reaction on Jesus' part: he knows that the crowds will take him and make him king and goes off alone to the hills. (John 6:15) The inadequate faith of the crowds is a danger for him, just as the inadequate faith and messianic expectations of Peter were a threat in the synoptic gospels.

John's account of the walking on the water is restrained. (John 6:16-21) Clearly he must report this tradition which is so closely tied to the previous miracle. Its reduced presentation may well be due to the fact that it is not utilised in the discourse which follows. There is the briefest of allusions to it when the crowd is surprised at finding Jesus with the disciples again. They had seen the disciples leave without him. Their question, 'Rabbi, when did you come here?' (John 6:25), is used by Jesus to challenge their reasons for wanting to see him again.

The faith of the crowd is inadequate. They simply want to have more bread. (John 6:26) Jesus challenges them to work for food which lasts, and 'remains for eternal life'. (John 6:27) To do the works of God they must have faith in the one God has sent.

In order to believe the crowd requires a sign. (John 6:30) They recall that their fathers had bread from heaven. What work will Jesus do? Jesus takes up their scriptural words and gives them new ones: 'Moses did not give you bread from heaven, but my Father gives you the true bread from heaven.' (John 6:32) The challenge is to move on from recalling the ancient gifts of God through Moses, and to recognise the new gift from heaven, the true bread given by God for the life of the world. (John 6:33)

The scene is set for the discourse proper to begin. Jesus says: 'I am the bread of life. The one who comes to me will never hunger, and the one who believes in me will never thirst.' (John 6:35) In the book of Ecclesiasticus chapter 24 it is personified wisdom who invites people to come, promising that those who eat will hunger for more and those who drink will thirst for more. Jesus offers the true wisdom. Faith in Jesus is acceptance of his wisdom. To those called by God in this way Jesus gives life. He repeatedly promises to raise to life on the last day those entrusted to him by the Father. (John 6:39, 6:40, 6:44, 6:54) Those who accept Jesus as bread of life, those who believe, will be raised to eternal life.

The reaction of the crowd points to Jesus' origins. How can he say that he is the bread from heaven? He is the son of Joseph, surely. (John 6:42) In response Jesus reiterates that he is sent by the Father to bring eternal life to believers.

The discourse then takes on clear eucharistic connotations. Jesus declares: 'I am the living bread which has come down from heaven. Whoever eats of this bread will live for ever, and the bread which I shall give is my flesh for the life of the world.' (John 6:51) To receive the bread of life is to receive not only the word and wisdom of Jesus. It is to eat his flesh and drink his blood. In the last supper tradition of St Paul and the synoptic gospels, Jesus gives the bread which is his body (Greek *soma*) and the cup of his blood (Greek *haima*). John by contrast speaks of the flesh (Greek *sarx*) and the blood. John may reflect earlier eucharistic language here for both Hebrew and Aramaic naturally speak of 'flesh and blood' as components of the human person. The alternative pair of words, 'body and blood', seems to arise from translating Jesus' words into suitable Greek equivalents. Just as the bread of the word is a pledge of eternal life, so the flesh and blood, the true food and true drink, are the nourishment of eternal life. (John 6:54) There is furthermore an intimate communion between the one who eats and drinks and Jesus himself. (John 6:56)

Jesus' statement of his origins from above had already upset the people. That he now speaks of giving his flesh to eat and blood to drink is a 'hard saying'. (John 6:60) Like the crucifixion of the Messiah, it is a scandal, an obstacle for belief. (John 6:61; 1 Corinthians 1:23) We are confronting the difficulties which John's community experienced with the Jews. They could not accept Jesus as the one sent by the Father, but even more difficult was the very idea that Jesus could give his flesh and blood in the eucharist.

In addition, John chapter 6 points to a major division within John's church. It is presented as a break provoked by Jesus himself owing to his difficult teaching on the bread of life. (John 6:66) The evangelist has cleverly relocated the division he experienced among Christians of his own community in the story of Jesus' ministry in Galilee.

Many go away, and Jesus challenges the twelve. Simon Peter's answer is the fourth gospel's version of his profession of faith in Jesus: 'Lord, to whom shall we go? You have the words of eternal life, and we have believed and come to know that you are the holy one of God.' (John 6:68-69) The disciples, who in John's account had reached full faith at the first Cana sign, welcome the further teaching of Jesus. But the evangelist warns us for the first time at this point that one of them will betray Jesus. Judas is described as a 'devil' (Greek *diabolos*). (John 6:70) While in Mark and Matthew, Peter had been addressed in this way by Jesus, in John Jesus now identifies the real threat.

The bread of life discourse reveals to us how the community in which John's gospel was developed understood the continuing presence of Jesus in the lives of believers. Jesus is their food as the word of God coming from God. Jesus is their food in their communion with him in the eucharist. Like the disciples at Emmaus, they were nourished on word and eucharist, the constant gifts of the Lord to believers through the centuries.

Living water and the light of the world
During the arguments with the people over the bread of life, there is no threat of violence. The atmosphere changes dramatically from John chapter 7. There has already been a comment by the evangelist earlier in the gospel concerning why the Jews sought to kill Jesus. Not only did he break the sabbath, but he also claimed equality with God. (John 5:18) From chapter 7 onwards there is open talk of killing Jesus. We can recall that, in a similar way in the synoptic gospels, there was an increasing focus on the coming death of Jesus once he began his journey to Jerusalem and during the Jerusalem ministry.

As chapter 7 begins, the relatives of Jesus encourage him to go to Jerusalem despite the risks. He refuses to give in to their pressure that he should go to Jerusalem to court popularity. He asserts that the time (Greek *kairos*), the right time, has not yet come. (John 7:6) He subsequently decides to go up for the feast of Tabernacles, but in secret. There is no mention of the disciples accompanying him, but they are present when he heals the blind man in Jerusalem. (John 9:2) Jesus will not return to Galilee before his death. As in the synoptic gospels, he goes knowingly to the place where he foresees his own martyrdom will take place.

The seventh and eighth chapters of John's gospel are complex. They contain a series of dialogues between Jesus and the Jews in Jerusalem. Crowds have gathered for the week-long feast of Tabernacles (Hebrew *sukkot*). This feast of thanksgiving for the grape harvest also commemorated the wilderness period of Moses and the people of Israel and was celebrated with lavish ceremony and great rejoicing. A major feature of the feast was the daily bringing of water libations from the pool of Siloam to be poured on the altar in the temple. It recalled the gift of water in the wilderness wandering of Moses and naturally led to

prayer for good rains as winter approached. At the climax of the
festival Jesus cries out: 'If anyone is thirsty let him come to me
and drink. For the one who believes in me, as scripture says,
rivers of living water will flow from his bowels.' (John 7:37-38)
In referring to the living water in the believer the text recalls
Jesus' words to the Samaritan woman that the water he gives
will become a spring of water in the believer welling up to eternal life. (John 4:14) The text of scripture is not identifiable, and it
is often interpreted as referring to Jesus rather than the believer,
for the evangelist will speak of water and blood flowing from
the pierced side of the dying Jesus. (John 19:34) It may, however,
be better understood to refer to the believer, for the evangelist
adds a comment that Jesus was speaking of the Spirit which
would be given to believers once Jesus was glorified in death.
(John 7:39)

The story of the woman caught in adultery breaks the flow of
dialogues between Jesus and the Jews. (John 8:2-11) Though it is
missing from the most reliable ancient manuscripts of the fourth
gospel, it is part of the gospel in use by the church from ancient
times. It seems to be a piece of tradition which had an indepen-
dent existence, and has been inserted in a context where it does
not belong.

A second feature of the ceremonial of the great feast of
Tabernacles was the lighting of huge gold candlesticks. The
practice recalls the pillar of fire which guided the Israelites by
night. In his very next words after speaking of living water,
Jesus declares: 'I am the light of the world. Whoever follows me
will not walk in the darkness, but will have the light of life.'
(John 8:12) Jesus brought living water to replace the water libations. He now takes the place of the pillar of fire. The theme of
Jesus replacing the feasts of Israel, which we have seen throughout the gospel so far, continues. As he brought a new passover,
so he replaces the feast of Tabernacles.

Another feature of these chapters is the sending of the temple
servants to arrest Jesus. (John 7:32) Later on they return without
him and exclaim: 'Never has any man spoken like this.' (John

7:46) They voice the truth that Jesus is no ordinary man. Jesus will only be arrested when the hour comes and he offers himself freely. As chapter 8 progresses Jesus uses the phrase 'I am' (Greek *ego eimi*). (John 8:24, 8:28) The words reflect God's revelation of the name of God to Moses. (Exodus 3:14) They are understood as a claim to divine status. He will use the same expression again at the end of the exchange.

To those who believe, Jesus promises that the truth (Greek *aletheia*) will make them free. (John 8:32) The suggestion that they are not free, that they are slaves, angers these Jews, who declare that they are the seed of Abraham and have never been slaves. (John 8:33) After more lengthy arguments Jesus declares that Abraham rejoiced to see his day. (John 8:56) The evangelist does not clarify how Abraham saw Jesus' day. Did he foresee it in his lifetime, or see it from his place in the life of the resurrection? The Jews understand Jesus' statement on an earthly level and scoff at the very idea that Jesus, who is not yet fifty years old, could have seen Abraham. Jesus makes his final statement: 'Before Abraham came to be, I am.' (John 8:58) The dialogue has reflected not the disputes of Jesus and the Pharisees but those raging between the Christians of John's community and groups of Jews who opposed the divine status being attributed to Jesus. At Jesus' assertion that he was always with God, an assertion which is blasphemous in their eyes, the Jews pick up stones to throw at him. Jesus leaves the temple, for the hour has not yet come. (John 8:59)

The man born blind and the good shepherd
The sixth of the seven great signs in John's gospel then follows. It has clear connections with the feast of Tabernacles. Jesus meets a man who was born blind. The question of the disciples whether it was the sin of the man or of his parents which caused the blindness allows Jesus to dismiss the causal link between suffering and sin. The man was born blind 'so that the works of God might be displayed in him.' (John 9:3) The man's cure is to be a sign that God offers healing and light. Jesus then reiterates

what he declared at the end of the feast. He is the light of the world. (John 9:5)

The healing of the man shows some primitive aspects. Two miracles in Mark's gospel showed Jesus employing healing techniques, such as the use of spittle. (Mark 7:31-37, 8:22-26) These healings were not reported by the later synoptic gospels probably due to the use of such methods. In the healing of the man born blind Jesus makes a paste with clay and spittle and smears it on the man's eyes. (John 9:6) He then sends him to wash in the pool of Siloam, from which the water libations had been brought during the feast. It is perhaps a little surprising that with such an exalted presentation of Jesus John retains the detailed description of the cure. The themes of light in darkness and life-giving water, themes of the feast, are evoked again as the man washes his eyes and returns able to see. The evangelist affirms that the name 'Siloam' means 'sent'. (John 9:7) There is an allusion here to John's constant description of Jesus as the one sent by God.

The story of the healing is over, but the story of the man born blind has only just started. This man is a model of honesty and courage. He seeks the truth. He admits it openly when there is something he does not know. He shows great courage in facing the Pharisees, who eventually throw him out of the synagogue, expelling him from their community. The man born blind is a model catechumen. It is no surprise that the story was used in preparation for baptism from the earliest centuries. The man is enlightened by Jesus and comes to full faith, worshipping him at the end of the chapter. The man provides encouragement for the members of the evangelist's community not to fear the expulsion from the synagogue which follows from their declaration of faith in Jesus.

The man makes a series of appearances as he is interrogated by different groups. They challenge his story, or are reluctant to side with him, fearing the consequences. At first his neighbours and those who had regularly seen him begging raise doubts whether he is the same man who was blind. The man kept saying: 'I am the one.' (John 9:9) He provides a detailed account for them of how 'the man called Jesus' cured him. (John 9:11) But he does not know where Jesus has gone.

The tension increases as the man is interrogated by the Pharisees. He recounts his story without hesitation. Since the cure had been worked on the sabbath, they declare Jesus to be a sinner. The man himself fearlessly defends Jesus: 'He is a prophet.' (John 9:17) Such a declaration was also a stage on the way to full faith for the Samaritan woman. (John 4:19)

The Pharisees, Jesus' frequent opponents in disputes during his ministry, give way in the narrative to the Jews. This change illustrates how the disputes of John's community with the Jews lie behind the development of this account. The Jews try a new line of investigation. They summon the man's parents. The parents refuse to get involved in the question of how he has received his sight: 'He is an adult. He will speak for himself.' (John 9:21) The evangelist explains in the next two verses that they took such an attitude for fear of being expelled from the synagogue.

The man is summoned again. By this time the Jews, having previously been divided on the issue, are unanimous: 'We know that this man is a sinner.' (John 9:24) The Jews interrogate him again. 'Why do you want to hear it again?' he says. 'Surely you do not want to become his disciples too?' (John 9:27) Despite the Jews' scornful words he continues to seek the truth and declares that Jesus must be from God to be able to do what he did. (John 9:33). The Jews turn on him again, vilify him as a sinner, and throw him out. (John 9:34)

The final scene involves Jesus and the bind man, with the Jews waiting in the wings. It is Jesus who seeks him out, when he learns that he has been thrown out. Jesus leads him to the further understanding, that he is the 'Son of Man', the title used in the fourth gospel to summarise the coming to earth and the saving work of the Son of God. The man's final words, omitted in some ancient copies of the gospel, are: 'Lord, I believe.' (John 9:38) They make explicit what the man's willingness to believe has already implied.

Jesus comes to give sight to those who are blind, and to bring blindness to those who think they see. The Pharisees mutter: 'Surely we are not blind?' (John 9:40) Jesus' final words are a profound challenge: 'If you were blind, you would have no sin. But since you say 'We see', your sin remains.' (John 9:41) The man once blind has struggled to full faith amid insults and ill treatment. His complacent opponents remain in their blindness. Faith in Jesus allows a new vision, but depends on a willingness to face new truths and even abusive treatment from others.

John chapter 10 follows on from the story of the man born blind without a break. Jesus speaks in this section about good and bad shepherds. (John 10:1-21) It attaches quite naturally to the last verses of chapter 9, where there is an implicit contrast between the attitude of the Pharisees and that of Jesus. Their attitude and behaviour contrast with the shepherding given by Jesus. The evangelist will provide a final reminder of the blind man at the end of the section. (John 10:21)

Jesus uses the image of the shepherd in a variety of ways. His words recall the speech of the prophet Ezekiel about the rulers of Israel. (Ezekiel 34) They are bad shepherds who have failed to care for the sheep. The prophet promised that God would become their shepherd, and that God would raise up a new shepherd. Jesus speaks of the thieves and brigands who do not enter by the gate, but break in to plunder and destroy. Jesus adds a new dimension to the imagery: 'I am the gate of the sheep.' (John 10:7) Through Jesus the sheep enter the pastures of life. By Jesus they are defended from thieves and brigands. Jesus declares: 'I have come that they may have life, and have it in abundance.' (John 10:10)

Another new dimension of the imagery of the shepherd follows: 'I am the good shepherd. The good shepherd lays down his life for the sheep.' (John 10:11) Jesus has been described as providing life in many ways. He is the bread of life. He provides living waters. Here he gives life by laying down his life. The Christian understanding of the death of Jesus as life-giving for all is expressed here. The servant in the second part of the book of Isaiah goes like a sheep to the shearing and gives his life as a sin offering for others. (Isaiah 53:7, 53:10) Here, it is the shepherd who freely allows others to take his life in defence of his sheep. There is an emphasis on the power of Jesus who not only lays down his life but will also take it up again. (John 10:18) There is a contrast here with the synoptic picture of God raising Jesus from death.

A further feature of this ideal shepherd is that he knows his sheep. There is a personal relationship between the Christian and the good shepherd. But the shepherd has others to seek out and bring in. A final allusion to the prophet Ezekiel is found in the reference to 'one flock and one shepherd'. (John 10:16) Ezekiel stresses the reunification of the tribes of Israel as one nation under one shepherd. (Ezekiel 34:23, 37:22-24)

These words on unity, like his teaching on the bread of life to be shared by all, provoke division (Greek *schisma*), a division experienced both in Jesus' ministry and in John's community. (John 10:19) Not all see the need to enter the fold of the good shepherd. In a clear echo of insults directed against Jesus in Mark's gospel, some Jews suggest Jesus is possessed. (John 10:20; Mark 3:22) But others disagree. (John 10:21)

After this there is something of a new start in Jesus' dialogues with the Jews. The evangelist, in a new introduction, tells us it is now the feast of Dedication in Jerusalem. This feast, known as *hanukkah,* commemorated the rededication of the temple in Jerusalem by Judas the Maccabee, after its profanation by Antiochus Epiphanes, the Seleucid ruler. (1 Maccabees 4 and 2 Maccabees 10) These events of the second century BC were celebrated with ceremonies of lights in the heart of winter. The issue of Jesus' identity is immediately raised. Jesus speaks again of the sheep entrusted to him by the Father. He then says: 'The Father and I are one.' (John 10:30) The words speak of a shared purpose. Jesus is sent by the Father to do what the Father wills. The words are a significant contribution to the developing understanding of the relationship of the Son to the Father. For the Jews they are another claim to divinity, for which they again try to stone Jesus. (John 10:31)

Jesus' reply recalls a looser use of the concept of divinity. Quoting a scriptural text, Jesus implies that God has called his people 'gods'. Why should they take offence, therefore, if the one actually consecrated by God claims to be the Son of God? (John 10:36) At this point the evangelist may be suggesting that Jesus, the consecrated one, replaces the rededicated temple. He would thus replace the feast of Dedication too. The Jews are angered by Jesus' insistence: 'The Father is in me and I am in the Father.' (John 10:38) Jesus once again eludes them. (John 10:39) The clear implication is that his hour has not yet come. The chapter ends on a note of hope. When Jesus returns from Jerusalem to the far side of the Jordan there are many who believe in him. (John 10: 42)

The resurrection and the life

The last of John's seven signs worked by Jesus is the raising of Lazarus from the dead. It comes as the climax of Jesus' ministry and is, in John's gospel, the cause of moves to arrest Jesus. In this sign Jesus gives not bread or water, light or healing, but life itself. It is for giving life to Lazarus that plots to end the life of Jesus will be made. While the synoptic gospels gave the accounts of the raising to life of Jairus' daughter and the widow's son at Nain, only the fourth gospel tells of the raising of Lazarus, the brother of Martha and Mary. The two sisters are mentioned in Luke's gospel providing hospitality for Jesus. (Luke 10:38-42) Mark's gospel refers to Jesus' lodging for the night in Bethany during the Jerusalem ministry (Mark 11:11), but only John gives the complete picture of Lazarus and his two sisters as friends of Jesus who lived at Bethany.

The evangelist tells us from the start that Lazarus was ill. (John 11:1) It is explained in what appears to be an editorial addition that Mary was the one who anointed Jesus' feet with ointment, a story still to come in John's gospel. (John 11:2, 12:1-8) It is reported to Jesus that 'the one you love' is ill. (John 11:3) The evangelist stresses Jesus' love not only for Lazarus but also for Martha and Mary. (John 11:5) Indeed, this chapter of John's gospel will lay a heavy emphasis on the emotions of Jesus. On receiving the news of Lazarus' illness Jesus makes a remark about the purpose of the illness, a remark which is rather similar to his statement about the blindness of the man born blind at the beginning of John chapter 9. Jesus says of Lazarus: 'This sickness is not for death, but for the glory of God, so that the Son of God may be glorified through it.' (John 11:4) Just as in his first sign in Cana of Galilee the disciples saw his glory, so here in the final one of the seven signs God's glory is revealed.

Jesus waits for two days before going to Bethany. Once again Jesus is supremely free and makes his own decisions. As at Cana he apparently disregarded his mother's concern about wine, so here he appears to neglect the need of Lazarus. The Son of God acts in his own time and with his own freedom both in working signs and in laying down his life. Furthermore, Jesus knows of the death of Lazarus without the news being reported. (John 11:14)

On arrival at the house of Lazarus, where mourners have gathered, Jesus meets first Martha and then Mary. While the earlier signs in John's gospel had been discussed and explained by Jesus after the event, the significance of this final sign is explained before Lazarus is raised, in the dialogues between Jesus and the sisters. Martha expresses her faith in Jesus that her brother would not have died had he been present. But she goes further: 'I know now that, whatever you ask of God, God will give you.' (John 11:22) Jesus asserts that Lazarus will rise again, and Martha expresses her belief in the resurrection at the last day, the belief held particularly by the Pharisees in Jesus' day. Jesus then declares: 'I am the resurrection and the life.' (John 11:25)

Jesus will demonstrate his power over death in the raising of Lazarus back to his mortal life. But the sign points beyond mortal life to the life of the resurrection. Jesus is the resurrection and the life. Whoever believes in him will never die. The one who gives life to anyone he chooses (John 5:21), the one who gives the bread of life so that a person may live and not die (John 6:51), now declares himself to be the resurrection and the life for those who believe. The response of Martha is to declare the fulness of Christian faith, as found at the conclusion of the gospel, that Jesus is both the Messiah and the Son of God. (John 11:27, 20:31)

When Mary comes to see Jesus she falls at his feet. She too, like her sister, affirms that had he been present her brother would not have died. The evangelist emphasises the distress of Jesus at seeing the weeping of Mary and of the mourners. The evangelist says he 'was deeply moved in spirit and greatly troubled'. (John 11:33) It happens rarely in the fourth gospel that we find a description of Jesus experiencing profound human emotion. He shares the anguish of Mary at the death of her brother and the distress of the Jews who mourned him. Approaching the tomb Jesus weeps. (John 11:35) The fourth gospel, with all its emphasis on the glory of God revealed in the Son of God, also provides precious awareness that the Word became flesh. We gain insight into the deep and full humanity and even the vulnerability of the Son of God.

The Son who does the work of the Father does not pray that God will hear him, for he is completely aware of what God has sent him to do. Instead, he thanks the Father for hearing his prayer. (John 11:41) The evangelist almost has Jesus make excuses for the prayer, which is for the benefit of those who hear Jesus. (John 11:42) Lazarus is summoned from death. He comes out still bound in his grave clothes. Perhaps the evangelist wants us to remember that Lazarus will die again, but that Jesus, whose grave clothes will be neatly laid aside in John's description of the empty tomb, will bestow immortal life on believers.

John chapter 11 ends with deliberations of the Sanhedrin: 'What are we doing now that this man is working so many signs?' (John 11:47) They fear a popular following of Jesus will provoke Roman intervention to crush and destroy the nation. It is Caiaphas, the high priest, who declares that it is better for one man to die for the people. (John 11:50) Whereas in the gospel of Mark it was Jesus' disturbance in the temple which led to the final plots to destroy him, here in the fourth gospel it is the popularity of Jesus due to the signs he worked. In both cases the religious authorities, who fear the uncompromising challenge of this new teacher, present Jesus to the Romans as a threat to the security and survival of the nation. John is cleverly telling the reader that the one who, according to Caiaphas, is put to death to save the people is in fact laying down his life for the world. As the evangelist makes clear, Jesus was to die 'not only for the nation, but also in order to gather together into one the scattered children of God'. (John 11:52)

The general ministry of Jesus concludes in John chapter 12. After that chapter Jesus will address his disciples in his extended farewell discourse. (John 13-17) John records the anointing of Jesus' feet by Mary, sister of Lazarus, before the feast of passover at the beginning of John chapter 12. In Mark and Matthew the head of Jesus was anointed before passover by an unnamed woman. In all these stories Jesus states that the anointing is a preparation for death. (Mark 14:8; Matthew 26:12; John 12:7) The entry of Jesus into Jerusalem retains many features of the synoptic accounts. As in Matthew, there is the reference to Zechariah chapter 9. The king comes in humility riding on an ass. The popularity of Jesus is linked explicitly to Jesus' raising of Lazarus. (John 12:17) The Pharisees become even more worried: 'Look, the world is going after him.' (John 12:19)

The evangelist neatly follows this cry of alarm with the arrival of certain Greeks who wish to see Jesus. (John 12:20-21) These men seem to be converts to Judaism who have been attracted by reports about Jesus. The evangelist shifts abruptly then to some words of Jesus. He speaks of the grain of wheat which dies and gives life. (John 12:24) In words reminiscent of the Gethsemane scene in the synoptic gospels, Jesus is troubled and asks: 'What shall I say? Father, save me from this hour? But it was for this that I came to this hour. Father, glorify your name!' (John 12:27-28) A voice from heaven is heard: 'I have glorified it, and I will glorify it.' (John 12:28) This evangelist, who has no voice of God earlier in the gospel, no baptism or transfiguration scene, in which the voice of God is heard in the synoptic tradition, saves the approving voice of God for the end of Jesus' public ministry. Jesus speaks of the approaching trial. When he is lifted up he will draw all to himself. (John 12:32) Both Jew and Gentile are called to the light.

John concludes the chapter with a survey of Jesus' ministry, recalling the blindness and hardness of heart of many and using words from Isaiah chapter 6 to suggest that God foresaw all this. But others did believe, says the evangelist, though they were afraid to speak openly for fear of expulsion from the synagogue. Once again John reflects the experience of his own community. The chapter concludes with a final public declaration of Jesus. (John 12:44-50)

CHAPTER 13

Death and Resurrection in John

The washing of the feet

Once we reach chapter 13 of the gospel of John the public ministry of Jesus is at an end. The evangelist has concluded his account of Jesus' signs and his disputes with the Jews with a summary of its impact. From chapter 13 until chapter 17, in these chapters which immediately precede the story of the death and resurrection of Jesus, Jesus will be in the company of his friends. He will leave them his last words.

John's gospel is quite different from the synoptic gospels in presenting an extensive speech of Jesus in the context of his final supper before he is arrested. Only Luke's gospel shows limited similarity, for this evangelist includes in the context of the last supper several pieces of teaching of Jesus concerning discipleship. (Luke 22:24-38) This section of John's gospel actually presents several speeches of Jesus. Jesus concludes a first speech at the end of chapter 14. Chapters 15 and 16 have him continue to speak as if there had been no interruption. In chapter 17 Jesus addresses a lengthy prayer to the Father.

The evangelist begins chapter 13 by reminding us of the approaching passover. He stresses Jesus' awareness that the hour has finally arrived for him to leave the world and return to the Father. He also stresses Jesus' love for his friends: 'he loved them to the end.' (John 13:1) To underline that the hour has truly come, John informs us that the devil has already put it in the heart of Judas to betray Jesus. (John 13:2) Luke had also shown a sensitivity to the role of Satan as the passion narrative began. (Luke 22:3) The gross injustice about to be perpetrated requires reference to some kind of evil source.

In stark contrast with the evil at work in Judas, Jesus shows only love and willingness to serve. Jesus performs the symbolic action of washing the disciples' feet. (John 13:2-15) The action symbolises his self-giving as a servant. There is once again a link with Luke's gospel, where Jesus had declared during the supper: 'I am among you as one who serves.' (Luke 22:27) In John's gospel this attitude is acted out in the washing of the feet. We should recall that John does not record Jesus' giving of the eucharistic gifts of bread and wine during his account of the farewell meal. The fourth gospel has provided its presentation of Jesus as offering his flesh and blood in John chapter 6. But there is a deep similarity between the washing of the feet in John and the gift of the eucharist in the synoptic gospels. Both present the self-giving of Jesus. Both prepare for his death. Both bring with them the command to 'do this in memory of me'. Jesus will say: 'I have given you an example (Greek *hypodeigma*) that you too should do as I have done to you.' (John 13:15) Jesus will be present in the community not only in the eucharistic bread and wine but also in the service of others. This symbolic action before he is arrested is a challenge to Christians. It is not by words alone, and certainly not by empty words, that the gospel will be lived. It is by actions of love and service. Jesus is the model for Christians in his washing of the disciples' feet. His example has been followed. It has also been disregarded.

The second preliminary to Jesus' farewell words concerns Judas' treachery and involves another symbolic action. Distress overcomes Jesus and he declares: 'one of you will betray me.' (John 13:21) John presents the scene in a different way from the synoptic gospels. We are introduced for the first time at this point to 'the disciple Jesus loved'. (John 13:23) This disciple is never named and will reappear during the final chapters of the gospel. (John 19:26, 20:2, 21:7, 21:20) Here, as elsewhere, he is close to Peter. Reclining next to Jesus he asks who the betrayer is. Jesus then performs a final symbolic action. He takes a morsel of bread and offers it to Judas. (John 13:26) In other contexts, in the stories of the feeding of the crowds and in the synoptic last supper narratives, Jesus takes bread and gives it to all. Here in John's last supper narrative, where no general giving of bread is reported, Jesus offers food to the one who most needs it. Even as the heart of Judas turns from him, Jesus offers love to Judas. But Jesus, as has been repeatedly emphasised, knows Judas' heart. It is Jesus who gives Judas leave to go and do what he plans. (John 13:27) And it was night.

For John, Jesus is now glorified. God will be glorified in the death and resurrection of the Son. Jesus' death in John is the revelation of the glory of God. (John 13:31-32)

The farewell speeches

The first farewell discourse begins with the words 'my little children'. (John 13:33) It is reminiscent of the words of a father about to die and leave his family behind. There will be interventions from Peter, Thomas, Philip and Judas (not Judas Iscariot) during the discourse. This speech will finish at the end of chapter 14 with Jesus' words, 'Arise, let us go.' (John 14:31) In a speech dominated by thoughts of Jesus' departure, the theme of the love of Jesus for the disciples and their love for each other constantly appears. Jesus announces his 'new commandment'. In the synoptic gospels Jesus had spoken of love of God and of neighbour as the chief commandments. (Mark 12:29-31) Here he commands the disciples to love each other as he has loved them. (John 13:34) 'Love your neighbour as yourself' is replaced by love which imitates Jesus' love. This is Jesus' command as he leaves the disciples. Peter interrupts to proclaim his fidelity. As in the synoptic tradition, his denial of Jesus is announced. (John 13:38)

Jesus' departure to the Father naturally raises the question of where he is going. He also announces his return to take them with him. Jesus assures them they know the way, but Thomas is not convinced. Jesus in answer declares: 'I am the way, the truth and the life.' (John 14:6) This is perhaps the most comprehensive of the 'I am' statements of Jesus. A similar image is that found in chapter 10, when Jesus asserts he is the 'gate of the sheep'. (John

10:7) Jesus is the way for he has revealed the Father to the world. As he returns to the Father he shows the way. He is the way because he is the truth. He has revealed the fulness of the truth of God. He is the way, because he leads his followers to life. The interruption from Philip to ask to see the Father shows how difficult it is to understand that in seeing the Son we see the Father. Jesus declares: 'I am in the Father and the Father is in me.' (John 14:10)

Nevertheless, Jesus is to depart. But he will not leave his children orphaned. (John 14:18) The Father will give, at Jesus' request, 'another advocate'. (John 14:16) We meet here for the first time the figure of the Paraclete (Greek *parakletos*). The Greek term means literally one who is 'called alongside', one called to assist. The term is translated in various ways. It seems to have the legal connotations of one called upon to defend an accused person. Jesus qualifies the term by referring to 'the Spirit of truth'. The Spirit of truth is the Spirit of Jesus, who is the truth. The Spirit is also 'another advocate', for Jesus has been the first advocate. (1 John 2:1) Jesus asserts that the disciples already know the Spirit, and that the Spirit is still to be sent. (John 14:16-17)

Jesus returns to the theme of the advocate whom the Father will send. This Spirit 'will teach you everything and remind you of everything I have said to you'. (John 14:26) The Spirit is called alongside to be the support of the disciples when Jesus leaves. The Spirit reminds them of the teaching of Jesus but also leads them on to new understanding. The process suggested here is at work in the writing of the gospels. Jesus and his teaching are remembered but they are also built upon, for the Spirit of Jesus helps believers to deeper understanding. Jesus has revealed the truth. The Spirit assists believers to understand and express it in new and changing circumstances.

With the presence of the advocate, the disciples are at peace as Jesus goes to the Father, the Father who is greater than the Son. (John 14:27-28) But the encounter with 'the prince of this world' is still to come. Jesus is ready to face his hour in full freedom. (John 14:30) This farewell discourse is at an end. The

following chapters show some overlap, and contain further
traditions of Jesus' farewell words to the disciples.

John chapter 15 is dominated by the image of the vine. This
section follows on from what precedes with no introduction.
The vine section is an allegory. Vine, branches and vine-dresser
symbolise Jesus, his disciples and the Father. The enduring connection between the disciples and Jesus is achieved now not by
the advocate, the Spirit of truth, but by the life which Jesus the
vine feeds to the branches. The vine image is used by the
prophet Isaiah as a symbol of Israel. (Isaiah 5:1-7) God is the
owner of the vine, who lavishes care upon it. What is new here is
that Jesus and the disciples are the vine and there is an intimate
bond between them. Intimacy of relationship was already expressed in chapter 14: 'You will know that I am in my Father,
and you in me and I in you.' (John 14:20) The intimacy between
Son and disciples is symbolised by the vine. As God punished
the vine in Isaiah chapter 5, so here the vine-dresser will cut off
and burn the unproductive branches. Jesus, the 'true vine', replaces the vine of Israel, just as Jesus the 'true bread' replaced
the manna. (John 15:1, 6:32)

The intimacy between the Son and the disciples is expressed
by repeated use of the word 'remain' (Greek *menein*). (John 15:4-
10) It is also translated as 'abide' or 'dwell'. Jesus reintroduces
the commandment to love: 'This is my commandment, that you
love one another as I loved you.' (John 15:12) With such an
intimate relationship of love between Jesus and the disciples
they are now 'friends' (Greek *philoi*) and no longer servants.
(John 15:15) Jesus chooses the disciples to be his friends and
sends them out to bear fruit. (John 15:16)

This intimate picture of loving communion is not the whole
picture. The world (Greek *kosmos*), used here, as often in John, of
the world which does not accept Jesus, has hated Jesus. It will
hate his friends too. Despite all the works Jesus has performed
the world continues to hate both Jesus and the Father. The
advocate, the Spirit of truth, will bear witness on Jesus' behalf,
as indeed will the disciples, but persecution and martyrdom are
foreseen. (John 15:26-16:2)

John chapter 16 contains many similarities of content with the first farewell speech in chapter 14. Jesus once more announces his departure and the sending of the advocate. This time the advocate has a clearly judicial role. The advocate is to convict the world about sin (Greek *hamartia*), about justice (Greek *dikaiosyne*) and about judgement (Greek *krisis*). (John 16:8) The Spirit will expose the sin of not believing that the Son has come from the Father. The Spirit will reveal true justice, for the Son has been vindicated by his return to the Father. The Spirit will speak of judgement, for the world which rejects the Son is already condemned.

The Spirit of truth has a further role, leading the disciples 'in all truth'. (John 16:13) There is a well-attested alternative reading, that the Spirit will lead the disciples 'into all truth'. There is little difference in the sense. The Spirit will assist believers in understanding the truth, in understanding the Son, who is the truth. The Spirit confirms and elucidates what Jesus reveals. As in previous descriptions of the Spirit, this advocate will provide the support and assistance given by Jesus during his life. Jesus continues to communicate through the Spirit.

Finally Jesus speaks of his return: 'In a short time you will no longer see me, and again in a short time you will see me.' (John 16:16) This statement produces confusion among the disciples. Jesus explains that after the time of sorrow he will return to them and they will have new insight. This recalls earlier statements in the gospel that after his resurrection the disciples would have new understanding. (John 2:22, 12:16) The disciples assert their faith that Jesus truly comes from God. (John 16:30) He ends the discourse reminding them that the hour has come. They will all be scattered. As in chapter 14, he offers them peace. His final words to them are: 'But have courage! I have conquered the world.' (John 16:33) These are the last words of Jesus to the group of disciples before his death. They are also a constant reassurance from the victorious Son who has been glorified in death and resurrection.

The discourses have come to an end. In chapter 17 Jesus

prays to the Father. Like the great patriarchs of the Old Testament, Jesus has delivered his farewell address. Like them, he concludes with a prayer invoking a blessing on those he leaves behind. (Genesis 49:1-28; Deuteronomy 33:1-29) But he begins by asking the Father to glorify him, so that he may glorify the Father. This revelation of God's power will bring eternal life for believers, life which consists in knowledge of the Father and the Son. Jesus speaks as one who has finished his work of making God known.

His prayer is firstly for believers, not for the world. (John 17:9) The world is once again those hostile to the Son, the world in which believers are immersed. Jesus prays: 'Holy Father, keep those you have given me in your name, so that they may be one as we are one.' (John 17:11) The emphasis on the unity of the disciples is accompanied by an emphasis on consecration in the truth. (John 17:17) Belief in Jesus is belief in the truth. It brings unity. It separates believers from the unbelieving world.

Jesus then prays for those who will believe on the basis of the word the disciples will proclaim. These too will be brought into unity, a unity which is the unity of Father and Son. This unity offers a witness to the world, so that the world too may believe. (John 17:21, 17:23) The final word is of love. It is the love of the Father for the Son which is extended to those to whom the Son is sent. (John 17:23) It is this love which binds all together and invites the world to know God. (John 17:26) Jesus reveals God as God of love. Jesus offers to believers the way of love.

Betrayal in the garden

The passion narrative of John's gospel is to be found in chapters 18 and 19. While, on the one hand, the evangelist does not hesitate to report the suffering of the Son of God, he also illustrates how Jesus faced his death in full freedom and with steady composure. The contrast between John's narrative and that of the synoptic gospels is never more marked than in the account of the events in the garden.

Jesus crosses the winter-flowing Kedron to reach the garden

where he often went with his disciples. (John 18:1-2) The group
brought by Judas to the place is described as a 'cohort' (Greek
speira) accompanied by servants of the high priests and Pharisees.
(John 18:3) The presence of Roman soldiers reported here is not
found in the synoptic accounts. John's version suggests prior
collusion of the Jewish authorities with the Romans. What is
totally missing from John's account of Jesus in the garden is any
reference to the prayer and pain of Jesus or to the sleeping disciples. And Judas simply stands among the enemies of Jesus.
(John 18:5)

In John's account of the meeting of Jesus with those who arrest him it is Jesus who takes the initiative. Jesus asks whom
they seek and declares his identity with the words 'I am' (Greek
ego eimi). (John 18:5) They fall to the ground as if to worship
Jesus. We recall how in arguments with the Jews the statement
of Jesus, 'I am', was understood as a claim to divinity. (John 8:24,
8:28, 8:58) The evangelist suggests here that the divine Son in
going to his death must first be acknowledged as such by his
enemies. Jesus insists that the others be allowed to go free. The
evangelist then curiously quotes from earlier words of Jesus in
the gospel as if he were quoting from the Old Testament scriptures: 'This was to fulfil the word he had spoken: I lost not one of
those you gave me.' (John 18:9, 6:39) The scene ends with the
attack on the high priest's servant. John identifies the attacker as
Peter and names the servant as Malchus. (John 18:10)

Peter's lies and Jesus' truth

Jesus is taken first to Annas, the father-in-law of the high priest
Caiaphas. John's gospel provides an account of Jesus' interrogation by Annas and only a passing reference to Caiaphas, who
earlier in the gospel had sanctioned the death of Jesus. (John
11:50) The interview with Annas is intertwined with the
interrogation of Peter in the courtyard outside.

Peter is admitted to the courtyard by 'another disciple'
(Greek *allos mathetes*) who is known to the high priest. (John
18:15) The identity of this disciple remains a mystery, though he

has constantly been identified as the disciple Jesus loved. (John 13:23, 19:26, 20:2, 21:7, 21:20) In fact, it is not possible to say who he is. Peter's denials are similar to those in the synoptic accounts. As in Luke's gospel Peter does not curse and swear. He simply lies: 'I am not.' (Greek *ouk eimi*). (John 18:17, 18:25)

Meanwhile Jesus offers Annas a way of discovering the truth about his disciples and his teaching. He should ask those who witnessed his teaching in the temple. While Peter gets away with his lies, Jesus is struck by a servant. (John 18:22)

As morning comes Jesus will bear witness to the truth before Pilate. A long section now begins in which Pilate dialogues repeatedly with the Jews and with Jesus. (John 18:28-19:16) In bringing Jesus to Pilate they are reluctant to enter the 'praetorium', the residence of the Roman prefect. The evangelist explains that the Jews did not wish to be defiled by entering a Gentile's house before the passover. For John's gospel the passover feast will begin in the evening as Jesus' body is taken down from the cross. The Jews who are bringing about the death of an innocent man are fastidious about avoiding defilement before they eat the passover lamb. The Jews remind Pilate that they have no authority to inflict the death penalty. They are clearly intent on nothing less. Once again the evangelist points to the fulfilment of Jesus' own words. (John 18:32)

The first private scene between the Roman prefect and Jesus has Pilate lose no time in focusing on the issue of investigation: 'Are you the king of the Jews?' (John 18:33) In the synoptic accounts of the trial before the Sanhedrin two charges emerged: that Jesus had threatened the temple, and that he had claimed to be the Messiah. In all four gospels Pilate's concern is with the latter charge. Does Jesus claim to be a king? In all four gospels Jesus does not give an affirmative reply. In John's gospel he counters with a question, but eventually declares: 'My kingdom is not of this world.' (John 18:36) This is the closest any evangelist comes to accepting some sort of regal authority for Jesus in the interviews with Pilate. He may be a king, but his kingship would not threaten Pilate or any other ruler of this world.

Pilate persists with the question: 'So you are a king?' (John 18:37) Jesus' reply is that given in all four gospels: 'You say that I am a king.' (John 18:37) The issue of being a king of this world is of no concern to Jesus. In the synoptic accounts of the trial before the Sanhedrin Jesus had countered the question about being the Messiah with a statement about the coming Son of Man. His identity was not to be found in worldly titles but as the Son of Man who, having been martyred, comes in triumph to his reward. Similarly in the fourth gospel Jesus counters Pilate's question about kingship with the declaration: 'I was born for this, I came into the world for this, that I should bear witness to the truth.' (John 18:37) Jesus consistently deflects attention from worldly acclaim to focus on the genuine truth. He comes to bear witness to the truth, and is martyred in the cause of truth. Jesus shows that the truth is worth dying for. He is the way, because he is the truth. He is the way, for he leads his followers to life. Pilate replies: 'What is truth?' (John 18:38) The two are worlds apart. Pilate does not have the insight to dialogue with Jesus. He does not understand the terms of the discussion.

One is reminded of Paul's words that the person without Spirit is not able to understand the things of the Spirit. (1 Corinthians 2:14) Surely the desperate search for the things of the Spirit evident in the world today is a search for the things of God, for the oxygen of true life, for what is trustworthy and true.

Pilate, while confused, is still convinced that Jesus should not be executed. As in the synoptic record, he offers the crowds the release of a prisoner, but this strategy fails. They cry out for Barabbas. (John 18:40) At this central point in the Pilate scenes Jesus is scourged, crowned with thorns and dressed in a purple robe. (John 19:1-2) As in the synoptic gospels, with the exception of Luke, the Roman soldiers mock this man who would be a king: 'Hail, king of the Jews!' (John 19:3)

Pilate brings out Jesus to the crowd and says: 'Behold the man!' (Greek *idou ho anthropos*; Latin *Ecce homo!*). (John 19:5) The suffering and bleeding figure of the Son of God is for all time a challenge and an appeal. This is what human beings in their

God-given freedom do to each other. The ultimate depths of incarnation are illustrated as we see the Son of God endure such treatment. In the face of Pilate's repeated declarations of Jesus' innocence, the crowds now accuse Jesus of claiming divine sonship: 'He must die for he made himself Son of God!' (John 19:7)

In the second private interview Pilate is fearful. His question about Jesus' origins is met with silence. Pilate would not be able to understand Jesus' answer. Pilate's fearful frustration is apparent in his assertion of his authority. (John 19:10) Jesus declares that such authority is ultimately from above. Despite Pilate's conviction of Jesus' innocence, the crowds prevail. They return to the question of kingship. In defending someone claiming kingship Pilate is no friend of the emperor. Pilate brings Jesus to the place of judgment, the location known as 'the pavement' (Greek *Lithostrotos;* Hebrew *gabbatha*). (John 19:13). He defiantly hails Jesus as king. It is the high priests who with blasphemous defiance retort: 'We have no king but Caesar!' (John 19:15) The struggle is lost: 'Then therefore he handed him over to them to be crucified.' (John 19:16) Jesus, witness to the truth, is condemned by lies. Jesus, the way, the truth and the life, is taken off on the way to death.

Death and burial

The fourth gospel stresses that Jesus carried his own cross to Golgotha, the place of the skull. (John 19:17) There is no mention of Simon of Cyrene. Jesus is crucified there with two others. John has made clear that this took place on the preparation day for the passover feast. (John 19:14) As Jesus is killed, the lambs for the passover are being killed by the temple priests. As the passover lamb's blood recalled the liberation of the exodus, this is the lamb of God who frees the world from sin.

John's gospel lays more emphasis than the synoptic gospels on the title affixed to the cross. The precise wording in this gospel reads 'Jesus the Nazarene, the king of the Jews'. (John 19:19) Only John refers to Jesus as Nazarene. Only John declares that the title was written in Hebrew, Latin and Greek. This allows the evangelist to show Pilate, the man confused about the truth, now proclaiming the truth about Jesus for the whole world to understand. Furthermore, it is only in John's gospel that the Jews object at the directness of the proclamation, giving Pilate the opportunity to defend the truth with his famous words 'what I have written I have written' (Greek *ho gegrapha gegrapha*). (John 19:22) Pilate has the last word.

Similarly John's gospel provides more detail on the sharing out of Jesus' garments. This gospel alone includes a quotation from Psalm 22 concerning the distribution of the just man's clothing. This gospel alone refers to his seamless tunic. (John 19:23) It has been suggested that this is an allusion to the seamless robe of the high priest. Is Jesus portrayed as a new high priest offering his sacrifice? It seems more likely that John is alluding to the garment as a symbol of unity. The theme of the untorn garment recalls the story of the prophet Ahijah in 1 Kings chapter 11. In a dramatic action Ahijah tears his cloak into twelve pieces to symbolise the coming break-up of the united kingdom of Solomon. The garment of Jesus is not torn. Jesus brings not division but unity. Had not the evangelist earlier proclaimed that Jesus would die not only for the people of Israel but also to gather into one the scattered children of God? (John 11:52)

The scene featuring the mother of Jesus and the beloved disciple is unique to John. The synoptic gospels mention women disciples who keep watch from afar as Jesus dies. (Mark 15:40) John challenges this with his reference to the women disciples by the cross (Greek *para to stauro*). (John 19:25) In particular only John's gospel refers to the mother of Jesus and the disciple Jesus loved standing by the cross. (John 19:26) It is most unlikely that they would have been permitted to stand close to the place of execution. John's scene makes a statement about the fidelity of the disciples and about the role of the mother. She who appeared previously only at Cana and was there, as here, addressed as 'woman' is now, at the end of Jesus' life, called 'mother'. She is mother to the disciple Jesus loves, as he is son to her. Jesus forms a new family, consisting of those who believe, and Mary is the first among these. It was her faith which facilitated the first sign of Jesus. She is present too in fidelity at the end with the disciple Jesus loved. In the synoptic gospels Jesus declares that his true family consists of those who do God's will. (Mark 3:35) Mary is the first of these. At his death in John's gospel she receives the primary role among believers. She is mother among the disciples, mother of believers.

Having established the new community of believers, Jesus knows all is accomplished. Jesus says: 'I thirst.' (John 19:28) The evangelist notes that he does this to fulfil the scriptures completely, and that to the very end Jesus is committed to doing the will of the Father. He is offered, as in the synoptic gospels, sour wine (Greek *oxos*). (John 19:29) The just man of Psalm 69 was offered vinegar to drink. Mark and Matthew say that the sponge was put on a reed to reach Jesus' lips. We can envisage a strong, long cane. John says the reed was hyssop, the plant used in the passover ritual to sprinkle the blood of the lamb on lintels and door-posts. (Exodus 12:22) The evangelist thus emphasises again that Jesus is the new lamb.

John's gospel cannot report the final words of Jesus as found in Mark and Matthew. The Jesus of John could never accuse the Father of abandoning him. Jesus is never left alone, for the Father is with him. (John 16:32) In John's gospel his final statement is 'It is finished' (Greek *tetelestai*). Jesus has completed the work the Father gave him. John then declares that 'bowing his head he gave up his spirit'. (John 19:30) The evangelist suggests a sharing of the Spirit of Jesus, which will be illustrated dramatically in the following verses.

Again John's gospel provides a different story once Jesus has died. There is no centurion to make a declaration about Jesus. There is no rending of the veil of the temple. But a soldier pierces the side of Jesus, out of which flow blood and water. (John 19:34) The intense reflection of Christians over the centuries has wondered at the symbolism, often suggesting allusions to baptism and to the eucharist. John may simply be communicating that in losing his life-blood Jesus also pours out the waters of new birth.

Jesus provides the life-giving waters of the Spirit for all to drink. The death of Jesus is life for believers. His followers will receive the gift of the Spirit. (John 7:39) Another reference to scripture fulfilled recalls that in the passover ritual not one bone of the lamb is to be broken. (Exodus 12:46) Not a bone of this lamb of God is broken. A final citation from the prophet Zechariah, in which people look upon one who has been slain, brings the scene of Jesus' death to an end. (Zechariah 12:10) It has provided rich material which originated from reflection on the meaning of the death of Jesus among John's believers.

The burial of Jesus is not done in haste as in the synoptic accounts. There is time to embalm Jesus' body with an extraordinary quantity of spices provided by Nicodemus. (John 19:39) The women's visit to the tomb will not be to bring spices, but to mourn the dead Jesus.

Resurrection in John

The story of the discovery of the empty tomb in John's gospel highlights the involvement of Mary Magdalene, Peter and the disciple Jesus loved. John seems to suggest that Mary came to the tomb alone. (John 20:1) She sees that the tomb is empty. That she also looked inside and that she was not alone is suggested by her words to the two disciples: 'They have taken the Lord from the tomb and we do not know where they have put him.' (John 20:2) When Peter and the beloved disciple reach the tomb the beloved disciple allows Peter to enter first. Unique to John's account is the reference to the grave clothes neatly laid aside. The absence of the body of Jesus and the presence of the clothes is enough to lead the beloved disciple to believe: 'He saw and he believed.' (John 20:8) He saw the empty tomb and the clothes. He did not see Jesus. He is the first of those who have not seen and yet believe. For this evangelist inner sight is more important than physical sight. The visit of Peter to the tomb is also reported in Luke. (Luke 24:12) There, as here, Peter does not understand. Luke stated that he went home wondering. A similar impression of Peter is given in John's gospel.

Matthew's gospel had told of the women at the tomb meeting and worshipping Jesus. (Matthew 28:9) John's account tells us that it was Mary Magdalene who was the first to meet Jesus. The discrepancies between the resurrection accounts witness to their authenticity. The impact of the experience of meeting the risen Jesus is evident in the variations in the reports given.

Mary first encounters two angel-messengers but it is not they who explain the empty tomb to her. As in the many of the accounts of the appearances of the risen Jesus, Mary does not at first recognise Jesus. (John 20:14) The good shepherd calls her by name, but does not allow her to cling to him. (John 20:17) The nature of the risen body of Jesus remains a mystery. Mary receives her mission to announce to the disciples that Jesus is going to the Father. Jesus declares that he goes 'to my Father and your Father, to my God and your God'. (John 20:17) The new family of believers will hear the good news from Mary Magdalene. She who was healed of severe illness by Jesus (Luke 8:2) is the first evangeliser.

We might recall the disciples' reluctance to believe the women that is reported in Luke's gospel. (Luke 24:11) The disciples in John too seem to remain doubtful. They are fearful of the Jews and stay behind closed doors. The account in John chapter 20 of Jesus' first appearance to the disciples in Jerusalem shows many similarities to the appearance of Jesus to the group of disciples in Luke chapter 24. It is the complete resurrection appearance. Jesus brings the disciples his peace. (John 20:19, 20:21; Luke 24:36) He shows his wounds to reassure them who he is. (John 20:20; Luke 24:39) Sent by the Father he sends them and bestows the Spirit on them. (John 20:22) In Luke he promises that they will receive power from on high. (Luke 24:49)

The gift of the Spirit is the gift of the glorified Christ. It was symbolised in the water from his wounded side. The Spirit is given to all who believe. What are we to make therefore of Luke's delaying the gift of the Spirit to report the extraordinary events of Pentecost fifty days later? In his account in the Acts of the Apostles chapter 2, Luke describes the powerful transforming presence of the Spirit among the early believers. The Jewish feast of Pentecost recalled the gift of the law on Sinai fifty days after leaving Egypt. For Christians the Spirit of Jesus replaces the law and brings it to fulfilment. John and Luke are giving different but complementary accounts of the dynamic effect of the Spirit of Jesus among the first believers. For John as for Luke Jesus brings forgiveness of sin. (John 20:23; Luke 24:46-47) The death of Jesus and the gift of his Spirit liberate people from the power of evil. Human beings are reconciled to God through the self-giving of the Son of God. John's gospel refers to a ministry given to the disciples to forgive and retain sin, a power exercised by certain individuals in the community. This was understood to refer not only to the conversion at baptism, but also to subsequent need for forgiveness. (1 John 2:1)

The chapter concludes with the second appearance of Jesus to the disciples, who on this occasion include Thomas. Remembered for his refusal to believe unless he saw and touched the wounds on Jesus' body, he should also be remembered as the disciple who voices the fullest declaration of the divinity of Jesus: 'My Lord and my God!' (John 20:28) Thomas is commended for his insight on seeing the risen Jesus. But Jesus declares blessed those who have the insight of faith without seeing him. (John 20:29) All Christians are thus declared blessed, more blessed than Jesus' own disciples. The beloved disciple, who in seeing the empty tomb had believed even before seeing the risen Jesus, is the model for all Christians. Like him, they are the disciples Jesus loves.

The solemn conclusion of the gospel of John follows. (John 20:30-31) It has been a gospel of signs, actions by which the true identity and reality of Jesus is revealed. The evangelist concludes: 'These signs have been written down so that you may believe that Jesus is the Messiah, the Son of God, and so that believing you may have life in his name.' (John 20:31)

Jesus' questions and Peter's truth

The final chapter of John's gospel is generally considered to be an appendix, an addition to an already finished gospel. The appearances of Jesus to the disciples have been narrated and they have been sent out to bring faith and forgiveness. A solemn conclusion has expressed succinctly the purpose of the writing of the gospel. Something like a fresh start, in a new location, is found in John chapter 21, which will in turn have its own solemn conclusion. This chapter, however, quite unlike the appendix to Mark's gospel, is found in all the ancient copies of the gospel. This addition was clearly made as the original gospel was completed.

Matthew reported a Galilee appearance of the risen Jesus to the twelve. (Matthew 28:16-20) The story of a Galilee appearance in John chapter 21 serves as another demonstration of Jesus' risen life, and also provides the context for a most significant dialogue between Jesus and Peter. It is a dialogue which emphasises the role of Peter as distinct from that of the others. It may well have been written when the death of Peter had already occurred.

In the narrative of the appearance of Jesus by the lake the disciples have gone fishing when Jesus appears. As in other accounts of appearances of the risen Jesus, the disciples do not recognise Jesus. (John 21:4) Not surprisingly it is the disciple whom Jesus loved who first recognises the Lord. (John 21:7) Interpreters have shown great ingenuity in trying to attribute some symbolic significance to the number of fish, but no suggestion has been convincing. It is possible that, as in the miraculous draught of fishes in Luke chapter 5, the fishing is to be related to the missionary activity of the disciples. The abundance of fish could therefore suggest the abundant number of believers. Jesus seems to confirm his identity by taking the bread and fish he has prepared and sharing them out among the disciples (John 21:13), surely a deliberate allusion to Jesus' continuing provision of the bread of the eucharist.

The writer concludes the story and attaches it to chapter 20

by saying: 'This was already the third time that Jesus was shown
to the disciples after being raised from the dead.' (John 21:14)
The climax of the chapter, in the dialogue with Peter, is still to
come. The text of the conversation has had enormous appeal
and has been used in many ways by believers, from illustrating
the qualities of pastoral leadership to explaining the role of the
successors of Peter. It is crucial to note from the outset that translations do not always reflect the variety of terms used in the
original Greek.

We begin with the three questions put to Peter by Jesus.
(John 21:15-17) He first asks: 'Do you love (Greek *agapas*) me?'
He asks the same question again: 'Do you love (Greek *agapas*)
me?' Finally Jesus asks: 'Do you love (Greek *phileis*) me?' It is frequently asserted that the different Greek terms for loving, using
the Greek verbs *agapan* and *philein,* are synonyms. No difference
of meaning is intended. It is simply a question of stylistic vari-
ation. It is true that earlier in John's gospel the word *philein* is
occasionally used where *agapan* might have been. Close scrutiny
of the gospel reveals, however, that the word *agapan* is much
more frequent than *philein.* This is no surprise, for *agapan* is the
verb based on the noun *agape,* which in Christian circles takes on
the meaning of self-giving love, or charity. In Christian circles
agapan will have a different sense from *philein.* While *agapan*
refers to self-giving love, *philein* still has connotations of self-
interest. One might say that *philein* speaks of human friendship
and human attachment, while *agapan* suggests something deeper.
While *philein* is without doubt a virtue, a praiseworthy quality,
agapan goes further.

A key to our understanding lies in the farewell discourse of
Jesus. The new commandment of Jesus is that disciples should
love (*agapan*) each other as Jesus loved. (John 13:34, 15:12) Jesus
also declares that the greatest love (*agape*) a person can show is
to give oneself in death. (John 15:13) As Paul affirms in the first
letter to the Corinthians, the greatest Christian gift is *agape,* self-
giving love, as shown in the self-giving of Jesus. (1 Corinthians
13:13)

Now let us turn our attention to Peter's replies. When asked whether he loves (*agapan*) Jesus more than the other disciples do, Peter replies that he does love Jesus, but Peter uses the word *philein*. When Jesus asks again, Peter replies in the same way. When Jesus asks if Peter loves him and this time uses the verb *philein*, Peter is understandably upset, but says for the third time that he loves (*philein*) Jesus. The apparent harshness of Jesus to Peter can be better understood when we connect these three questions which elicit totally honest replies from Peter to the three questions asked of him in the court of the high priest. Peter had lied each time. He had denied Jesus three times. His three true answers here make up for his three lies earlier.

The third element in the dialogue is the commissioning Jesus gives to Peter. Peter's true and honest replies to the painful repeated questioning of Jesus are followed each time by a command, and each command is different. Once again scholars are inclined to consider the differences as unimportant. But as with Jesus' question, it is far more likely in such a solemn context that every word is carefully chosen. Even if some of these words are used loosely earlier in the gospel, in chapter 21 this does not seem to be the case. The writer of this appendix has chosen his words most carefully.

The first command to Peter is 'Feed (Greek *boske*) my lambs (Greek *arnia*).' The second is 'Shepherd (Greek *poimaine*) my sheep (Greek *probata*).' The third reads 'Feed (Greek *boske*) my little lambs (Greek *probatia*).' Not all the ancient manuscripts are in agreement on the order of the words. The different ways of referring to the shepherd's activity suggest the completeness of the task of Peter, his total oversight of the community. Peter is called to provide the fulness of pastoral care. The recipients of this care, the sheep, the lambs and the little lambs, whatever combination and order they came in in the original text, represent the whole people of Jesus. We should note also that the sheep and lambs always belong to Jesus, not to Peter. It is Jesus who is the chief shepherd. (1 Peter 5:4)

Recognition of the changing vocabulary in John 21:15-17 allows us to appreciate more fully its most profound message. Peter who lied three times is now determined to speak the truth. He dares not claim for himself more than what he knows in his heart to be true. He cannot claim unselfish and self-giving love of Jesus. But he does love him. The repeated questioning of Jesus allows Peter to be rehabilitated as a man of truth. He is no longer a man of lies. Like all disciples he is to become a man of truth and love. Both have to be learnt. He has now journeyed far on the way of truth. He still has some distance to go on the way of love.

But there is more. Verse 18, with its solemn introduction, flows logically from the preceding dialogue. Jesus affirms that Peter will one day reach the practice of *agape*. Until now he has been free to go where he wished. But when he is old he will be taken where he would rather not go. He will be taken to the cross and offer his life in selfless and self-giving love. He will lay down his life in love, as Jesus did. Like the good shepherd, who gives his life for his sheep, Peter's shepherding will also end in martyrdom. (John 10:11) It is no doubt with a knowledge that Peter has already been martyred in Rome in the persecution of Nero that this speech of Jesus is added to the gospel. This part of the dialogue ends with two words of Jesus, words used in the calling of the disciples in the synoptic gospels: 'Follow me!' (John 21:19)

Peter is curious to know of the fate of the beloved disciple, who is standing close by. They were together at the empty tomb. They are together in this scene. Jesus replies: 'What if I wish him to remain until I come, what is it to you?' (John 21:22) These words of Jesus seem to have given rise to a rumour that Jesus would return before the beloved disciple died. (John 21:23) We might recall at this point the confusion about Jesus' words on the time of the end in Mark chapter 13. Jesus declared that only the Father knew the time of the end. Subsequent Christian teachers had attempted to make his words more precise. Here too the evangelist dismisses speculation about the time of Jesus' return.

The dialogue between Jesus and Peter has enormous relevance. Jesus asks Peter for love. The honest replies of Peter are poignant. But Peter's as yet inadequate love does not disqualify him from Christian pastoral leadership. He is still called to care for the people of Christ. Jesus does not require perfect disciples, but he does require that they be people of love, and people of truth, willing to be led by the Spirit on the way of truth, willing to learn a deeper love. Faithful love and truth, the qualities of the Father revealed in the Son with which the gospel began (John 1:14), are both gift and challenge to the disciple as this gospel ends.

A second conclusion brings chapter 21 and this extraordinary gospel to an end. The disciple Jesus loved is the one who bears witness to what is recorded in the gospel. (John 21:24) He will be identified in the tradition as John, the son of Zebedee, known to us from the synoptic tradition. (Mark 1:19) The gospel 'according to John' seems to have its origin in him. The end of the gospel suggests that so much more could have been written about Jesus. If everything experienced during his time on earth had been written down, the world could not contain it. (John 21:25) One might say that disciples beloved of Jesus have written of him throughout two millennia and are still writing about him, talking about him, and above all learning his way of truth and love, discovering that it is the way to abundant life.

CHAPTER 14

Trustworthy and True?

Four gospels

We have completed our survey of the four gospels, the four gospels accepted and treasured by the church as the good news of Jesus Christ. It is particularly fortunate that we receive from the church not one, but four gospels, for each gospel provides a new vision of Jesus and suggests we can never exhaust the possibilities of understanding the one who was Son of the Father and became the man, Jesus of Nazareth. Having not one written gospel but four helps us to appreciate that the gospels provide both historical basis and catechetical explanation. On firm historical foundations the communities of faith and their evangelists developed their understandings of Jesus, his life, death and resurrection. They give us portrayals of Jesus which are mutually enriching. Their gospels were recognised by the whole church as accurate, as guided by the Spirit and as faithfully reflecting the faith of the first believers. These gospels were thus set apart. They became 'canonical', officially recognised, treasured and preserved for future generations. They were recognised as trustworthy and true.

The fact of having four different documents, each called a gospel, *euaggelion,* 'good news', helps us to appreciate the nature of a written gospel. Gospels give us an accurate record of what Jesus did on earth together with that fuller understanding which the disciples enjoyed due to their experience of the risen Jesus and the gift of the Spirit of truth.

If, then, the gospels show differing portrayals and a developing understanding of Jesus, would it not be better to preserve the latest and most developed account? This has not been the tradition among Christians, for the Spirit of Jesus invites us to value each gospel, each different insight, each distinct but complementary portrait. Just as the masterly portrayal of Jesus by Michelangelo would not lead us to reject earlier portrayals by artists such as Giotto, so we preserve and value each written record. On the other hand, gospels written later by groups who claimed new and strange understandings of Jesus were rejected by the church, because they did not reflect the faith of the early believers. In this way the Spirit of Jesus assisted the church in declaring canonical those gospels which were indeed trustworthy and true.

Our survey has clearly demonstrated that Mark gives us the earliest gospel. The tradition that a certain Mark was Peter's companion in Rome, attested in 1 Peter 5:13, may well be a reliable pointer. This gospel emphasises the humanity and vulnerability of Jesus, that Jesus went as a martyr to the place of execution, and that he was faced with misunderstanding from his friends. Such a scenario reflects many features of the persecuted and martyred church of Rome in the reign of the emperor Nero.

Clearly Matthew's gospel used Mark as a major source, adopting and modifying its structure. The Jesus of Matthew is a teacher greater than Moses, who proclaims significant teaching in five great discourses. The evangelist is most concerned to demonstrate the connections between Jesus and the faith of his ancestors. The traditional title of the gospel, 'according to Matthew', suggests the presence and preaching of the apostle Matthew in the church, perhaps that of Antioch in Syria, in which the gospel was later produced.

Luke too uses Mark, modifying the structure of Mark's gospel with the extended journey to Jerusalem. For Luke Jesus reaches out with the compassion of God, to the poor and to sinners, to Samaritans and Gentiles. The man named Luke went beyond the gospel record and gave us in the Acts of the Apostles an account of the early church, with particular emphasis on the missionary work of Peter and of Paul.

The fourth gospel takes us by another path. Of all the gospels it is the one which lays heaviest stress on the divine origins of Jesus. It complements and completes the picture of Jesus, who in all the gospels is proclaimed 'Son of God'. John's gospel clearly contains something less of the historical deeds and historical words of Jesus. His signs are vehicles for a christology which uses rich imagery to proclaim the truth about Jesus. His words express the christological insights of the community which claimed its origins in the preaching of John, son of Zebedee. The beloved disciple, the mysterious figure who provides an ideal model, was quickly identified with John, though there can be no certainty about this.

Emphasis on the different presentations of Jesus allows us to appreciate the many features of his person. But the complete gospel picture of Jesus is a harmonious whole. Insights of later evangelists are found to be present in earlier gospel material in less developed ways. As understanding of Jesus grew, the Spirit of Jesus reminded the disciples of what he had said and took them forward on the way of truth.

Jesus and his Jewish roots
He brings with him the religious and cultural traditions of Judaism. Each gospel tells us of his Jewish roots. Matthew and Luke construct genealogies to affirm his identity as a son of Abraham and a son of David. The same evangelists, in their different infancy stories, display the world of Jewish faith and life from which he came and which nourished him. As he begins to preach, it is clear that he has learnt from his Jewish faith to call God his Father, to treasure the law and the prophets, and to await the kingdom of God when God would gather people into the life of the resurrection. He joins John the Baptist, the prophet and preacher of repentance, who offers Israel a new beginning.

But the new prophet from Nazareth also challenges his people to move on, to think new thoughts, to be open to the coming of the kingdom and to the new presence of God. He comes to bring the law and prophets to fulfilment. He teaches on his own authority that his people should move on from what the ances-

tors said to receive his new words. He comes to replace the practices and festivals of Judaism, to be living water, new manna,
light of the world. He brings the Spirit of God.

He rejects some aspects of his contemporaries' faith. They fail
to see the finger of God at work in his exorcisms and healings.
They are angry at his disregard for their cherished views and
practices. Above all he will not accept the popular conceptions
of the Messiah to be sent by God. For him power in this world is
a temptation to be fiercely rejected. For the true anointed one of
God is to go as a lamb to the slaughter, as a servant to lay down
his life for others. It is profoundly ironic that the charge against
him which led to his death was that he made himself a king.
Despite his rejection of worldly titles he is condemned for claiming one. His trial and execution distort the truth, to which his life
bears witness. Love and truth, the qualities of the God of Israel,
are his legacy and challenge.

His disciples will adopt, and continue to treasure, his Jewish
roots. Christians will preserve the great gifts of Judaism, the
scriptures and the developing faith. But they will move on.

Jesus and the present challenge

He brings a challenge for the present. It is the challenge to welcome the kingdom of God. It is a challenge to a change of heart
and to belief in the good news. It is a challenge to follow him.
The challenge is urgent, for the hour is not known. The word of
the gospel is sown. An abundant harvest is assured. But not all
will bear fruit.

He reaches out to those considered outsiders. He comes to
call sinners. He goes out to meet the prodigal son. He comes to
seek out and save what is lost. He calls sinners to a change of life.
He brings good news to the poor, to those who rely on God. He
declares blessed both those in situations of need and loss, and
those who live lives of gentleness and peace. He heals the sick
with his acts of power.

He challenges the righteous. He goes out to speak to the elder
son who has slaved for so many years. He offers a new way and

a stern rebuke to those whose hearts are closed. His call to discipleship brings about a new family of all those who hear the
word of God and do it. His own mother and the disciple he loves
are first among these. His disciples form a new community, a
new gathering of God, a church. They are nourished by the
word of scripture and the eucharist of his presence.

They are called not to be served but to serve, to wash each
other's feet, to grow in truth and love. They are called to reach
out to the hungry, the thirsty, the stranger and those sick or in
prison, to serve the Lord in serving the least of his brothers and
sisters. They are called to go out to all nations of the world, to
transcend national boundaries and particular cultural expressions, to teach what he taught. They are called to speak of a more
abundant justice, to serve the poor, to challenge the idolatry of
wealth and power, pleasure and war. They are called to offer a
better way for the pain and hopelessness of the world.

They remain attached to him as branches to the vine. The
Spirit, who is sent and called to assist them, leads them to all
truth and gives strength in their witness. They will suffer for the
truth. Many will lose their lives in witness, taken where they
would rather not go. In losing their lives they will keep them for
the eternal life.

Jesus and the future hope

He brings hope for the future. The kingdom is already present
but is still to come in its fulness. He assures his disciples that he
will return, but only the Father is aware of the day and the hour.
All must wait with oil in their lamps. But his return to gather his
people from the ends of the earth is assured.

The life of the resurrection, the new gift of life from God, is
the future hope. He himself spoke of that life. He spoke of God
raising him to the life of the resurrection. He confirmed the truth
of that hope by his coming to his friends after his resurrection.
This reality witnessed by the disciples profoundly changed their
lives. They went out to proclaim what they had experienced,
that the one who had been crucified had been raised to new life

by God. The Spirit of truth was his gift to them to proclaim the new life, the liberation from evil, the new hope. Through his Spirit he is with believers. The one who came as the Immanuel, the Word from the Father, is with his church all the days until the end of the age.

Beyond 2000

Jesus of Nazareth gave us a vision, a vision of life, a vision of God. He came from God to bring to completion the revelation given to the people of God. He came to confirm the God-given instincts of our hearts, about love and truth, about life and hope, about God and about what is truly of value. He came as one who is trustworthy and true to show the way.

Our exploration of the four gospels has allowed us to see how they too are trustworthy and true. They have a unique God-inspired power which speaks to every age, and keeps us in touch with the good news of the one who came from God. They lead us on to new vision, to new insights. I offer this book to my fellow Christians, that it may help them on their way of truth and love. I offer it to those who are not Christians, that it may invite them to read the gospels and to discover the one who is trustworthy and true in the time beyond 2000.

Suggested Further Reading

R. E. Brown, *An Introduction to the New Testament*, New York, Doubleday, 1997

W. J. Harrington,
   Mark: Realistic Theologian, Dublin, Columba, 1996
   Luke: Gracious Theologian, Dublin, Columba, 1997
   Matthew: Sage Theologian, Dublin, Columba, 1998
   John: Spiritual Theologian, Dublin, Columba, 1999

More detailed works on the gospels:

R. A. Culpepper, *The Gospel and Letters of John* (Interpreting Biblical Texts), Nashville, Abingdon Press, 1998

C. F. Evans, *Saint Luke* (TPI New Testament Commentaries), London, SCM Press, 1990

D. J. Harrington, *The Gospel of Matthew* (Sacra Pagina), Collegeville, The Liturgical Press, 1991

M. D. Hooker, *The Gospel according to St Mark* (Black's New Testament Commentaries), London, A and C Black, 1991

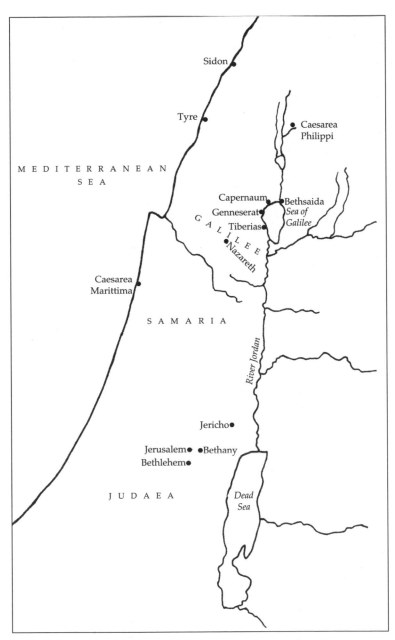

Palestine in Jesus' Day

Index of gospel passages and gospel people